丛书主编：常俊跃

世纪CBI内容依托系列英语教材

An Introduction to English Lexicology

英语词汇学教程

夏洋 邵林 主编

图书在版编目(CIP)数据

英语词汇学教程 / 夏洋,邵林主编. —北京:北京大学出版社,2017.7
(21世纪CBI内容依托系列英语教材)
ISBN 978-7-301-28218-2

Ⅰ.①英… Ⅱ.①夏…②邵… Ⅲ.①英语—词汇—高等学校—教材 Ⅳ.①H319.34

中国版本图书馆CIP数据核字(2017)第065347号

书　　　名	英语词汇学教程 YINGYU CIHUIXUE JIAOCHENG
著作责任者	夏 洋 邵 林 主编
责 任 编 辑	刘文静
标 准 书 号	ISBN 978-7-301-28218-2
出 版 发 行	北京大学出版社
地　　　址	北京市海淀区成府路205号　100871
网　　　址	http://www.pup.cn　新浪微博:@北京大学出版社
电 子 邮 箱	编辑部 pupwaiwen@pup.cn　总编室 zpup@pup.cn
电　　　话	邮购部 62752015　发行部 62750672　编辑部 62754382
印 刷 者	北京虎彩文化传播有限公司
经 销 者	新华书店 787毫米×1092毫米　16开本　13.5印张　320千字 2017年7月第1版　2024年8月第6次印刷
定　　　价	52.00元

未经许可,不得以任何方式复制或抄袭本书之部分或全部内容。
版权所有,侵权必究
举报电话:010-62752024　电子邮箱:fd@pup.cn
图书如有印装质量问题,请与出版部联系,电话:010-62756370

编委会

丛书主编：常俊跃

主　　编：夏　洋　邵　林

副 主 编：李　佳　刘　宓

前　言

随着我国英语教育的快速发展，英语专业长期贯彻的"以语言技能训练为导向"的课程建设理念及教学理念已经难以满足社会的需要。专家教师们密切关注的现行英语专业教育与中学英语教学脱节，语言与内容教学割裂，单纯语言技能训练过多，专业内容课程不足，学科内容课程系统性差，高低年级内容课程安排失衡及其导致的学生知识面偏窄、知识结构欠缺、思辨能力偏弱、综合素质发展不充分等问题日益突显。

针对上述问题，大连外国语大学英语专业在内容与语言融合教育理念的指导下确定了如下改革思路：

（一）**遵循全新教学理念，改革英语专业教育的课程结构**。改变传统单一的语言技能课程体系，实现内容课程与语言课程的融合，扩展学生的知识面，提高学生的语言技能。

（二）**开发课程自身潜力，同步提升专业知识和语言技能**。课程同时关注内容和语言，把内容教学和语言教学有机结合。以英语为媒介，系统教授专业内容；以专业内容为依托，在使用语言过程中提高语言技能，扩展学生的知识面，提高思辨能力。

（三）**改革教学方法手段，全面提高语言技能和综合素质**。依靠内容依托教学在方法上的灵活性，通过问题驱动、输出驱动等方法调动学生主动学习，把启发式、任务式、讨论式、结对子、小组活动、课堂展示、多媒体手段等行之有效的活动与学科内容教学有机结合，提高学生的语言技能，激发学生的兴趣，培养学生的自主性和创造性，提升思辨能力和综合素质。

本项改革突破了我国英语专业英语教学大纲规定的课程结构，改变了英语专业通过开设单纯的听、说、读、写、译语言技能课程提高学生语言技能的传统课程建设理念，对英语课程及教学方法进行了创新性的改革。首创了具有我国特色的英语专业内容与语言融合的课程体系；开发了适合英语专业的内容与语言融合的课程；提高学生综合运用语言的能力，扩展学生的知识面，提高学生的综合素质，以崭新的途径实现英语专业教育的总体培养目标。

经过十年的实验探索，改革取得了鼓舞人心的结果。

（一）**构建了英语专业内容与语言融合教学的课程体系**。课程包括美国历史文化、美国自然人文地理、美国社会文化、英国历史文化、英国自然人文地理、英国社会文化、澳新加社会文化、欧洲文化、中国文化、跨文化交际、《圣经》与文化、希腊罗马神话、综合英语（美国文学经典作品）、综合英语（英国文学经典作品）、综合英语（世界文学经典作品）、综合英语（西方思想经典）、英语视听说（美国经典电影）、英语视听说（英国经典电影）、英语视听说（环球资讯）、英语视听说（专题资讯）、英语短篇小说、英语长篇小说、英语散文、英语诗歌、英语戏剧、英语词汇学、英语语言学、语言与社会、语言与文化、语言与语用等。这些课程依托专业知识内容训练学生综合运用的语言能力，扩展学生的知识面，提高学生的多元文化意识，提升学生的综合素质。

（二）系统开发了相关国家的史、地、社会、文化、文学、语言学课程资源。在内容与语言融合教育理念的指导下，开发了上述课程所需要的教学课件及音频视频资源。开发的教材系统组织了教学内容，设计了新颖的栏目板块，设计的活动也丰富多样，在实际教学中受到了学生的广泛欢迎。在北京大学出版社、华中科技大学出版社、北京师范大学出版社、上海外语教育出版社的支持下，系列教材已经陆续出版。

（三）牵动了教学手段和教学方法的改革，取得了突出的教学效果。在内容与语言融合教育理念的指导下，教师的教学理念、教学方法、教学手段得到更新。通过问题驱动、输出驱动等活动调动学生主动学习，把启发式、任务式、讨论式、结对子、小组活动、课堂展示、多媒体手段等行之有效的活动与学科内容教学有机结合，激发学生的兴趣，培养学生自主性和创造性，提高学生的语言技能，提升思辨能力和综合素质。曾有专家教师担心取消、减少语言技能课程会对学生的语言技能发展产生消极影响。实验数据证明，内容与语言融合教学不仅没有对学生的语言技能发展和语言知识的学习产生消极影响，而且还产生了多方面的积极影响，对专业知识的学习也产生了巨大的积极影响。

（四）提高了教师的科研意识和科研水平，取得了丰硕的教研成果。开展改革以来，团队对内容与语言融合教学问题进行了系列研究，活跃了整个教学单位的科研气氛，教师的科研意识和科研水平也得到很大提高。课题组已经撰写研究论文70多篇，撰写博士论文3篇，在国内外学术期刊发表研究论文40多篇，撰写专著2部。

教学改革开展以来，每次成果发布都引起强烈反响。在中国外语教学法国际研讨会上，与会的知名外语教育专家戴炜栋教授等对这项改革给予关注，博士生导师蔡基刚教授认为本项研究"具有导向性作用"。在全国英语专业院系主任高级论坛上，研究成果得到知名专家博士生导师王守仁教授和与会专家教授的高度评价。在中国英语教学研究会年会及中国外语教育改革论坛上，本成果引起与会专家的强烈反响，教育部外指委石坚教授、仲伟合教授、蒋洪新教授等给予了高度评价。本项改革的系列成果两次获得大连外国语大学教学成果一等奖，两次获得辽宁省优秀教学成果奖一等奖，一次获得国家教学成果二等奖。目前，该项改革成果已经在全国英语专业教育领域引起广泛关注。它触及了英语专业的教学大纲，影响了课程建设的理念，引领了英语专业的教学改革，改善了教学实践，必将对未来英语专业教育的发展产生积极影响。

《英语词汇学教程》依照内容与语言融合的外语教学理念编写，强调语言所传达的知识和信息，在获得信息的同时学习语言。

《英语词汇学教程》教材共分15单元，每单元设置主课文一篇，补充阅读课文2~3篇。

前 言

课文的选择兼顾英语词汇学知识体系以及学生新词汇和语言知识的输入。教材内容主要涵盖词汇学核心概念、英语词汇发展史、英语构词法、语义关系、语义变化和英语谚语等内容。教材的主要目的是使学生掌握有关英语词汇学的基础知识，并同步提升英语学习者词汇学习能力和相关语言技能。

教材在每单元设置一定量基于内容与语言融合教学理念的练习，其中既包含语言知识和技能的运用，也包含对英语词汇学知识的巩固。练习的设置有助于学生在使用教材的过程中，实现知识体系构建和语言技能训练的同步提高。

编者在教材编写过程中，强调在保证英语词汇学知识体系完整的前提下，整合多样的语言输入和输出内容，以期培养学生的语言知识的技能和交际能力。因此该教材在每一单元都精心设计了旨在对学生在语法、词汇、篇章结构、语言功能等方面进行全面严格培养的基本技能练习。同时，编者设计出与英语词汇学相关的、学生参与度较高的课堂和课外活动。这些活动的设置是本教材的亮点之一，它使得课堂教学得以延伸，也能激发学生的学习热情，这也是内容与语言融合教学理念在本教材中的最好体现。

基于内容与语言融合教学理念的《英语词汇学教程》不仅可以作为我国高校英语词汇学必修或选修课程教材，同时也适用于对英语词汇学相关话题感兴趣的英语学习者自学。

本教材是我国英语专业语言学系列课程改革的一项探索，凝聚了全体编写人员的艰苦努力。然而由于水平所限，还存在疏漏和不足，希望使用本教材的老师和同学们能为我们提出意见和建议。您的指导和建议将是我们提高的动力。

编者

于大连外国语大学

2017 年 3 月 30 日

Contents

Unit 1	An Invitation to Lexicology	1
	Text A What Is Lexicology?	2
	Text B The Secrets of a Word	9
	Text C The Synonyms of Word	10
	Text D Morphology	11
Unit 2	Historical Development of English Vocabulary	14
	Text A English Vocabulary: A Historical Perspective	15
	Text B The Growth of Present-Day English Vocabulary	23
	Text C A Brief History of English	25
Unit 3	Foreign Elements of English Vocabulary	28
	Text A The Sources of English Vocabulary	29
	Text B Latin and Greek Borrowings	35
	Text C French Borrowings	36
	Text D Borrowings from Other Languages	38
Unit 4	Classification of English Vocabulary	40
	Text A Content Words and Function Words	41
	Text B Stylistic Classification of the English Vocabulary	42
	Text C Colloquialism in Literature	49
	Text D The Importance of Function Words	51
Unit 5	Morphological Structure of English Vocabulary	53
	Text A Morphemes	54
	Text B Latin and Greek Roots and Affixes in English Vocabulary	62
	Text C Roots and Stems	66
Unit 6	Major Word Formations in English	68
	Text A English Compound	69
	Text B Derived Words	77
	Text C Conversion	79
	Text D Deriving Nouns from Verbs: Names for People	83
Unit 7	Minor Word Formations in English	87
	Text A Minor Process of Word Formation	88
	Text B Acronymy	95
	Text C Reduplication	96
	Text D Eponyms	97

Unit 8	Word Meaning and Motivation	99
	Text A Word Meaning in the English Language	100
	Text B Motivation of Words	102
	Text C Aspects of Meaning	107
	Text D Onomatopoeia	108
Unit 9	Sense Relations Between Words	111
	Text A Synonymy	112
	Text B Antonymy	113
	Text C Hyponymy	118
	Text D Oxymoron	120
Unit 10	Polysemy and Homonymy	124
	Text A Polysemy and Homonymy	125
	Text B Lexical Relations: Hyponymy and Homonymy	132
	Text C Fun with Homonyms	134
Unit 11	Semantic Changes	137
	Text A Semantic Changes and the Causes	138
	Text B Semantic Shift	145
	Text C The History of Semantic Change	146
	Text D Metaphor and Metonymy	147
Unit 12	Figurative Use of Words	151
	Text A What Is Figurative Speech?	152
	Text B Literal and Figurative Language	153
	Text C Synecdoche and Metonymy	158
	Text D Taboos and Euphemisms	159
Unit 13	Meaning and Context	162
	Text A Context as the Key to Unlocking Word Meaning	163
	Text B Ambiguity	171
	Text C Context and Context of Situation	174
	Text D Decoding Meaning Through Context	175
Unit 14	English Idioms	179
	Text A English Idioms—Cream of the Language	180
	Text B Major Sources of English Idioms	182
	Text C Animals and English Idioms	187
	Text D Food and English Idioms	190
Unit 15	English Vocabulary and Greek Mythology	193
	Text A English Words of Greek Mythological Origins	194
	Text B The English Word Roots and Mythology	200
	Text C Words in Astronomy of Greek Mythological Origins	202
	Text D The Adventures of Odysseus	204

Unit 1

An Invitation to Lexicology

> Without grammar, very little can be conveyed; without vocabulary, nothing can be conveyed.
>
> —— D. A. Wilkins
>
> No matter how well the student learns grammar, no matter how successfully he masters the sounds of a second language, without words to express a wide range of meanings, communication in that language cannot happen in any meaningful way.
>
> —— McCarthy

Unit Goals

- To have a glimpse of major issues involved in English lexicology
- To be familiar with the relationship between English lexicology and other disciplines
- To understand the definitions of word, vocabulary and lexicology
- To know the difference between word and lexeme

Before You Read

1. English is crazy! Here are some funny facts about the English language and some unique language oddities to wrap your mind around. How do you account for these language oddities? Please share your explanations with your partner.

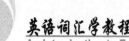

1) A guinea pig is neither from Guinea nor is it a pig.
2) You fill in a form by filling it out.
3) Do you have noses that run and feet that smell?
4) If a vegetarian eats vegetables, what does a humanitarian eat?
5) Why is it that writers write, but fingers don't fing and hammers don't ham?
6) When the stars are out, they are visible, but when the lights are out, they are invisible.
7) Do you notice that there is no egg in eggplant? Or ham in the hamburger? Nor apple or pine in pineapple!

2. What are the Chinese equivalents of the following idioms? Share your explanations with your partner, and discuss whether the meaning of each idiom is the combination of meanings of its components.

English Idioms	Chinese Equivalents
service station	
dressing room	
sporting house	
black stranger	
white man	
yellow book	
red tape	
green fingers	
blue stocking	
American beauty	
Dutch courage	
French leave	
Greek gift	
Spanish athlete	

Start to Read

Text A What Is Lexicology?

Lexicology and Its Major Concerns

    Lexicology, as a sub-branch of general linguistics, is derived from *lexikós* (word) plus *logos* (learning or science), hence the science of words.

    Like general linguistics, lexicology can be both **diachronic** (historical) and **synchronic** (contemporary), the former dealing with the origin and development of the form and meaning of the words in a particular language across time, whereas the latter studying the vocabulary of a language as a system at a particular point of time. But there are many interrelated areas in lexicology, where one cannot be studied in isolation, without regard to the other.

The definitions suggest that lexicologists should be concerned about:
- morphology (structure and form)
- etymology (origins, sources and history)
- semantics (meaning and sense relations)
- lexicography (dictionary making)

Morphology is the study of word formation, of the structure of words.

Some observations about words and their structure: Some words can be divided into parts which still have meaning. Many word-parts have meanings by themselves. But some word-parts have meanings only when used with other words. Each word has a relation in the grammatical system of a language and belongs to some parts of speech. Lexicology studies this relationship in terms of the grammatical meanings as also their relationship with the lexical meaning. In the field of word formation, lexicology is still more closely related to grammar. Both study the patterns of word formation.

The word **etymology** is derived from the Greek *etumos* which means real or true. The ending *-ology* suggests the study/science of something, as in *biology* or *geology*. And that is the etymology of *etymology*. It is the study of the origins of words and how words evolved. Here is another example. The Ancient Greek word *hippos* means *horse*. And *potamus* means *river*. Hence *hippopotamus* literally means *river horse*. A few other parts of words derived from Ancient Greek are *tele* (long distance), *micro* (small), *phone* (speak), and *scope* (look). From these come such words as *telephone*, *telescope*, *microphone*, and *microscope*.

Semantics is the study of meaning. It is a wide subject within the general study of language. An understanding of semantics is essential to the study of language acquisition (how language users acquire a sense of meaning, as speakers and writers, listeners and readers) and of language change (how meanings alter over time). The study of semantics includes the study of how meaning is constructed, interpreted, clarified, negotiated and paraphrased. The types of meaning and sense relations such as polysemy, homonymy, synonymy, antonymy, hyponymy and semantic field all fall into the scope of semantic study.

Lexicography is the art and science of dictionary making. In lexicography word is studied as an individual unit in respect of its meaning and use from the practical point of learning the language or comprehending texts, or for any other purpose like checking correct spelling, pronunciation, etc. Different dictionaries serve very different purposes. Some only give information about semantics (word meanings, descriptions or definitions) and orthography (standard spellings). Others give information about etymology, variants and change of meaning over time. Besides, a dictionary also serves as a clearing  house of information. In order that these functions be performed adequately, the information in the dictionaries should be collected from as many sources as possible, and should be authentic and easily retrievable. Lexicography in this way is an applied science.

Some Confusing Terms in Lexicology

As noted above, lexicologists study words on a mass scale. We will also use the word **vocabulary** interchangeably with **lexis**. Take note that *lexis* and *vocabulary* are uncountable nouns; if you need to refer to individual items, you should talk about **lexical items** or **vocabulary items**. You might also encounter the term **lexicon**, which can be used in a couple of ways: It can be used as a more technical version of *lexis* on the one hand and many people use it synonymously with **dictionary** on the other. In practical applications, such as language learning, the lexicon is represented by a dictionary, which lists words alphabetically and provides definition. What must be remembered is that any dictionary can never be comprehensive in its listing of the lexis of a particular language.

Practice 1:
Do you know the specific meaning of "vocabulary" in each context?

Contexts	Meanings
A. His Chinese *vocabulary* is rather limited.	(1) The total number of the words in a language.
B. Most technical jobs use a specialized *vocabulary*.	(2) All the words used in a particular historical period.
C. Modern English *vocabulary*.	(3) All the words of a given dialect, a given book, a given discipline.
D. The English *vocabulary* is one of the largest and richest.	(4) All the words that an individual person knows, learns, or uses.

Another issue that sometimes arises is whether *bring* and *brought* are two separate words. We shall say that they are two separate **word-forms**, but that they represent one lexeme.

A **lexeme** is an abstract representation of morphological analysis in linguistics, which roughly corresponds to a set of forms taken by a single word. For example, in the English language, *look*, *looks*, *looked* and *looking* are concrete forms of the same lexeme, conventionally written as *look*. A lexeme exists regardless of any inflectional endings it may have.

Some lexemes (such as *put up with*) consist of more than one word. Thus, *fibrillate, rain cats and dogs*, and *come in* are all lexemes, as are *elephant, jog, cholesterol, happiness, face the music*, and thousands of other meaningful items in English. The headwords in a dictionary are all lexemes.

We have used the word **word** extensively, and there is commonsensical obviousness to it. At this stage we will take the orthographic definition of *word*, and say that it is an item that, in writing, is usually separated from other items by spaces.

Practice 2:
What is the definition of WORD?

Please examine the following items, and share your answers to the questions with your partner.

    (1) Semantics (2) dis-
    (3) tlentzmsth (4) the

1. Why do you think item (1) is a word, but item (2) is not?
2. Do you think item (3) is a word in English? How do you pronounce it?
3. Do you think both item (1) and item (4) are words? Are they meaningful?
4. What is your definition of WORD?

Leonard Bloomfield, one of the greatest American linguists, introduced the concept of "minimal free forms" in 1926. Words are thought of as the smallest meaningful unit of speech that can stand by themselves. For example, *child* is a word. We cannot divide it up into smaller units that can convey meaning when they stand alone. On the basis of this assumption, a tentative definition of **word** could be "a minimal free form of a language that has a given sound and meaning and performs syntactic function."

After You Read

Knowledge Focus

1. Discuss the following questions with your partner.
   1) What is lexicology?
   2) How do you understand that lexicology can be both diachronic and synchronic?
   3) What are the sub-branches in linguistics that are related to lexicology?
   4) What is morphology?
   5) What is the etymology of the word *etymology*?
   6) What does the study of semantics include?
   7) How is word studied in lexicography?
   8) What is the difference between word and vocabulary?
   9) What is the difference between word-forms and lexeme?
   10) How do you understand "a minimal free form"?

2. Each of the statements below is followed by four alternative answers. Choose the one that would best complete the statement.
   1) Morphology is the branch of grammar which studies the structure or forms of words, primarily through the use of _____ construct.
      A. word   B. form
      C. morpheme   D. root
   2) A word is _____ of a language that has a given sound and meaning, and performs certain syntactic function.
      A. a smallest form   B. a minimal free form
      C. a constituent form   D. a part
   3) _____ is traditionally defined as the study of the origins and history of the form and meaning of words.
      A. Semantics   B. Linguistics
      C. Etymology   D. Stylistics
   4) Semantics is the study of meaning of different _____ levels: lexis, syntax, utterance, discourse, etc.
      A. linguistic   B. grammatical
      C. arbitrary   D. semantic
   5) Lexicography shares with lexicology the same problems: the form, meaning, origins and usages of words, but they have a _____ difference.
      A. spelling   B. semantic   C. pronunciation   D. pragmatic

6) *Take* is the _____ of *taking, taken* and *took*.
   A. lexis   B. word-form
   C. lexeme   D. lexical item
7) We can use the word *vocabulary* interchangeable with _____.
   A. *lexis*   B. *lexeme*
   C. *word*   D. *morpheme*
8) _____ refers to the system of spelling in a language.
   A. Lexicology   B. Morphology
   C. Lexicography   D. Orthography
9) Many people use the word _____ synonymously with *dictionary*.
   A. *lexicology*   B. *lexicon*
   C. *lexeme*   D. *lexical*
10) which of the following is NOT a lexeme?
    A. *hope*   B. *-ceive*
    C. *rely on*   D. *put up with*

3. Match the English terms in Column I with the Chinese meanings in Column II.

I	II
A. lexis	a. 词位
B. lexeme	b. 词汇
C. lexicon	c. 词汇、词典
D. lexicology	d. 语义学
E. morphology	e. 词源学
F. etymology	f. 词典学
G. semantics	g. 词态学
H. lexicography	h. 词汇学

Language Focus

1. **Fill in the blanks with the following words you have learned in the text. Change the forms where necessary.**

| tentative | diachronic | minimal | commonsensical | authentic |
| lexical | acquisition | derive | orthography | retrievable |

1) In dictionaries, words are listed according to their _____.
2) Fragmentation can slow your computer and render lost files less _____. Windows comes with a perfectly fine defragger.
3) I don't know if the painting is _____.
4) Any translator will make _____ errors as well as errors of tone and spirit while working on a book.
5) We are devising our Five-Year Plan and have some _____ ideas regarding the excessive trade surplus.

6) Thousands of English words are _____ from Latin.
7) The ancient theories of child language _____ explore the dilemma of nature versus nurture; that is, whether language is inherent and God-given or learned from environment.
8) We stayed with friends, so our expenses were _____.
9) The only _____ solution would be to divide the children into groups according to age.
10) This article traces the development of translation theories through a _____ analysis of perceptions of meaning in different periods of history.

2. Proofreading & Error Correction.

Now, it is clear that the decline of a language must ultimately have political and economical causes: it is not due simply to the bad influence of this or that individual writer. But an affect can become a cause, reinforce the original cause and producing the same effect in an intensified form, and so on indefinitely. A man may take drink because he feels himself to be a failure, and then fail all the most completely because he drinks. It is rather the same thing that is happening to the English language. It becomes ugly and inaccurate because our thoughts are foolish, but the sloven of our language makes it easier for us to have foolish thoughts.

The point is that the process is irreversible. Modern English, especially written English, is full of bad habits which are spread by imitation and which can be avoided if one is willing to take the necessary trouble. If one gets rid of these habits one can think more clearly, and think clearly is a necessary first step towards political regeneration: so that the fight, against bad English is not frivolous and is not the exclusive concerning of professional writers.

I will come back to this present, and I hope that by that time the meaning of what I have said here will have become clearer.

1) _____
2) _____
3) _____
4) _____
5) _____

6) _____

7) _____

8) _____

9) _____

10) _____

3. Translate the following paragraph into Chinese.

Lexicography is the art and science of dictionary making. In lexicography word is studied as an individual unit in respect of its meaning and use from the practical point of learning the language or comprehending texts, or for any other purpose like checking correct spelling, pronunciation, etc. Different dictionaries serve very different purposes. Some only give information about semantics (word meanings, descriptions or definitions) and orthography (standard spellings). Others give information about etymology, variants and change of meaning over time.

Comprehensive Work

1. Do some research and find out the etymology of the following words.
   1) butterfly
   2) eternal
   3) fantastic
   4) tranquility
   5) umbrella

2. How many letters does the word have?

> What is a word made up of 4 letters yet is also made up of 3. Although is written with 8 letters, and then with 4. Rarely consists of 6, and never is written with 5.

3. Writing

For English learners, vocabulary learning seems to be an insurmountable problem. Describe your personal experience of learning English vocabulary and offer some vocabulary learning tips to beginners of English learning. Below are some sample tips.

- **Tip One: Learn words in context.** Most vocabulary items are learned in context. The more words you're exposed to, the larger vocabulary you will have. While you are reading, pay close attention to words you don't know. First, try to figure out their meanings from context. Then look the words up. Read and listen to challenging material so that you'll be exposed to many new words in context.
- **Tip Two: Make up as many associations and connections as possible.** Read the word aloud to activate your auditory memory. Relate the word to words you already know. For example, the word *gargantuan* (very large) has a similar meaning to the words *gigantic*, *huge*, *large*, etc. You could make a sequence: *small, medium, large, very large, gargantuan*. List as many things as you can that could be considered gargantuan: Godzilla, the circus fat lady, the zit on your nose, etc. Create pictures of the word's meaning that involve strong emotions. Think "the gargantuan creature was going to rip me apart and then eat me!"
- **Tip Three: Practice and review.** Learning a word won't help very much if you promptly forget it. Research shows that it takes from 10 to 20 repetitions to really make a word part of your vocabulary. It helps to write the word—both the definition and a sentence you make up using the word—perhaps on an index card that can later be reviewed. As soon as you learn a new word, start using it. Review your index cards periodically to see if you have forgotten any of your new words.

Read More

Text B The Secrets of a Word

For some people studying words may seem uninteresting. But if studied properly, it may well prove just as exciting and novel as unearthing the mysteries of Outer Space.

It is significant that many scholars have attempted to define *word* as a linguistic phenomenon. Yet none of the definitions can be considered totally satisfactory in all aspects. It is equally surprising that, despite all the achievements of modern science, certain essential aspects of the nature of the word still escape us.

We do not know much about the origin of language and, consequently, of the origin of words. We know almost nothing about the mechanism by which a speaker's mental process is converted into sound groups called "words," nor about the reverse process whereby a listener's brain converts the acoustic phenomena into concepts and ideas, thus establishing a two-way process of communication.

The list of unknowns could be extended, but it is probably high time to look at the brighter side about the nature of the word.

First, we do know that a word is a unit of speech which serves the purposes of human communication. Thus, the word can be defined as a unit of communication. Secondly, a word can be perceived as the total of the sounds which comprise it. Third, a word, viewed structurally, possesses both the external structure and the internal structure.

The external structure means the morphological structure of a word. For example, in the word *post-impressionists* the following morphemes can be distinguished: the prefixes *post-*, *im-*, the root *press*, the noun-forming suffixes *-ion*, *-ist*, and the grammatical suffix of plurality *-s*. All these morphemes constitute the external structure of the word *post-impressionists*.

The internal structure of the word, or its meaning, is nowadays commonly referred to as the word's semantic structure. This is certainly the word's main aspect, in that words can serve the purposes of human communication solely due to their meanings. The area of lexicology specializing in word meaning is called semantics.

Another structural aspect of the word is its unity. The word possesses both external (or formal) unity and semantic unity.

Formal unity of the word is sometimes inaccurately interpreted as indivisibility. The example of *post-impressionists* has already shown that the word is not, strictly speaking, indivisible. Yet, its component morphemes are permanently linked together in opposition to word-groups, whose components possess a certain structural freedom, e. g. *bright light, to take for granted*.

The formal unity of the word can best be illustrated by comparing a word and a word-group comprising identical constituents. The difference between a *blackbird* and a *black bird* is best explained by their relationship with the grammatical system of the language. The word *blackbird*, which is characterized by unity, possesses a single grammatical framing: *blackbird/s*. The first constituent *black* is not subject to any grammatical changes. In the word-group a *black bird*, each constituent can acquire grammatical forms of its own: the *blackest birds* I've ever seen. Other words can be inserted between the components which is impossible, so far as the word is concerned, since it

would violate its unity: a *black night bird*.

The same example may be used to illustrate what we mean by **semantic unity**. In the word-group a *black bird*, each of the meaningful words conveys a separate concept: *bird—a kind of living creature; black—a color*. The word *blackbird* conveys only one concept: *the type of bird*. This is one of the main features of any word: it always conveys one concept, no matter how many components it may have in its external structure.

So far we have only underlined the word's major peculiarities, but this suffices to convey the general idea of the difficulties and questions faced by the scholar attempting to give a detailed definition of the word. The difficulty does not merely consist in the considerable number of aspects that are to be taken into account, but also in the essential unanswered questions of word theory which concern the nature of its meaning.

All that we have said about the word can be summed up as follows. The word is a speech unit used for the purposes of human communication, materially representing a group of sounds, possessing a meaning, susceptible to grammatical employment and characterized by formal and semantic unity.

Questions for Discussion or Reflection
1. How do you understand the external structure of a word?
2. Do you think *greenhouse* is a word? Why or why not?
3. How do you explain the semantic unity of a word?

Text C   The Synonyms of Word

Lexicon, in its most general sense, is synonymous with vocabulary. In its technical sense, however, lexicon deals with the analysis and creation of words, idioms and collocations. **Word** is a unit of expression which has universal intuitive recognition by native-speakers, whether it is expressed in spoken or written form. This definition is perhaps a little vague as there are different criteria with regard to its identification and definition. It seems that it is hard, even impossible, to define *word* linguistically. Nonetheless it is universally agreed that the following three senses are involved in the definition of *word*, none of which, though, is expected to cope with all the situations: (1) a physically definable unit (it could be represented both phonologically and orthographically); (2) the common factor underlying a set of forms (there lies the common factor in *checks, checked, checking*, etc.); (3) a grammatical unit (every word plays a grammatical part in the sentence).

According to Leonard Bloomfield, a word is a minimum free form. There are other factors that may help us identify words: (1) stability (no great change of orthographic features); (2) relative uninterruptibility (we can hardly insert anything between two parts of a word or between the letters).

To make the category clearer we can sub-classify words into a few types: (1) grammatical (e.g. *to, in, the*) and lexical words (e.g. *table, chair, gigantic*). By lexical words we mean the words that carry a semantic content, e.g. nouns, verbs, adjectives and many adverbs; (2) closed-class and open-class words. Open-class words allow for new words to be added to nouns, verbs, adjectives and adverbs as they become necessary, and develop our language alongside our ever changing society. For example, the computer age has introduced words such as *blue-tooth*; we have incorporated others like *chav, alcopop, Rambo* and many others. Only very rarely does one find new closed-class words. These can be seen as words that allow us to build our language grammatically—things like pronouns, prepositions, conjunctions and determiners. These are also called structural words, function words, or grammatical words, and they allow us to deploy open class words in a system that has consistency.

In order to reduce the ambiguity of the term *word*, the term **lexeme** is postulated as the abstract unit, which refers to the smallest unit in the meaning system of a language that can be distinguished from other smaller units. A lexeme can occur in many different forms in actual spoken or written texts. For example, *write* is the lexeme of the following words: *write, writes, wrote, writing,* and *written*. **Vocabulary** usually refers to all words or lexical items a person has acquired. Vocabulary is also used to mean word list or glossary.

Exercises

1. Please define the following terms and illustrate with examples.
   1) Lexicon: _____
   2) Word: _____
   3) Lexeme: _____
   4) Vocabulary: _____

2. Group Discussion

Could you define grammatical words and lexical words with examples? Some claim that the importance of lexical words outweighs that of grammatical words, while others hold polarized opinion. As a language user, in your opinion, which category plays a more important role in daily communication? Please have a group discussion and share your views with your classmates.

Text D Morphology

Morphology, in linguistics, is the study of the forms of words, and the ways in which words are related to other words of the same language. Formal differences among words serve a variety of purposes, from the creation of new lexical items to the indication of grammatical structure.

If you ask most non-linguists what the primary thing is that has to be learned if one is to "know" a language, the answer is likely to be "the words of the language." Learning vocabulary is a major focus of language instruction, but what is involved in knowing the words of a language?

Obviously, a good deal of this is a matter of learning that *cat* is a word of English, a noun that refers to a "feline mammal usually having thick soft fur and being unable to roar." The notion that the word is a combination of sound and meaning was the basis of the theory of the linguistic sign developed by Ferdinand de Saussure at the beginning of the 20th century. But if words like *cat* were all there in language, the only thing that would matter about the form of a word would be the fact that it differs from the forms of other words (i.e., *cat* is pronounced differently from *mat, cap, dog,* etc.). Clearly there is no more specific connection between the parts of the sound of *cat* and the parts of its meaning: the initial [k], for example, does not refer to the fur. The connection between sound and meaning is irreducible here.

But of course *cat* and words like it are not the end of the story. Another word of English is *cats*, a single word in pronunciation but one that can be seen to be made up of a part *cat* and another part *–s*, with the meaning of the whole made up of the meaning of *cat* and the meaning of *–s* ("plural"). *Cattish* behavior is that which is similar to that of a cat; and while a *catbird* is not itself a kind of cat, its name comes from the fact that it sometimes sounds like one. All of these words are clearly connected with *cat*, but on the other hand they are all words in their own right.

We might, of course, simply have memorized *cats, cattish* and *catbird* along with *cat*, even though the words seem to have some sort of relation to one another. But suppose we learn about a new animal, a *wug*, say "a large, hairy bovine mammal known for being aggressive and braying". We do not need to learn independently that two of these are *wugs*, or that *wuggish* behavior is likely to involve attacking one's fellows, or that a *wugbird* (if there were such a thing) might be a bird with a braying call. All of these things follow from the knowledge we have not just of the specific words of our language, but of their relations to one another, in form and meaning. The latter is our knowledge of the morphology of our language.

In some languages, the use of morphology to pack complex meanings into a single word is much more elaborate than in English. In West Greenlandic, *tusaanngitsuusaartuaannarsiinnaanngivipputit* is a single word meaning "you simply cannot pretend not to be hearing all the time." Other languages do much less of this sort of thing: Chinese and Vietnamese are often cited in this connection, though Chinese does have rather exuberant use of compounding (structures like *catbird* made up of two existing items). Despite this variation, however, morphology is an aspect of the grammar of all languages, and in some it rivals syntax in the expressive power it permits.

For Fun

Works to Read

1. ***Words, Meaning and Vocabulary: An Introduction to Modern English Lexicology*** by Howard Jackson and Etienne Z. Amvela

   This textbook is a systematic and accessible introduction to the lexicology of modern English. The book provides an account of the sources of modern English words and studies the development of vocabulary over time. *Words, Meaning and Vocabulary* is an essential introduction to lexicology for undergraduate students.

2. ***Word Myths: Debunking Linguistic Urban Legends*** by David Wilton

   Word Myths takes on these linguistic urban legends, not just debunking them, but also examining why they are told and what they tell us about ourselves. The book examines the patterns underlying these legends and comes to conclusions about such things as why we attach morbid tales to children's rhymes, why newspapers keep promulgating false origins for terms like the Windy City, or why so many words have false nautical origins. *Word Myths* is an entertaining, yet authoritative, look at these and other linguistic legends.

Websites to Visit

1. http://www.vocabulary.com/
   This website offers the quickest and most intelligent way to improve your vocabulary.
2. http://www.etymonline.com/
   This website not only gives the definitions of words but also provides the origins of words and how words evolved.
3. http://www.englishvocabularyexercises.com/vocab-categories.htm
   This website features over 500 gap-fill exercises to learn and review over 1500 items of general vocabulary in English.

Unit 2
Historical Development of English Vocabulary

> Words play an enormous part in our lives and are therefore deserving of the closest study.
>
> —— Aldous Huxley
>
> What the elements are to chemistry, what the sounds are to music, are words to language. However, words are not only the elements of a language but also of the history of the people speaking it. They are important milestones along the way leading to the majestic Palace of Human Knowledge.
>
> —— Dr. Ernest Klein

Unit Goals

- To have a rough idea of the history of English language
- To grasp the branches of the Indo-European language
- To identify the stages of English vocabulary development
- To develop your skills of analyzing and generalizing linguistic phenomena in your learning experiences

 ### Before You Read

1. English is a member of _____.
   ☐ Sino-Tibetan Family
   ☐ Indo-European Family
   ☐ Austronesian Family
   ☐ Altaic Family

2. How many languages does the Indo-European family include? Please label the following languages that you think belong to the Indo-European family.

Languages	Yes	No
French		
Japanese		
Czech		

Languages	Yes	No
Hindi		
Chinese		
Scottish		
Russian		
Finnish		
German		
Greek		

Start to Read

Text A   English Vocabulary: A Historical Perspective

Have you ever wondered why some of the basic words in various European languages seem so similar? Why do doctors and botanists use so many words that are derived from Latin? Why are some words associated with the law based on French borrowings (*treason, judge, court*)? Why do the French themselves use English borrowings like *le weekend* or *le parking*? Why did Shakespeare and Chaucer use *thou* and *thee* and why don't we today? Why are there these strange inconsistencies in English where *-ough* can be pronounced so many ways (*bough, cough, tough, though, thorough, through*)?

The answers to these and other questions lie in where English words come from. The study of the historical development of the English vocabulary should not be treated in isolation from the history and the growth of the English language itself. Understanding the history may give us an insight into the nature of English: extremely rich and heterogeneous, a heavy borrower, full of synonyms, a global language. As useful preliminaries, we shall first place English in the context of world languages and discuss the historical development of English vocabulary from the Old English to the modern English periods.

The Indo-European Language Family

The 5,000 or so languages of the world can be grouped into about 300 language families, on the basis of similarities in their basic word stock and grammars. One of these families, the Indo-European includes most of the European languages spoken today, and English is also a member of this family. The Indo-European family includes several major branches: In the Eastern set, there are the Slavic languages (Russian, Polish, Czech etc.); the Baltic languages of Latvian and Lithuanian; the Indo-Iranian languages (Persian, Hindi etc.). In the Western set, there are the Germanic languages (Swedish, German, English etc.); the Italic languages (Portuguese, Spanish, French etc.); the Celtic languages (Scottish, Welsh, Irish etc.); Hellenic (Greek).

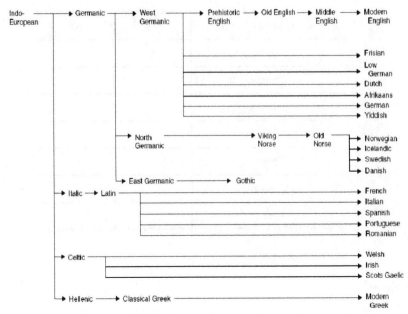

Of these branches of the Indo-European family, two are of paramount importance, the Germanic and the Romance languages. English is a member of the Germanic group of languages. It is believed that this group began as a common language in the Elbe river region about 3,000 years ago. By the second century BC, this Common Germanic language had split into three distinct sub-groups:

• East Germanic was spoken by peoples who migrated back to southeastern Europe. No East Germanic language is spoken today, and the only written East Germanic language that survives is Gothic.

• North Germanic evolved into the modern Scandinavian languages of Swedish, Danish, Norwegian, and Icelandic.

• West Germanic is the ancestor of modern German, Dutch, Flemish, Frisian, and English.

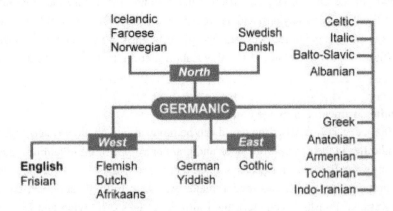

Before 449 AD, the primary inhabitants of the British Isles were Celts, who had invaded from the east hundreds of years earlier and driven out earlier, non-Indo-European tribes. They spoke Celtic languages: Welsh, Manx, Gaelic, and Briton. In fact, before the Roman Empire began to seriously expand around 125 BC, most of Europe was inhabited by Celts.

In 55 BC the Romans finally got around to invading Britain. Caesar's first invasion wasn't successful, but a century later Romans came again. They ruled southern Britain from 43 AD to 410 AD. The Celtic Britons under Roman rule were converted to Christianity by Roman missionaries, but they otherwise retained their own essentially separate identities and language during this period. The Romans left Britain in the late 4th and early 5th centuries, partly because their empire was under attack in mainland Europe from rebelling Germanic tribes: Goths, Franks and Vandals, all former Roman allies, were now attacking the Romans. In 410, Visigoths, led by their king, Alaric, burned Rome.

The departure of the Romans left the Britons without the military shield they'd become used to. In that same year, 410, they were being attacked by Picts and Scots, other Celtic tribes who lived in Scotland. The Britons begged Rome for military aid, but Rome had no resources to spare.

The beleaguered Britons, looking around for allies, noticed that just across the Channel, three Germanic tribes—the Jutes, Saxons, and Angles—had military strength to spare. In 449 the Britons invited them to come over and help protect Britain against the northerners, in exchange for a piece of land in the east.

Old English (450–1100)

West Germanic invaders from Jutland and southern Denmark, the Angles (whose name is the source of the words *England* and *English*), Saxons, and Jutes, began to settle in the British Isles in the 5th and 6th centuries AD. They spoke a mutually intelligible language, similar to modern Frisian—the language of the northeastern region of the Netherlands—that is called Old English, which has a vocabulary of 50,000 to 60,000. Four major dialects of Old English emerged, Northumbrian in the north of England, Mercian in the Midlands, West Saxon in the south and west, and Kentish in the Southeast.

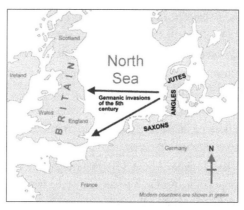

These invaders pushed the original, Celtic-speaking inhabitants out of what is now England into Scotland, Wales, Cornwall, and Ireland, leaving behind a few Celtic words. These Celtic languages survive today in the Gaelic languages of Scotland and Ireland and in Welsh. Cornish, unfortunately, is, in linguistic terms, now a dead language.

Also influencing English at this time were the Vikings. Norse invasions and settlement, beginning around 850, brought many North Germanic words into the language, particularly in the north of England. One example is the word *dream*, which had meant *joy* until the Vikings imparted its current meaning on it from the Scandinavian cognate *draumr*.

The majority of words in modern English come from foreign, not Old English roots. In fact, only about one sixth of the known Old English words have descendants surviving today. But this is deceptive; Old English is much more important than these statistics would indicate. About half of the most commonly used words in modern English have Old English roots. Words like *be*, *water*, and *strong*, for example, derive from Old English roots.

Old English, also known as Anglo-Saxon, whose best known surviving example is the poem "Beowulf", lasted until about 1100, shortly after the most important event in the development and history of the English language, the Norman Conquest.

Middle English (1100–1500)

William the Conqueror, the Duke of Normandy, invaded and conquered England and the Anglo-Saxons in 1066. The new overlords spoke a dialect of Old French known as Anglo-Norman.

Prior to the Norman Conquest, Latin had been only a minor influence on the English language, mainly through vestiges of the Roman occupation and from the conversion of Britain to Christianity in the 7th century (ecclesiastical terms such as *priest*, *vicar*, and *mass* came into the language this way), but now there was a wholesale infusion of Romance (Anglo-Norman) words.

The influence of the Normans can be illustrated by looking at two words, *beef* and *cow*. *Beef*, commonly eaten by the aristocracy, derives from the Anglo-Norman, while the Anglo-Saxon commoners, who tended the cattle, retained the Germanic *cow*. Many legal terms, such as *indict*, *jury*, and *verdict* have Anglo-Norman roots because the Normans ran the courts. This split, where words commonly used by the aristocracy have Romantic roots and words frequently used by the Anglo-Saxon commoners have Germanic roots, can be seen in many instances.

Sometimes French words replaced Old English words; *crime* replaced *firen*, and *uncle* replaced *eam*; other times, French and Old English components combined to form a new word, as the French *gentle* and the Germanic *man* formed *gentleman*; other times, two different words with roughly the same meaning survive into modern English. Thus we have the Germanic *doom* and the French *judgment*, or *wish* and *desire*.

In 1204, King John lost the province of Normandy to the King of France. This began a process where the Norman nobles of England became increasingly estranged from their French cousins. England became the chief concern of the nobility, rather than their estates in France, and consequently the nobility adopted a modified English as their native tongue. About 150 years later, the Black Death (1349-1350) killed about one third of the English population. And as a result of this the laboring and merchant classes grew in economic and social importance, and along with them English increased in importance compared to Anglo-Norman.

This mixture of the two languages came to be known as Middle English. The most famous example of Middle English is Chaucer's *Canterbury Tales*. Unlike Old English, Middle English can be read, albeit with difficulty, by modern English-speaking people.

By 1362, the linguistic division between the nobility and the commoners was largely over. In that year, the *Statute of Pleading* was adopted, which made English the language of the courts and it began to be used in Parliament.

The Middle English period came to a close around 1,500

with the rise of Modern English.

Early Modern English (1500–1800)

The transition from Middle to Modern English is not marked by any specific cultural event but rather by a linguistic event: the Great Vowel Shift. This shift resulted in vowels either being raised on the vowel chart or becoming diphthongs. One way that vowels can be classified is according to how high the tongue is placed in the mouth when the vowel is articulated. What happened between Middle and Early Modern English is that in certain words, vowels began to be replaced by vowels pronounced higher in the mouth.

From the 16th century the British had contact with many peoples from around the world. This, together with the Renaissance of Classical learning, meant that many new words and phrases entered the language.

The invention of printing also meant that there was now a common language in print. Books became cheaper and more people learned to read. Printing also brought standardization to English. Spelling and grammar became fixed, and the dialect of London, where most publishing houses were, became the standard. In 1604 the first English dictionary was published.

Late Modern English (1800–Present)

The main difference between Early Modern English and Late Modern English is vocabulary. Late Modern English has many more words, arising from two principal factors: firstly, the Industrial Revolution and technology created a need for new words; secondly, the British Empire at its height covered one quarter of the earth's surface, and the English language adopted foreign words from many countries.

The industrial and scientific revolutions created a need for neologisms to describe the new creations and discoveries. For this, English relied heavily on Latin and Greek. Words like *oxygen*, *protein*, *nuclear*, and *vaccine* did not exist in the classical languages, but they were created from Latin and Greek roots. Such neologisms were not exclusively created from classical roots, though, English roots were used for such terms as *horsepower*, *airplane*, and *typewriter*.

Also, the rise of the British Empire and the growth of global trade served not only to introduce English to the world, but to introduce words into English. Hindi, and the other languages of the Indian subcontinent, provided many words, such as *pundit*, *shampoo*, *pajamas*, and *juggernaut*. Virtually every language on Earth has contributed to the development of English, from Finnish (*sauna*) and Japanese (*tycoon*) to the vast contributions of French and Latin.

With the continued development and prosperity of the colonies in America, India, Australia, Canada, New Zealand, and Africa, English became a true world language. Despite the variety, speakers of English are able to communicate with more people now than has ever before been possible. Among modern languages, English is now one of the superpowers.

After You Read

Knowledge Focus

1. **Tell whether the following statements are true or false according to the knowledge you learned and why.**
   1) English, in origin, is closer to French than German. (   )
   2) English belongs to the West-Germanic language group of Indo-European language family. (   )
   3) The Germanic tribes were considered to be the first peoples known to inhabit the British Isles. (   )
   4) Celtic is generally known as Old English.(   )
   5) Old English lasted until about 1100, shortly after the most important event in the development and history of the English language, the Norman Conquest.(   )
   6) Middle English lasted for more than three hundred years.(   )
   7) What happened between Middle and Early Modern English is that in certain words, vowels began to be replaced by vowels pronounced lower in the mouth.(   )
   8) French, Celtic and English existed simultaneously for over a century.(   )
   9) Middle English is much more readable than Old English by the modern people.(   )
   10) English, German, Irish and Flemish all belong to the Germanic.(   )

2. **Each of the statements below is followed by four alternative answers. Choose the one that would best complete the statement.**
   1) Greek is the modern language derived from _____.
      A. Italic   B. Hellenic
      C. Celtic   D. Germanic
   2) _____ and _____ are the two most important branches in the Indo-European family.
      A. Germanic and Italic   B. Germanic and Celtic
      C. Italic and Celtic   D. Italic and Hellenic
   3) The five Romance languages, namely, _____, Spanish, French, Italian, and Romanian, all belong to the Italic through an intermediate language Latin.
      A. English   B. Norwegian
      C. Dutch   D. Portuguese
   4) The early inhabitants of the British Isles were _____.
      A. Germans   B. Celts
      C. Scandinavians   D. Romans
   5) Unfortunately, _____ is, in linguistic terms, now a dead language.
      A. Scottish   B. Welsh
      C. Cornish   D. Irish
   6) Old English has a vocabulary of about _____ words.
      A. 30,000 to 40,000   B. 50,000 to 60,000
      C. 70,000 to 80,000   D. 80,000 to 90,000
   7) Old English began to undergo a great change when the _____ invaded England in 1066.
      A. Romans   B. Angles   C. Danes   D. Normans

8) Prior to the Norman Conquest, _____ had been only a minor influence on the English language, mainly through vestiges of the Roman occupation and from the conversion of Britain to Christianity in the 7th century.
   A. Latin   B. Scandinavian
   C. French   D. Greek
9) Greater changes in the pronunciation of long vowels occurred during the period of Early Modern English and continued through the 8th century. These changes have been called _____.
   A. the Great Vowel Shift   B. the Great Depression
   C. the Renaissance   D. the Colonization
10) The main difference between Early Modern English and Late Modern English is _____.
   A. pronunciation   B. grammar
   C. vocabulary   D. spelling

3. Complete the following statements with proper words and expressions.
   1) Norwegian, Icelandic, Danish and _____ are generally known as Scandinavian languages.
   2) No East Germanic language is spoken today and the only written East Germanic language that survives is _____.
   3) The name of Angles is the source of the words _____.
   4) Norse invasions and settlement, beginning around 850, brought many _____ words into English, particularly in the north of England.
   5) Only about _____ of the known Old English words have descendants surviving today.
   6) Now people generally refer to _____ as Old English.
   7) As a result of the influence of the Normans, words commonly used by the aristocracy have _____ roots and words frequently used by the Anglo-Saxon commoners have _____ roots.
   8) In 1362, _____ was made the language of the courts and it began to be used in Parliament.
   9) _____ brought standardization to English. Spelling and grammar became fixed, and the dialect of London, where most publishing houses were, became the standard.
   10) The industrial and scientific revolutions created a need for neologisms to describe the new creations and discoveries. For this, English relied heavily on _____ and _____.

Language Focus
1. Fill in the blanks with the following words you have learned in the text. Change the forms where necessary.

| impart | heterogeneous | aristocracy | articulate | beleaguer |
| albeit | inconsistency | preliminary | estrange | intelligible |

1) Being able to clearly _____ a differing perspective should be central to your business plan.
2) Her presence _____ an air of elegance to the ceremony.
3) Some other Asians believe that because Asia is so big and _____ there is no set of values which are shared by all Asians.
4) For starters, the _____ financials should finally begin contributing to the earnings recovery.
5) There was a great _____ between what he said and what he did.

6) There are a lot of _____ to be gone through before you can visit foreign countries.
7) Historically, China's minority nationalities have been _____ to a high degree from the Han nationality.
8) I tried, _____ unsuccessfully, to contact him.
9) His lecture was readily _____ to all the students.
10) Many members of the _____ were guillotined in France during the Revolution.

2. Proofreading & Error Correction.

  Although the Norman French borrowings were very significant, expanded the total recorded vocabulary of English from about 35,000 to 45,000 words, that number seems small when compared the influx of words that was to come. Under the reign of the Tudors, culminating with Elizabeth I, English really came into its own as a language of culture and literature. With the advent of the printing press, inventing by Gutenberg in 1452 and brought to England by Caxton in 1476, literacy in a wide scale became possible, and a much larger population began to write books as well as to read them.

  The Renaissance was a period of renewed interest in classic Greek and Roman culture, and the huge collection of learning they had amassed. In the Renaissance, any university-educated man was familiar to both Greek and Latin, and would often choose to write in the later. Newton, for example, composed of his *Principia Mathematica* entirely in Latin (although his later work *Opticks* was in English). Writers who are now considered masters of English prose or poetry, like John Milton and John Donne, also wrote in Latin. Scholars associated literary and rhetorical excellence with Latin, the standard educating language of Europe.

1) _____
2) _____
3) _____
4) _____
5) _____
6) _____
7) _____
8) _____
9) _____
10) _____

3. Translate the following paragraph into Chinese.

  The majority of words in modern English come from foreign, not Old English roots. In fact, only about one sixth of the known Old English words have descendants surviving today. But this is deceptive; Old English is much more important than these statistics would indicate. About half of the most commonly used words in modern English have Old English roots. Words like *be, water,* and *strong,* for example, derive from Old English roots.

Comprehensive Work

1. **Here is a sample text chosen from the *Declaration of Independence*. Work in a group and pick out all the words of Greek or Latin origin from the text. What insight does this give you about borrowings from Greek and Latin?**

   When in the course of human events, it becomes necessary for one people to dissolve the political bonds which have connected them with another, and assume among the powers of the earth separate and equal station to which the laws of nature and nature's God entitle them, a decent respect to the opinions of mankind requires that they should declare the causes which impel them to the separation.

2. **Writing**

   Ungelivable and *gelivable* are newly-coined words by Chinese internet users. Why do Chinese people coin such English words? What does it indicate?

   _____
   _____
   _____

Read More

Text B The Growth of Present-Day English Vocabulary

Since the beginning of 20th century, particularly after World War II, the world has seen breathtaking advances in science and technology. As a result, thousands and thousands of new words have been created to express new ideas, inventions, and scientific achievements. Although borrowing remained an important channel of vocabulary expansion, yet more words are created by means of word-formation.

In fact English has adopted words from almost every known language in the course of its historical development. This has made the English vocabulary extremely rich and heterogeneous. English is supposed to have the most copious vocabulary of all the languages, estimated at more than a million words. It is also noted for its wealth of synonyms and idioms, a fact no doubt due to its sharing so many common words with other languages.

After World War II, neologisms sweep in at a rate much faster than any other historical period. The main reasons for the frequent appearance of neologisms are three:

Marked progress of science and technology: Since the end of World War II, tremendous new advances in all fields of science and technology have given rise to the creation in the English language of tens of thousands of new words. The great majority of these are technical terms known only to the specialists, but a certain number of them have become familiar to the public and passed into general use, like words used in connection with the nuclear bomb: *chain reaction, radioactivity, fall-out, clean bomb, overkill, neutron bomb* and *medium–range ballistic missile* and so on; and words connected with the exploration of space: *astronaut, countdown, capsule, launching pad, spaceman, space suit, space platform* and *space shuttle*, etc.

Socio–economic, political and cultural changes: These changes necessitate the introduction of new words: words that connect with new social habits and new living conditions, like *hire purchase*, *credit card*, *fringe benefit*, *chore*, *house sitter*, *house sitting*, *pressure cooker*, *microwave oven*, *instant noodle*, *supermarket*, etc; drug addiction, like *upper*, *downer*, etc.; some subculture, like *hippie*, *yuppie*, *gay*, *lesbian*, etc; Women's Liberation Movement, like *Ms*, *chairperson*, *spokeswoman*, *saleswoman*, *feminism*, *male chauvinism*, and *sexism* as well as changes in education, like *open classroom*, *Open University*, etc.

The influence of other cultures and languages: English is characterized by a marked tendency to go outside her own linguistic resources and borrow from other languages. Although this borrowing has slowed down, it is still an important factor in vocabulary development. For example, *discotheque* from French, *sputnik* from Russian, *mao tai* from Chinese and so on.

The development of science, the rapid changes in society, the receptive and flexible nature of English with regard to the influence of other cultures and languages—all these have resulted in a dramatic increase in vocabulary, the development mode of which can be divided into three kinds: creation of roots, affixes and other elements, e.g. *supercomputer*, *workaholic*; semantic change, i.e., old form + new meaning, such as *break*, *web*, *mouse*; and borrowing, which is also known as loaned word. Reviving archaic or obsolete words also contributes to the growth of English vocabulary though quite insignificant. They all in turn contribute to the richness and resourcefulness of the English language.

Indeed, English has now inarguably achieved global status. Whenever we turn on the news to find out what's happening in East Asia, or the Balkans, or Africa, or South America, or practically anywhere, local people are being interviewed and telling us about it in English. According to the *Ethnologue: Languages of the World*, English is one of approximately 6,900 living languages in the world and many of these languages have relatively few speakers; a small subset of them is widely spoken. The table below lists some of the most commonly spoken languages, and the number of individuals who speak them as a first or second language. Figures in this table are given in millions and are based on information in *Gordon* (2005), *the World Almanac, and Wikipedia*'s "List of Languages by Number of Native Speakers."

Most Widely Spoken Languages			
Language	First Language Speakers	Second Language Speakers	Total
Chinese (Mandarin)	873 (83%)	178 (17%)	1,051
English	340 (25–40%)	500–1,000 (60–75%)	840–1,340
Hindi	370 (76%)	120 (24%)	490
Spanish	360 (86%)	60 (14%)	420
Russian	167 (60%)	110 (40%)	277
Arabic (standard)	206 (90%)	24 (10%)	230
Portuguese	203 (95%)	10 (5%)	213
Bengali	207 (98%)	4 (2%)	211

Most Widely Spoken Languages			
Language	First Language Speakers	Second Language Speakers	Total
Indonesian	23 (14%)	140 (86%)	163
Japanese	126 (99%)	1 (1%)	127
German	95 (77%)	28 (23%)	123
French	65 (57%)	50 (43%)	115

It is important to remember, however, that the widespread use of English has little to do with the language itself but more with the fact that British colonization spread English around the world, a phenomenon that was followed by the emergence of the United States (which has the highest percentage of native speakers) as a political and economic force. Had world events been different, English might be still a language spoken only in Great Britain, where it had its origins over 1,500 years ago.

Questions for Discussion or Reflection
1. What are the reasons for the frequent appearance of neologisms?
2. What are the three kinds of development modes of the English vocabulary?
3. Why is the English language widely spoken?

Text C A Brief History of English

The language we call English was first brought to the North Sea coasts of England in the 5th and 6th centuries A.D., by seafaring people from Denmark and the northwestern coasts of present-day Germany and the Netherlands. These immigrants spoke a cluster of related dialects falling within the Germanic branch of the Indo-European language family. Their language began to develop its own distinctive features in isolation from the continental Germanic languages, and by 600 AD had developed into what we call Old English or Anglo-Saxon, covering the territory of most of modern England.

New waves of Germanic invaders and settlers came from Norway and Denmark starting in the late 8th century. The more violent of these were known as Vikings, sea-faring plunderers who retained their ancient pagan gods and attacked settlements and churches for gold and silver. They spoke a northern Germanic dialect similar to, yet different in grammar from Anglo-Saxon. In the 11th century, the attacks became organized, state-sponsored military invasions and England was even ruled for a time by the kings of Denmark and Norway. The Scandinavian influence on the language was strongest in the north and lasted for a full 600 years, although English seems to have been adopted by the settlers fairly early on.

The Norman Invasion and Conquest of 1066 was a cataclysmic event that brought new rulers and new cultural, social and linguistic influences to the British Isles. The Norman French ruling minority dominated the church, government, legal, and educational systems for three centuries. The Norman establishment used French and Latin, leaving English as the language of the illiterate and powerless majority. During this period English adopted thousands of words from Norman French and from Latin, and its grammar changed rather radically. By the end of that time, however, the aristocracy had adopted English as their language and the use and importance of French gradually faded. The period from the Conquest to the reemergence of English as a full-fledged literary language is called Middle English. Geoffrey Chaucer wrote his masterpiece, *The Canterbury Tales*, in Middle English in the late 1300s.

William Caxton set up the first printing press in Britain at the end of the 15th century. The arrival of printing marks the point at which the language began to take the first steps toward standardization and its eventual role as a national language. The period from 1500 to about 1650 is called Early Modern English, a period during which notable sound changes, syntactic changes and lexical enrichment took place. The Great English Vowel Shift, which systematically shifted the phonetic values of all the long vowels in English, occurred during this period. Word order became more fixed in a subject-verb-object pattern, and English developed a complex auxiliary verb system. A rush of new vocabulary from the classical languages, the modern European languages, and more distant trading partners such as the countries of Asian minor and the Middle East entered the language as the renaissance influences of culture and trade and the emerging scientific community of Europe took root in England.

Shakespeare wrote prolifically during the late 1500s and early 1600s and, like Chaucer, took the language into new and creative literary territory. His influence on English drama and poetry continued to grow after his death in 1616 and he has never been surpassed as the best known and most read poet/playwright of modern English.

The King James Bible was published in 1611, the culmination of at least a century of efforts to bring a Bible written in the native language of the people into the Church establishment and into people's homes. Among the common people, whose contact with literature often did not go far past the Bible, the language of the scriptures as presented in this version commissioned by King James I was deeply influential, due in part to its religious significance, but also to its literary quality. Its simple style and use of native vocabulary had a surpassing beauty that still resonates today.

By the 1700s almost all of the modern syntactic patterns of English were in place and the language is easily readable by modern speakers. Colonization of new territories by the newly united Kingdom of Great Britain spread English to the far corners of the globe and brought cargoes of still more loanwords from those far-flung places. At this point English began to develop its major world dialectal varieties, some of which would develop into national standards for newly independent colonies. By the 21st century, as the language of international business, science, and popular culture, English has become the most important language on the planet.

Exercises

Fill in the blanks with the details from the text.

1. The Norman Invasion and Conquest of _____ was a cataclysmic event that brought new rulers and new cultural, social and linguistic influences to the British Isles.
2. Geoffrey Chaucer wrote his masterpiece, _____, in Middle English in the late 1300s.
3. _____ set up the first printing press in Britain at the end of the 15th century.
4. _____ has never been surpassed as the best known and most read poet/playwright of modern English.
5. Published in 1611, _____ was brought into people's homes because of its simple style and use of native vocabulary.

For Fun

Works to Read

1. *A History of the English Language* by Albert Croll Baugh and Thomas Cable

    This classic exploration of the history of the English language combines internal linguistic history and external cultural history—from the Middle Ages to the present. Students are encouraged to develop both an understanding of present-day English and an enlightened attitude toward questions affecting the language today.

2. *Language Change: Progress or Decay?* by Jean Aitchison

    This book gives a lucid and up-to-date overview of language change, discussing where our evidence about language change comes from, how and why changes happen, and how languages begin and end. It considers both changes that occurred long ago, and those currently in progress. The work remains nontechnical in style and accessible to the reader with no previous knowledge of linguistics.

Websites to Visit

1. http://www.wordorigins.org/

    This website is devoted to the origins of words and phrases. It is full of folklore and historical lessons.

2. http://takeourword.com/

    This is a fun website for browsing through and learning about etymologies in a more entertaining, less structured way.

Unit 3

Foreign Elements of English Vocabulary

> English is such a deliciously complex and undisciplined language, we can bend, fuse, distort words to all our purposes. We give old words new meanings, and we borrow new words from any language that intrudes into our intellectual environment.
> —— Dr. Willard Gaylin
>
> We don't just borrow words; on occasion, English has pursued other languages down alleyways to beat them unconscious and rifle their pockets for new vocabulary.
> —— Booker T. Washington

Unit Goals

- To understand the foreign elements in English vocabulary
- To be familiar with the distinction between native words and borrowed words
- To know Latin, Greek and French borrowings
- To have a glimpse of borrowings from other languages

 ### Before You Read

1. All the following English words are borrowed from other languages. Do you know the meanings and origins of them?

Word	Meaning	Origin
kindergarten		
marijuana		
Yamen		
tsunami		
mansion		
maneuver		
catastrophe		
concerto		

2. **List some words that you think are English borrowings. It's better to list some English words borrowed from your second foreign language. Share your word list with your classmates.**

Start to Read

Text A The Sources of English Vocabulary

Ordinarily we pay little attention to the words we speak. We concentrate instead on the meaning we intend to express and are seldom conscious of how we express that meaning. Only if we make a mistake and have to correct it or have difficulty remembering a word do we become conscious of our words. This means that most of us don't know where the words we use come from and how they come to have the meanings they do. Since words play such an important role in our lives, making our life easy or difficult depending on which words we choose on a given occasion, exploring their nature and origin should provide an interesting adventure.

English words come from several different sources. They develop naturally over the course of centuries from ancestral languages, they are also borrowed from other languages, and we create many of them by various means of word formation. Each of these sources have made a material impact on the vocabulary available to us today.

It has been estimated, however, that the present English vocabulary consists of more than 1 million words, including slang and dialect expressions and scientific and technical terms, many of which only came into use after the middle of the 20th century. The English vocabulary is more extensive than that of any other language in the world, although some other languages—Chinese, for example—have a word-building capacity equal to that of English.

Internal processes have led to the creation of many new words as well as to the establishment of patterns for further expansion. For example, the process of onomatopoeia, or the imitation of natural sounds, has created such words as *burp* and *beeper*. Affixation, or the addition of prefixes and suffixes, such as *mis-*, *ex-*, *-ness*, and *-ist*, has given English such words as *mislead*, *exchange*, *forgetfulness*, and *machinist*. The process of blending parts of words produces new words such as in *brunch*, composed of parts of *breakfast* and *lunch*. The formation of compounds yields such words as *lighthouse* and *downpour*. These processes that have probably added the largest number of words to English are derivation and conversion.

Throughout its history English has come into contact with a great number of languages. Extensive and constant borrowing from every major language—especially from Latin, Greek, French, and the Scandinavian languages—has also provided numerous words.

In some occasions, the idea to be named already exists in other cultures by speakers of other languages. The easiest way of appropriating the idea so that it can be discussed in English is to borrow the word, and the word is then a **loan-word** in English.

The Anglo–Saxon Base

Germanic settler tribes (Angles, Saxons, Jutes and Frisians) entered Britain in 449 AD onwards and displaced the original Celtic-speaking inhabitants. If we can assume that the lexicon reflects the preoccupations of the language users, we would not be surprised that the original Anglo-Saxon lexicon is concerned about basic, down-to-earth matters. The Anglo-Saxons were originally not a settled group; there was a settled civilization, but not very literate or sophisticated.

Many of the words are still used today. Some are grammatical words (such as *be, in, that*) while others are lexical words (*sing, live, go*). Anglo-Saxon words are usually short and concrete. Although Anglo-Saxon lexemes form only a relatively small proportion of the modern lexicon, in any passage of English, there is a relatively high density of Anglo-Saxon-derived lexemes, and indeed the 100 most frequently used items are almost all Anglo-Saxon.

There are a number of items that pertain to down-to-earth, everyday matters. Many of the words that we described as "core" earlier seem to be from Anglo-Saxon. These words are of parts of the body (*arm, bone, chest, ear, eye, foot, hand, heart*), the natural environment (*field, hedge, hill, land, meadow, wood*), the domestic life (*door, floor, home, house*), the calendar (*day, month, moon, sun, year*), animals (*cow, dog, fish, goat, hen, sheep, swine*), common adjectives (*black, dark, good, long, white, wide*) and common verbs (*become, do, eat, fly, go, help, kiss, live, love, say, see, sell, send, think*).

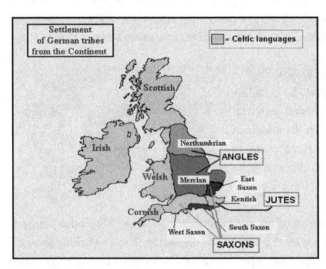

Celtic Borrowings

When the Anglo-Saxons took control of Britain, the original Celts moved to the northern and western fringes of the island. This explains why the only places where Celtic languages are spoken in Britain today are in the west (Welsh in Wales) and north (Scottish Gaelic in the Scottish Highlands). Celtic speakers seem to have been kept separate from the Anglo-Saxon speakers. Those who remained in other parts of Britain must have merged in with the Anglo-Saxons. The end result is a surprising small number of Celtic borrowings. Some of them are dialectal such as *cumb* (deep valley) or *loch* (lake). Reminders of Britain's Celtic past are mainly in the form of Celtic-based place names including river names such as *Avon, Severn* and *Thames*. Town names include *Kent, Leeds, London* and *York*.

Scandinavian Borrowings

The Scandinavian influence on Britain can be thought of in terms of three episodes.

Firstly, we can think of the period 750–1016 when the Vikings (Scandinavians) began attacking the northern and eastern shores of Britain and settling in those parts of Britain. There was a state of enmity between the Anglo-Saxons and the Vikings, so unsurprisingly, not many Scandinavian borrowings took place; these include *husbonda* (husband) and *lagu* (law).

Secondly, we can consider the period 1016–1050, where the conditions were more or less similar to the earlier period, only that King Alfred the Great had succeeded in uniting the Anglo-Saxons through actively promoting the English language (among other things). There were more borrowings, including *cnif* (knife) and *diegan* (die).

Finally, we have the period 1050–1480. The French-speaking Normans took over Britain in 1066, and both the English and Scandinavians were given the same fate and were subdued by the Normans. Naturally, the English and the Scandinavians came together and interacted with each other more closely. Therefore, there is a massive influence of the Scandinavian languages on English, in both grammar and vocabulary.

Unless you are a specialist, it is very difficult to pick out Scandinavian loan-words in English. This is because they seem to have the same quality and texture as Anglo-Saxon words. They are ordinary, everyday words, and quite often monosyllabic and include grammatical words (like the verb *are*, or the pronouns *their, them* and *they*) and some of the commonest words in English today (like *bag, dirt, fog, knife, flat, low, odd, ugly, want, trust, get, give, take, raise, smile* and *though*). A good number of *sc-* or *sk-* words today are of Scandinavian origin (*scathe, scorch, score, scowl, scrape, scrub, skill, skin, skirt, sky*). Scandinavian loan-words are therefore more usefully considered as core items. Why is this so?

- The English and Scandinavian belong to the same Germanic racial, cultural and linguistic stock originally and their language, therefore, shared common grammatical features and words. But changes had occurred in the languages during the couple of centuries of separation of the two sets of people.
- The Scandinavians came to settle, rather than conquer or pillage. They lived alongside the Anglo-Saxons on more or less equal terms.
- Under the Norman French, particularly, the two different groups fashioned a common life together as subjects.

Under these conditions,

a. the English word sometimes displaces the cognate Scandinavian word: *fish* instead of *fisk; goat* instead of *gayte*;

b. the Scandinavian word sometimes displaces the cognate English word: *egg* instead of *ey, sister* instead of *sweoster*;

c. both might remain, but with somewhat different meanings: *dike–ditch, hale–whole, raise–rise, sick–ill, skill–craft, skirt–shirt*;

d. the English word might remain, but takes on the Scandinavian meaning: dream (originally "joy" "mirth" "music" "revelry").

After You Read

Knowledge Focus

1. Below is a list of terms mentioned in the text. Work with your partner to provide two examples to each term and then match each term with its corresponding definition.

	Terms	Examples	Definition
1)	Dialects		A. Combining parts of words to produce a new word
2)	Cognates		B. Addition of prefixes or suffixes
3)	Onomatopoeia		C. Words that share the same origin
4)	Affixation		D. Variants of a language
5)	Blending		E. Borrowed words
6)	Loan words		F. Imitation of natural sounds

2. **Tell whether the following statements are true or false according to the knowledge you learned and why.**
   1) The processes that have probably added the largest number of words to English are derivation and blending. (   )
   2) The word *brunch* is an example of the formation of compounding. (   )
   3) The original Anglo-Saxon lexicon is concerned about basic, down-to-earth matters. (   )
   4) Many of the original Anglo-Saxon words are still used today. Some are lexical words (such as *be, in, that*) while others are grammatical word (*sing, live, go*). (   )
   5) The only places where Celtic languages are spoken in Britain today are in the east and north. (   )
   6) More Scandinavian borrowings took place during the period 750–1016 than 1050–1480. (   )
   7) The Scandinavian languages have a massive influence on English largely due to the Norman Conquest of 1066. (   )
   8) Both Anglo-Saxon words and Scandinavian loan-words in English are ordinary, everyday words, and quite often monosyllabic and include grammatical words and some of the commonest words in English today. (   )
   9) Many Scandinavian words displaced the cognate English words, but not vice versa. (   )
   10) A good number of *sc-* or *sk-* words today are of French origin. (   )

3. **Identify the mutual cognates in English and German.**

German	Meaning	English Cognate
Feder	bird covering	
Milch	white baby food	
Brennen	to consume by fire	
Haar	head fluff	
Blut	red body liquid	
Fuss	lower body part	
Mutter	female parent	
Machen	create something	
Wasser	basic liquid	

Language Focus

1. Fill in the blanks with the following words you have learned in the text. Change the forms where necessary.

| enmity | obsolete | sophisticated | pertain | merge |
| yield | density | appropriate | subdue | pillage |

1) Our research has only recently begun to _____ important results.
2) I'm afraid that your remark does not _____ to the question.
3) Some of the opposition party's policies have been _____ by the government.
4) Police managed to _____ the angry crowd.
5) We can _____ our two small businesses together into one larger one.
6) The horse-drawn plow is now _____ in most European countries.
7) The town had been _____ and burned.
8) Mark is a smart and _____ young man.
9) Personal _____ must be forgotten at a time of national crisis.
10) These forests are largely intact because of low population _____ and poor accessibility.

2. Proofreading & Error Correction.

Loanwords are words adapted by the speakers of one language from a different language (the source language). A loanword can also be called a borrowing. The abstract noun borrowing refers to the process of speakers adopted words from a source language into their native language.

Borrowing is a consequence of cultural contact between two language societies. Borrowing of words can go in all directions between the two languages in contact, because often there is an asymmetry, such that more words go from one side to the other. In this case the source language community has some advantage of power, prestige and/or wealth that makes the objects and ideas it brings undesirable and useful to the borrowing language community. For example, the Germanic tribes in the first few centuries adopted numeral loanwords from Latin whereas they adopted new products via trade with the Romans. Few Germanic words, on the one hand, passed into Latin.

The actual process of borrowing is complex and involves many usage events. Generally, some speakers of the borrowing language know the source language too, or at least enough of it to

1) _____
2) _____
3) _____
4) _____
5) _____
6) _____
7) _____
8) _____
9) _____

utilize the relevant word. They adopt the new word when speaking the borrowing language, because it most exactly fits the idea they are trying to express. If they are bilingual in the source language, that is often the case, they might pronounce the words the same or similar to the way they are pronounced in the source language.

10) _____

3. Translate the following paragraph into Chinese.

When the Anglo-Saxons took control of Britain, the original Celts moved to the northern and western fringes of the island, which is why the only places where Celtic languages are spoken in Britain today are in the west (Welsh in Wales) and north (Scottish Gaelic in the Scottish Highlands). Celtic speakers seem to have been kept separate from the Anglo-Saxon speakers. Those who remained in other parts of Britain must have merged in with the Anglo-Saxons. The end result is a surprising small number of Celtic borrowings.

Comprehensive Work
Discussion & Writing

Work in a group. Choose one topic to discuss and write a report after your investigation and exploration.

1. Major influence of a particular language on English.
- Choose one of the languages from which English has borrowed considerable numbers of words (French, Old Scandinavian, Latin or Greek).
- Discuss the set(s) of loanwords taken from this language into English, and the social and cultural contact that was the backdrop to this influence. (If there was more than one period of major influence, you can either concentrate on a particular period or discuss the influence of the language through various periods of history).
- Consider aspects such as relative status of the languages in contact, differences in sphere of usage of the languages in the society, particular cultural or institutional domains in which influence was greatest, and any other interesting aspects of the contact you can think of (e.g. parallels with language contact more recently in history).

2. Loanwords from lesser-known sources.
- Write about loanwords from a language or language family that is not one of the major sources of borrowings in English. For example, what Arabic loanwords does English have, and how did they get into the language?
- Describe the cultural connections that facilitated the borrowing of the loanwords (in more than one period if there is more than one layer of borrowing from the language).
- Kinds of information you might give include observations on typical forms and changes in forms, particular interesting etymologies, etc.
- Loanword source languages worth investigating include Arabic, Japanese, Sanskrit/Hindi, American Indian languages, African languages, Chinese, other languages you know.

3. **English loanwords in Chinese**
   - Find some examples of English loanwords in Chinese. (e.g. *romance, marathon, cocaine, rifle, golf, milkshake, hippies,* etc.)
   - Discuss the pros and cons of borrowing English words into Chinese.
   - Do you think some incorrect or non-standard usage of English loanwords in Chinese could bring about misunderstanding or inconvenience? Do you think it could be named "language pollution"? Justify your opinion.

Read More

Text B Latin and Greek Borrowings

Latin Borrowings

Latin, being the language of the Roman Empire, had already influenced the language of the Germanic tribes even before they set foot in Britain. Latin loanwords reflected the superior material culture of the Roman Empire, which had spread across Europe: *street, wall, candle, chalk, inch, pound, port, camp.*

The native Celts had also learned some Latin, and some of these were borrowed by the Anglo-Saxons in Britain: *sign, pearl, anchor, oil, chest, pear, lettuce.*

Latin was also the language of Christianity, and St Augustine arrived in Britain in 597 AD to christianise the nation. Terms in religion were borrowed: *pope, bishop, monk, nun, cleric, demon, disciple, mass, priest, shrine.* Christianity also brought with it learning: *not* (note), *paper, scol* (school).

Many Latin borrowings came in during the early Modern English period. Sometimes, it is difficult to say whether the loan-words were direct borrowings from Latin or had come in through French (because, after all, Latin was also the language of learning among the French). One great motivation for the borrowings was the change in social order, where scientific and philosophical empiricism was beginning to be valued. Many of the new words are academic in nature therefore: *affidavit, apparatus, caveat, corpuscle, compendium, equilibrium, equinox, formula, inertia, incubate, momentum, molecule, pendulum, premium, stimulus, subtract, vaccinate, vacuum.* This resulted in the distinction between learned and popular vocabulary in English.

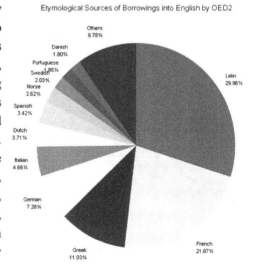

Greek Borrowings

Greek was also a language of learning, and Latin itself borrowed words from Greek. Indeed the Latin alphabet is an adaptation of the Greek alphabet.

Many of the Greek loan-words were through other languages: through French—*agony, aristocracy, enthusiasm, metaphor*; through Latin—*ambrosia, nectar, phenomenon, rhapsody*. There were some general vocabulary items like *fantasy, cathedral, charismatic, idiosyncrasy* as well as more technical vocabulary like *anatomy, barometer, microscope, homoeopathy*.

During the Renaissance and after, there were modern coinages from Greek elements (rather than borrowings). For example, *photo–* yielded *photograph, photogenic, photolysis* and *photokinesis*; *bio–* yielded *biology, biogenesis, biometry, bioscope*; *tele–* yielded *telephone, telepathy, telegraphic, telescopic*. Other Greek elements used to coin new words include *crypto–, hydro–, hyper–, hypo–, neo–* and *stereo–*.

Exercises

Figure out the meanings of the word roots in the table below. They have all been borrowed, directly or indirectly (via French), from Greek and Latin. Think about the meanings that all the examples have in common.

Examples	Meaning
scribe, in**scribe**, **scrib**ble, **scrip**ture	
temporal, **temp**orary, con**temp**orary	
solar, **sol**arium, **sol**stice	
cardinal, **card**iac, **cord**ial, ac**cord**	
vision, **vis**ual, in**vis**ible, tele**vis**ion	
dental, **dent**ist, **dent**ifrice, **dent**ate	
octopus, **oct**agon, **oct**ette, **Oct**ober	
population, **popul**ar, **popul**ous	

Text C French Borrowings

The Norman Conquest of 1066 left England as a trilingual country, although most people would only speak one or two of the dominant languages. Latin was the language for record keeping, learning and the church. French was the language of the Norman aristocracy and therefore also the language of prestige, government and polite social intercourse. English was the language of the common folk and menials.

When the Normans took over England, they changed the language of government and the court almost overnight and disregarded existing institutions. Instead, they took on almost wholesale institutions derived from France, including the feudal system which guaranteed strong control by the king.

There were three periods of French borrowings. The first, from about 1066 to 1250 represents the height of Norman power. The language spoken by the Normans, known as Norman French was the language of the King's court, the nobles' castles and the courts of law. Norman French was therefore the language of honour, chivalry and justice. Indeed, Matthew of Westminster said, "Whoever was unable to speak French was considered a vile and contemptible person by the common people." There were not many French borrowings, since English continues to be used, largely in its own, low-level arenas and French and English speakers were kept separate.

The second period, roughly from 1250 to 1400 represents the period of English-French bilingualism in individuals. The number of French loanwords ballooned in this period.

In 1204, Normandy was acquired by the French king. Among other things, it meant that the Norman aristocracy in England couldn't travel back and forth between their lands in England and France anymore. They had to choose whether they wanted to remain in England or in France. Those who remained in England began to see England as their home. This led to the reassertion of English as the language of the realm. Other reasons for the reassertion of English are:

- The Normans in England belonged to the Capetian dynasty spoke Norman French; this became non-prestigious in France as the variety spoken by the Angevin dynasty in France, Parisian French, became the prestige variety; because Norman French was seen as socially inferior, it was less difficult to abandon it in favour of English;
- Subsequently, England became at war with France in the Hundred Years War (1337–1453).

Even as English was on its way, the gaps in English vocabulary had to be filled by loanwords from French. These include items pertaining to new experiences and ways of doing things introduced by the Normans. So while the English already had *kings*, *queens* and *earls*, terms taken from French include *count*, *countess*, *sire*, *madam*, *duke*, *marquis*, *dauphin*, *viscount*, *baron*, *chevalier*, *servant* and *master*. Other domains that became enriched with French loanwords include:

- Government: *country, crown, government, parliament, chancellor*
- Finance: *treasure, wage, poverty*
- Law: *attorney, plaintiff, larceny, fraud, jury, verdict*
- War: *battle, army, castle, tower, siege, banner*
- Religion: *miracle, charity, saint, pardon*
- Morality: *virtue, vice, gentle, patience, courage, mercy, courtesy, pity*
- Recreation: *falcon, covert, scent, chase, quarry*
- Art and fashion: *apparel, costume, gown, art, beauty, colour, image, design, cushion, tapestry*
- Cuisine: *stew, grill, roast, bacon, mutton, pork, veal, venison*
- Household Relationships: *uncle, aunt, nephew, cousin*

The third period of the French borrowings is from around 1400 onwards. The borrowings of the first two periods tend to be more elegant and sophisticated but yet not too far away from the core and several became quite native (*dance, April, native, fine, line, punish, finish*). The later borrowings were more distant from the core, with attention being 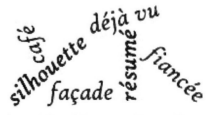 explicitly called to their sophisticated, well-bred, cultivated, even arty "French" texture. The spellings and pronunciations of such words as *ballet, tableau, statuesque, cliché, motif, format, trousseau, lingerie, soufflé, hors d'oeuvre, rouge*, and *etiquette* are very much French.

Exercises

Fill in the missing information in the following chart to summarize the three periods of French borrowings illustrated in the text.

Period	Time	Features
1	1066 to 1250	
2	1250 to 1400	
3	1400 onwards	

Text D Borrowings from Other Languages

Although English owes its greatest lexical debt to Greek and Latin, it has borrowed generously from other languages as well: Scandinavian, Hindi, Yiddish, various East European languages and, of course, North American native languages.

The long colonial rule of the British in India not only developed the British palate for tea, it resulted in the import of many words from Hindi and the other languages of India, such as *cummerbund*, *punch*, *shampoo*, and *thug*. Arabic has contributed several words to English, such as *algebra*, *alcohol*, *assassin*, *mosque*, and *orange*. The Slavic nations (Russia, Czech Republic, Poland, etc.) have also made a contribution through the millions of immigrants to the English-speaking nations from that part of Europe. Here are a few: *commissar*, *polka*, *robot*, *troika*, *tsar*, and *vodka*. Word borrowings for Yiddish are not widely used but they are common in the dialects around New York. A few of them are *knish*, *kvetch*, *-nik* (as in *peacenik*, a suffix meaning "-er, -ist"), and *schlep*.

English has also borrowed from Italian, especially musical and culinary terms. The English-speaking peoples have a special place on their menus for Italian food, so much so that words like *spaghetti* and *macaroni* seem like native words now. The same is true of *piano*, *cello*, and *maestro*. The following words were all taken from the Italian language: *bimbo*, *broccoli*, *violoncello*, *opera*, *maestro*, *minestrone*, *pasta*, and *pizza*.

In North America, English borrowed from Native American languages many words in the semantic fields of artefacts (e.g. *wampum* and *toboggan*) and animals (e.g. *caribou* and *coyote*). But an even more important group of loans was the place names (e.g. mountains like the *Appalachians* and the *Alleghenies*; the Great Lakes: *Erie*, *Ontario*, *Huron*, *Michigan* and *Superior*; and states, such as *Massachusetts* and *Oklahoma*).

As a result of empire and trade contacts, the lexicon of English continued to acquire terms from other languages including the following:

- Australian: *wallaby, kangaroo, boomerang*
- Arabic: *saffron, sequin, tamarind, alchemy, zenith*
- Persian: *naphtha, jasmine, chess, lilac*
- Japanese: *samurai, kimono, tsunami*
- Other Asian regions: *avatar, yoga, karma, curry, bangle, chop, catamaran, mandarin, ketchup, kowtow*

For Fun

Works to Read

1. ***English Vocabulary Elements*** by Keith Denning, Brett Kessler & William R. Leben

   This is the best introduction to the study of English words available. This linguistically-informed and highly readable text has a dual focus: on the one hand it systematically covers topics ranging from word formation and word analysis, to etymology, meaning change, and growth of the English vocabulary; at the same time, there is an emphasis throughout on developing word-awareness and on incremental vocabulary expansion.

2. ***Origins of the English Language*** by Joseph M. Williams

   This book highlights the history of the English language from the evolution of man clear through to Modern English that we speak today, providing enough knowledge for anyone to completely understand the origin of English.

Websites to Visit

1. http://www.krysstal.com/borrow.html

   This website is a collection of tables listing hundreds of English words borrowed from 146 languages.

2. http://www.macroevolution.net/root-word-dictionary.html#.VN3Oetx5JL4

   This website is one of the most comprehensive online dictionaries of word roots. Here, you will find the meanings of all the Greek and Latin root words commonly used in constructing biological and medical terminology.

3. http://www.collinsdictionary.com/words-and-language/word-origins/

   This website provides examples of loanwords from Arabic, French, Latin and other languages that will help you learn more about the origins of the English words.

Unit 4
Classification of English Vocabulary

> People say jargon is a bad thing, but it's really a shortcut vocabulary professionals use to understand one another.
> —— Erin McKean

Unit Goals

- To understand the differences between content words and function words
- To be familiar with the classification of English vocabulary
- To get to know some slang words in English
- To be able to use colloquial words in conversation

 Before You Read

1. Read the following stanza taken from "Ode on a Grecian Urn," and pick out the words that are no longer in current use. Are you able to understand these archaic words?

   Heard melodies are sweet, but those unheard
   Are sweeter; therefore, ye soft pipes, play on;
   Not to the sensual ear, but, more endeared,
   Pipe to the spirit ditties of no tone.
   Fair youth, beneath the trees, thou canst not leave
   Thy song, nor ever can those trees be bare;
   Bold love, never, never canst thou kiss,
   Though winning near the goal—yet do not grieve:
   She cannot fade, though thou hast not thy bliss,
   For ever wilt thou love, and she be fair!

2. Guess the meanings of the underlined words.
   1) I am not going to work for <u>peanuts</u>.
      A. crazy people					B. agricultural companies
      C. very small amount of money
   2) This music is <u>groovy</u>.
      A. pleasant					B. bad
      C. latest
   3) It's a good exercise to strengthen your <u>abs</u>.
      A. abcd alphabets					B. abdominal muscles
      C. basic knowledge

4) Would you like your whiskey on the rocks?

A   B

5) My sister has three rugrats.

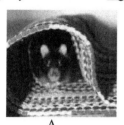   

A   B

Start to Read

Text A　Content Words and Function Words

The English vocabulary consists of different kinds of words, which may be classified according to different criteria. By notion, words can be classified into two categories—content words and function words.

Nouns, verbs, adjectives, adverbs, and numerals are the **content words**. These words denote concepts such as objects, actions, attributes, degree, quantity, and ideas that we can think about like *children*, *soar*, *fragile*, *gracefully*, and *seven*. Content words are sometimes called the **open class** words because we can and regularly do add new words to these classes. A new word, *steganography*, which is the art of hiding information in electronic text, entered English with the Internet revolution. Verbs like *disrespect* and *download* entered the language quite recently, as have nouns like *byte* and *email*.

There are other classes of words that do not have clear lexical meaning or obvious concepts associated with them, including conjunctions such as *and*, *or*, and *but*; prepositions such as *in* and *of*; the articles *the*, *a/an*, and pronouns such as *it* and *he*. These kinds of words are called **function words** because they have a grammatical function. For example, the articles indicate whether a noun is definite or indefinite—*the* boy or *a* boy. The preposition *of* indicates possession as in "the book *of* yours," but this word indicates many other kinds of relations, too.

Function words are sometimes called **closed class** words. It is difficult to think of new conjunctions, prepositions, or pronouns that have recently entered the language. The small set of personal pronouns such as *I*, *me*, *mine*, *he*, *she*, and so on are part of this class. With the growth of the feminist movement, some proposals have been made for adding a neutral singular pronoun that would be neither masculine nor feminine and that could be used as the general, or generic, form. If such a pronoun existed, it might have prevented the department chairperson in a large university from making the incongruous statement: "We will hire the best person for the job regardless of his sex." Others point out that *they* and *their* are already being used as neutral third-person singular forms, as in "Anyone can do it if *they* try hard enough" or "Everyone can do *their* best." The use of the various forms of *they* is standard on the BBC as pronoun replacements for *anyone* and *everyone*, which may be regarded as singular or plural.

Text B Stylistic Classification of the English Vocabulary

By level of usage, the English vocabulary can be classified into three main categories: common words, special literary words and special colloquial words.

1. Common Words

Common words consist of neutral words, common literary words, and common colloquial words.

Neutral words, which form the bulk of the English vocabulary, are used in both literary and colloquial language. Neutral words are the main source of synonymy and polysemy. It is the neutral stock of words that is so prolific in the production of new meanings.

Common literary words are chiefly used in writing and in polished speech. By contrast, **common colloquial words** are mainly used in spoken English, as in conversation among friends and colleagues.

The following synonyms illustrate the relations that exist between the neutral, literary and colloquial words in the English language:

Colloquial	Neutral	Literary
dad/ mom	father/ mother	parent
chap	fellow	associate
get out	go away	retire
go on	continue	proceed
teenager	boy/girl	youth
flapper	young girl	maiden
get going	start	commence

There are very few absolute synonyms in English just as there are in any language. The main distinction between synonyms remains stylistic. But stylistic difference may be of various kinds: it may lie in the emotional tension connoted in a word, or in the sphere of application, or in the degree of the quality denoted. Colloquial words are always more emotionally colored than literary ones. The neutral words, as the term itself implies, have no degree of emotiveness, nor have they any distinctions in the sphere of usage.

2. Special Literary Words

Special literary words consist of technical terms, poetical words, and archaic words.

Technical Terms

Technical terms or terminologies are mostly and predominantly used in special works dealing with the notions of particular disciplines and academic areas as in medicine: *hepatitis*, and *tuberculosis*, in chemistry: *pasteurization* and *melamine*, in mathematics: *calculus* and *factorial*, in music: *allegro* and *sonata*, in linguistic: *lexicology* and *semantics*, etc. Therefore, it may be said that technical terms belong to the style of academic  language. But their use is not confined to this style. They may as well appear in other styles—in newspaper style, and practically in all other existing styles of language. But their function in this case changes. They do not always fulfill their basic function of bearing exact reference to a given concept.

Here is an example of a moderate use of special terminology bordering on common literary vocabulary.

> There was a long conversation—a long wait. His father came back to say it was doubtful whether they could make the loan. Eight percent, then being secured for money, was a small rate of interest, considering its need.
>
> (Theodore Dreiser, *The Financier*)

Such terms as *loan* and *rate of interest* are widely known financial terms which to the majority of the English and American reading public need no explanation. It will suffice if the reader has a general idea of the actual meaning of the terms used.

Poetical Words

Poetical words are words that are traditionally used only in poetry. They are mostly archaic or very rarely used highly literary words which aim at producing an elevated effect. They have a marked tendency to detach themselves from the common literary word-stock and gradually assume the quality of terms denoting certain definite notions and calling forth poetic diction. Examples are as follows:

- He kneels at *morn* and noon and eve. (Samuel Taylor Coleridge "The Rime of the Ancient Mariner")
- Youths and maidens all *blithe* and full of glee, carried the luscious fruit in plaited baskets. (Homer, "The Iliad")
- Thus quietly thy summer goes,/ Thy days declining to *repose*. (Philip Freneau, "The Wild Honey Suckle")

In the above lines, *morn* "morning," *blithe* "happy," and *repose* "rest" are all poetical words. They are called upon to sustain the special elevated atmosphere of poetry. This may be said to be the main function of poetical words.

It must be remembered though, that not all English poetry makes use of poetical words, as they might be named. In the history of English literature there were periods which were characterized by protests against the use of such conventional symbols. The literature trends known as classicism and romanticism were particularly rich in fresh poetical words.

Archaic Words

The word-stock of a language is in an increasing state of change. Words change their meaning and sometimes drop out of the language altogether. New words spring up and replace the old ones.

Archaic words are primarily and predominantly used in the creation of a realistic background to historical novels. Besides, they are frequently to be found in the style of official documents. Among the obsolescent elements of the English vocabulary preserved within the style of official documents, the following may be mentioned: *aforesaid*, *hereby*, and *hereinafter*.

The function of archaic words and constructions in official documents is terminological in character. They are used here because they help to maintain that exactness of expression so necessary in this style.

It should be noted that some words are both archaic and poetical. The most common poetical archaic words are found in pronominal forms:

2nd Person	Nominative	Objective	Possessive	Possessive
singular	*thou* "you"	*thee* "you"	*thy* "your"	*thine* "yours"
plural	*ye* "you"			

3. Special Colloquial Words

Special colloquial words include slang and jargon.

Slang

There is hardly any other term that is as ambiguous and obscure as the term slang. Slang seems to mean everything that is below the standard of usage of present-day English.

The *New Oxford English Dictionary* defines slang as follows: a) the special vocabulary used by any set of persons of a low or disreputable character; language of a low and vulgar type; b) the cant or jargon of a certain class or period; c) language of a highly colloquial type considered as below the level of standard educated speech, and consisting either of new words or of current words employed in some special sense.

We can find many examples of slang in teenagers' dialogues. Girls and boys in Britain like to create their own world of words. Here are two examples:

a. Crumbs! That girl is really choong, blud.

b. Safe, man! You're looking buff in your fresh creps.

In order to fully understand the above two sentences, we must know the neutral equivalents of some slang words:

crumbs – wow

choong; *buff* – attractive

blud; *man* – friend

safe – hi

creps – trainers

Now let's look at the same sentences with common words:

a. Wow! That girl is really attractive, friend.

b. Hi, friend! You're looking attractive in your fresh trainers.

Jargon

Jargon is a recognized term for a group of words that exists in almost every language and whose aim is to preserve secrecy within one or another social group. They are generally old words with entirely new meanings imposed on them. They may be defined as a code within a code, that is, special meanings of words that are imposed on the recognized code—the dictionary meaning of the words. Thus the word *grease* means "money"; *loaf* means "head"; *a tiger hunter* is "a gambler"; *a lexer* is "a student preparing for a law course".

In Britain and in the US almost any social group of people has its own jargon. The following jargon is well known in the English language: the jargon of criminals, generally known as **cant** or **argot**; the jargon of jazz people; the jargon of the army, known as military slang; the jargon of sportsmen, and many others.

After You Read

Knowledge Focus

1. Discuss the following questions with your partner.
   1) By notion, how many categories can the English vocabulary be classified into? What are they?
   2) What kinds of words are content words?
   3) What kinds of words are function words?
   4) By level of usage, how many main categories can the English vocabulary be classified into? What are they?
   5) What is the function of technical terms?
   6) Why are archaic words used in official documents?
   7) What do special literary words consist of?
   8) What do special colloquial words include?
   9) What is slang?
   10) Why is jargon created?

2. Tell whether the following statements are true or false according to the knowledge you learned and why.
   1) Conjunctions are content words. (   )
   2) Function words do less work of expression in English on average than content words. (   )
   3) Function words can express the relation between notions, the relation between words as well as between sentences. (   )
   4) Content words are sometimes called closed class words. (   )
   5) Technical terms belong to common words. (   )
   6) The literature trends known as realism and naturalism were particularly rich in fresh poetical words. (   )
   7) Archaic words are frequently to be found in the style of official documents. (   )
   8) Archaic words are generally old words with entirely new meanings imposed on them. (   )

9) Slang refers to the specialized vocabularies by which members of particular arts, sciences, trades and professions communicate among themselves such as in business. (   )
10) From the definition in the *New Oxford English Dictionary*, slang is represented both as a special vocabulary and as a special language. (   )

3. **Mark the choice that can best complete the statement.**

   1) Words may fall into content words and function words by _____.
      A. use frequency   B. notion   C. origin   D. sound
   2) Content words denote clear notions and thus are known as _____ words. They include nouns, verbs, adjectives, adverbs and numerals.
      A. functional   B. notional   C. empty   D. formal
   3) Function words do not have notions of their own. Therefore, they are also called _____ words. Prepositions, conjunctions, auxiliaries and articles belong to this category.
      A. content   B. notional   C. empty   D. new
   4) In "What did you think about him," the word _____ is a content word.
      A. *think*   B. *you*   C. *about*   D. *him*
   5) In this sentence, "I don't like action movies. They're too violent," _____ is a function word.
      A. *action*   B. *movies*   C. *they*   D. *violent*
   6) Terminology consists of _____ terms used in particular disciplines and academic areas.
      A. technical   B. artistic   C. different   D. academic
   7) _____ refers to the specialized vocabularies by which members of particular arts, sciences, trades, and professions communicate among themselves.
      A. Slang   B. Jargon   C. Dialectal words   D. Argot
   8) _____ belongs to the sub-standard language, a category that seems to stand between the standard general words including informal ones available to everyone and in-group words.
      A. Jargon   B. Argot   C. Dialectal words   D. Slang
   9) Argot generally refers to the jargon of _____. Its use is confined to the sub-cultural groups and outsiders can hardly understand it.
      A. workers   B. criminals   C. businessmen   D. policemen
   10) Archaisms are words or forms that were once in _____ use but are now restricted only to specialized or limited use.
       A. common   B. little   C. slight   D. great

4. **Label the following words that you think are content words.**

Words	Yes	No
smile		
child		
and		
on		
the		
blue		

Words	Yes	No
slowly		
with		
hope		
if		

Language Focus

1. Fill in the blanks with the following words you have learned in the text. Change the forms where necessary.

denote	neutral	incongruous	predominantly	suffice
prolific	connote	demarcation	obsolescent	ambiguous

1) Electronic equipment quickly becomes _____.
2) The city's population is _____ Irish.
3) I shall not attempt to draw a precise line of _____ between the two methods.
4) "Look at those pretty little girls' dresses" is _____, because it is not clear whether the girls or the dresses are "pretty."
5) Picasso was extremely _____ during his Cubist years.
6) The British government acted as a _____ observer during the talks.
7) His private opinions were _____ with his public statements.
8) Very soon "Third World" came to _____ poverty.
9) In algebra, the sign x usually _____ an unknown quantity.
10) One example will _____ to illustrate the point.

2. Proofreading & Error Correction.

Archaisms are words which are no longer used in everyday speech, which have ousted by their synonyms. Archaisms remain in the language, but they are used as stylistic devices to express solemn. Most of these words are lexical archaisms and they are stylistic synonyms of words which ousted them from the neutral style. An archaism can be a word, a phrase, or the use of spelling, letters, or syntax that have passed out use. Because they are both common and dated, archaisms draw attention to themselves when using in general communication.

Writers of historical novels, as well as historians and film makers, for example, do his best to avoid unintentional archaisms. Creating a fictional character from times past may require extensive research of and knowledge of archaisms. An example of a fairly common archaism

1) _____

2) _____

3) _____
4) _____
5) _____

6) _____

7) _____

involves spelling and letters is businesses that include *Ye Olde* in their name. The word *Ye* does not actually start from a *y*, as it may appear; it begins with the letter *thorn* which has passed out of use. *Thorn* was a letter used to spelling the sound we now spell with the consonant digraph *th*. Hence, *Ye* is pronounced as and means *the*. *Olde* reflects a spelling from Middle English of the word we now write as *old*.

8) _____

9) _____

10) _____

3. Translate the following paragraph into Chinese.

Nouns, verbs, adjectives, adverbs, and numerals are the content words. These words denote concepts such as objects, actions, attributes, degree, quantity, and ideas that we can think about like *children*, *soar*, *fragile*, *gracefully*, and *seven*. Content words are sometimes called the open class words because we can and regularly do add new words to these classes. A new word, *steganography*, which is the art of hiding information in electronic text, entered English with the Internet revolution. Verbs like *disrespect* and *download* entered the language quite recently, as have nouns like *byte* and *email*.

Comprehensive Work
Discussion & Writing

The following are the lyrics of Eric Bogle's "The Silly Slang Song." Work in groups of four or five students, pick out the slang words in the song as many as you can and compare their original meanings with their modern meanings. Reflect on what happened to the English language. Is it a progress or a regress? Discuss with your group members and write an essay on it.

Do you remember the day when if you said that you were gay
It meant with joy, you could sing and shout
A fairy was enchanting and dressing up and camping
Was something you did with the Scouts
That carefree age when an urgent case of aids
Was powdered milk we sent to the Sahara.
A fruit was something nice to eat
A poof was something for your feet
And a queen was an old tart in a tiara
*Ah look what we've done to the old mother tongue
It's a crime the way we've misused it
It's been totally diswoggled, crumbed, blonged and golly-woggled

> And we've strangled, fangled, mangled and abused it*
> Ah those far off times when a bong meant a chime
> And a buzz was a noise insecticidal
> A joint was something between bones and getting really stoned
> Only happened to bad people in the Bible
> When if you had a bad trip it meant you fell and broke your hip
> Cold turkey just meant Christmas at Aunt Dottie's
> Coke was something that you burned
> Smack was something that you earned
> From your mumsy-wumsy when you had been naughty
> **
> The years have gone I'm afraid when only eggs got laid
> And only the rhinoceros got horny
> Only kangaroos jumped and only camels humped
> Getting stuffed meant a little taxidermy
> Swinging was for trapezes or Tarzan's chimpanzees
> Tossing off was something Scotland did with cabers
> Now it means something quite obscene
> And a heavy ugly scene
> Is any movie starring Arnold Schwarzenegger
> **
> They're only words, and words are what we use
> When we've got sod all to say

Read More

Text C Colloquialism in Literature

In literature, colloquialism is the use of informal words and phrases in a piece of writing.

Colloquial expressions tend to sneak in as writers, being part of a society, are influenced by the way people speak in that society. Naturally, they are bound to add colloquial expressions in their vocabulary. However, writers use such expressions intentionally too as it gives their works a sense of realism. For instance, in a fiction story depicting American society, a greeting "What's up?" between friends will seem more real and appropriate than the formal "How are you?" and "How do you do?".

John Donne uses colloquialisms in his poem "The Sun Rising":

> Busy old fool, unruly Sun,
> Why dost thou thus,
> Through windows, and through curtains, call on us?
> Must to thy motions lovers' seasons run?
> Saucy pedantic wretch, go chide
> Late school boys and sour prentices,

Go tell court huntsmen that the king will ride,
Call country ants to harvest offices,
Love, all alike, no season knows nor clime,
Nor hours, days, months, which are the rags of time.

The poet addresses the sun in an informal and colloquial way as if it were a real human being. He asks the sun in a rude manner why he had appeared and spoiled the good time he was having with his beloved. Not finishing there, he commands the "saucy pedantic sun" to go away.

The use of colloquial expressions can also be seen in *Burro Genius* by Victor Villasenor:

"I don't understand!" roared my father, putting his money back in his pocket. "Hell, I've forgotten more than you or most people will EVER UNDERSTAND!"

"Salvador," said my mother as quietly as she could, "why don't you and Mundo go outside and let me talk to this woman alone."

"Damn good idea!" said my father.

In this scene, the character Salvador uses colloquial words like "Hell" and "Damn" that gives insight into his aggressive and harsh nature. The idea of using colloquialisms is to put in diversity into the characters.

Yet another instance of colloquialism can be seen in *Of Mice and Men* by John Steinbeck:

"Sure I will, George. I won't say a word."

"Don't let him pull you in—but—if the son-of-a-bitch socks you—let 'im have it."

"Never mind, never mind. I'll tell you when. I hate that kind of guy. Look, Lennie, if you get in any kind of trouble, you remember what I told you to do?"

Lennie raised up on his elbow. His face contorted with thought. Then his eyes moved sadly to George's face. "If I get in any trouble, you ain't gonna let me tend the rabbits."

The above colloquial expressions are realistic enough as they are uttered by middle aged men of a working class who are not well educated and refined.

To sum up, colloquial expressions, in a piece of literature, may give us deep insights into the writer's society. They tell us about how people really talk in their real life. Therefore, they help a writer to form strong connections with readers. Colloquial expressions impart a sense of realism to a piece of literature which again attracts readers as they identify it with their real life.

Questions for Discussion and Reflection

1. What is colloquialism? Give examples.
2. What is the function of colloquialism in literature?
3. Can you think of other examples of colloquialism in literary works?
4. Can you use colloquialism to rewrite the following sentences?
   1) He was dismissed for stealing money from the till.
   2) She broke up with her boyfriend.
   3) What a stupid person I was to leave my suitcase on the train!

4) Just go away and leave me alone!
5) I've been feeling a little sad.

Text D The Importance of Function Words

In English there are about 500 function words, and about 150 are really common. Content words—nouns, verbs, adjectives, and most adverbs—convey the guts of communication. They are how we express ideas. Function words help shape and shortcut language. People require social skills to use and understand function words, and they are processed in the brain differently. They are the key to understanding relationships between speakers, objects, and other people. When we analyze people's use of function words, we can get a sense of their emotional state and personality, and their age and social class.

Pronouns tell us where people focus their attention. Take this simple, pronoun-heavy sentence "I don't think I buy it" as an example. Why did you say "I don't think I buy it" instead of "I don't buy it" or even "That's ridiculous"? If someone uses the pronoun *I*, it is a sign of self-focus. For instance, if someone asks "What's the weather outside," you could answer "It's hot" or "I think it's hot." The *I think* may seem insignificant, but it is quite meaningful. It shows you are more focused on yourself. Depressed people use the word *I* much more often than emotionally stable people. People who are lower in status use *I* much more frequently.

We can even tell if someone is lying by their use of function words. A person who is lying tends to use *we* more or use sentences without a first-person pronoun at all. Instead of saying "I didn't take your book," a liar might say "That's not the kind of thing that anyone with integrity would do". People who are honest use exclusive words like *but* and *without* and negations such as *no*, *none*, and *never* much more frequently.

There are gender differences in how people use function words. Most people think men use *I* more because men are more narcissistic and self-congratulatory. But across studies and cultures, we found that women use *I*, *me*, and *mine* more. Women are more self-attentive and aware of their internal state. Men use more articles: *a*, *an*, and *the*. That means men talk about objects and things more. They use articles when they are referring to concrete objects because articles precede concrete nouns. Women also use more third-person pronouns—*he*, *she*, and *they*—because women talk more about people and relationships, and they are better at managing them.

Questions for Discussion or Reflection
1. What kinds of people use the pronoun *I* more?
2. What are the differences between liars and honest people in respect of the use of function words?
3. What kind of function words men use more? What about women?

For Fun

Works to Read

1. ***500 Years of New Words*** by Bill Sherk

    This book takes you on an exciting journey through the English language from the days before Shakespeare to the first decade of the 21st century. All the main entries are arranged not alphabetically but in chronological order based on the earliest known year that each word was printed or written down.

2. ***The Secret Life of Pronouns: What Our Words Say about Us*** by James W. Pennebaker

    The smallest, most commonly used, most forgettable words serve as windows into our thoughts, emotions, and behaviors. The ways people use pronouns, articles, and other everyday words are linked to their personality, honesty, social skills, and intentions. Anyone who reads this book will become much more conscious about how he or she uses words when talking to friends, when talking to the public, or when writing for the public.

Websites to Visit

1. http://www.internetslang.com/
    On this website you will find a list of slang terms, acronyms and abbreviations as used in website, on Twitter, ICQ chat rooms, blogs, SMS and internet forums.
2. http://www.theofficelife.com/business-jargon-dictionary-A.html
    The website is the ridiculous business jargon dictionary. You may browse by letter.
3. http://www.waywordradio.org/dictionary-listing/?gclid=CNujnc7GxcMCFQ6maQodoaIAvw
    The website is a web lexicon of new words and fringe English.

Unit 5

Morphological Structure of English Vocabulary

> All the great things are simple, and many can be expressed in a single word: freedom, justice, honor, duty, mercy, hope.
> —— Winston Churchill

Unit Goals

- To understand the definitions of morpheme, allomorph, affix, and root
- To grasp the classification of morphemes
- To be familiar with the distinction between free morphemes and bound morphemes
- To comprehend how morphemes differ from phonemes and syllables
- To understand how the base differs from the stem and the root

 Before You Read

1. Can the following words be broken down into smaller units?

   1) airplane
   2) steamship
   3) train
   4) automobile
   5) truck
   6) bicycle
   7) omnibus

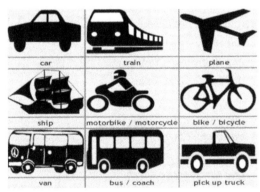

2. Match the English terms in Column I with the Chinese meanings in Column II.

I	II
A. morpheme	a. 词根
B. affix	b. 词基
C. root	c. 词缀
D. stem	d. 词素
E. base	e. 词干

Start to Read

Text A Morphemes

Words are usually treated as the basic and minimal units of a language. However, structurally a word is not the smallest unit because many words can be separated into even smaller meaningful units. For example:

> girls = girl + s
> kicked = kick + ed
> coolness = cool + ness
> reintroduce = re + introduce
> bookworm = book + worm

In linguistic terminology, a **morpheme** is the smallest meaningful linguistic unit of language, not divisible or analyzable into smaller forms. A single word may be composed of one or more morphemes:

> one morpheme: *nation*
> two morphemes: *nation* + *al*
> three morphemes: *inter* + *nation* + *al*
> four morphemes: *inter* + *nation* + *al* + *ist*
> more than four morphemes: *inter* + *nation* + *al* + *ist* + *s*

Morphemes and Allomorphs

A morpheme may take various shapes or forms. When we look at the plural morpheme, we will notice that they are often but not always predictable. Here are a few examples.

> one map – two maps
> one dog – two dogs
> one rose – two roses

but

> one mouse – two mice
> one man – two men
> one ox – two oxen
> one sheep – two sheep

In the first group, the plural morpheme has three different phonological forms, /s/, /z/, and /ɪz/. In the second group, a vowel change instead of a suffix marks the plural in *mice* and *men*, in *oxen* the suffix we encounter is rather exotic (meaning this word is virtually the only one that takes the *-en* ending) and in the last example there is no visible plural marking at all.

The three different phonological forms, /s/, /z/, and /ɪz/, are variants of the same morpheme *-s*. And the different forms, *-s*, *-en* and zero suffix in *dogs*, *ox<u>en</u>* and *sheep* respectively, are variants of the plural morpheme. They are called allomorphs. An **allomorph** is any of the variant forms of a morpheme as conditioned by position or adjoining sounds. For another example, *im-*, *ir-*, and *il-* in <u>im</u>*polite*, <u>ir</u>*responsible* and <u>il</u>*legal* are allomorphs of the morpheme *in-*, a common negative prefix.

The English language has many different kinds of morphemes that can be classified in various ways. In general, there are two main types of classification.

A. Free Morphemes and Bound Morphemes

Free morphemes can stand by themselves (i.e., they are what we conventionally call words) and either tell us something about the world (free lexical morphemes) or play a role in grammar (free grammatical morphemes). *Man*, *pizza*, *run* and *happy* are instances of free lexical morphemes, while *and*, *but*, *the* and *to* are examples for free grammatical morphemes. It is important to note the difference between morphemes and phonemes: morphemes are the minimal meaning-bearing elements that a word consists of and are principally independent from sound. For example, the word *zebra* consists of five phonemes and two syllables, but it contains only a single morpheme. *Ze-* and *-bra* are not independent meaning-bearing components of the word *zebra*, making it mono-morphemic.

Not all morphemes can be used independently, however. Some need to be bound to a free morpheme. In English, the morpheme *-s* indicating "plural number" cannot stand alone and is usually attached to a noun. Similarly, the morpheme *-er*, used to describe "someone who performs a certain activity" (e.g. a *dancer*, a *teacher* or a *baker*) cannot stand on its own, but needs to be attached to a free morpheme (a verb in this case). Morphemes which cannot occur as separate words are **bound morphemes**.

Bound Morpheme	Examples	Function
{-s}	two dogs, toys	turns nouns from singular to plural
{-ed}	looked, desired, played	turns verb into past tense
{un-}	untie, undo, unhappy, unpleasant	"negative" morpheme: denotes the reversal of an action if used with verbs, and the opposite quality if used with adjectives
{-ness}	happiness, tiredness	turns adjectives into nouns
{-er}	Londoner, New Zealander, New Yorker	denotes inhabitant of a city, region or country

Bound morphemes come in two varieties, derivational and inflectional. And the core difference between the two is that the addition of derivational morphemes creates new words while the addition of inflectional morphemes merely changes word form.

Derivational Morphemes

The signature quality of derivational morphemes is that they derive new words. In the following examples, derivational morphemes are added to produce new words which are derived from the parent word.

happy – happiness – unhappiness
frost – defrost – defroster
examine – examination – reexamination

In all cases the derived word means something different from the parent and the word class may change with each derivation. As demonstrated in the examples above, sometimes derivation will not cause the word class to change, but in such a case the meaning will usually be significantly different from that of the parent word, often expressing opposition or reversal.

probable – improbable
visible – invisible
tie – untie

create – recreate

Independently of whether or not word class changes and how significantly meaning is affected, derivation always creates new words from existing ones.

Inflectional Morphemes

Inflectional morphemes, by contrast, indicate the syntactic relationships between words and function as grammatical markers. For instance, the word *girls* consists of two morphemes: the free lexical morpheme *girl* that describes a young female human being and the inflectional morpheme *-s* that denotes plural number.

Examples for the morphological encoding of other grammatical categories are tense (past tense *-ed* as in *walked*), aspect (progressive aspect as in *walking*), case (genitive case as in *Mike's car*) and person (third person *-s* as in *Mike drives a Toyota*). More examples of inflectional morphemes are shown in the following:

Inflectional morphemes	Examples	Names
1. {-s pl.}	dog*s*, ox*en*, m*ice*	1. Noun plural
2. {-s sg ps}	boy*'s*	2. Noun singular possessive
3. {-s pl ps}	boys*'*, men*'s*	3. Noun plural possessive
4. {-s 3d}	vacate*s*	4. Present third-person singular
5. {-ING vb}	discuss*ing*	5. Present participle
6. {-D pt}	chew*ed*, rode	6. Past tense
7. {-D pp}	chew*ed*, eat*en*, sw*u*m	7. Past participle
8. {-ER cp}	bold*er*, soon*er*, near*er*	8. Comparative
9. {-EST sp}	bold*est*, soon*est*, near*est*	9. Superlative

B. Roots and Affixes

A root is the basic unchangeable part of a word, and it conveys the main lexical meaning of a word. Take the following set of words for example, *talk, talkative, talker, talks, talked* and *talking*, the root in each word is *talk*, which is the basic unchangeable part, carrying the main lexical meaning. Roots can be classified into free roots and bound roots.

Free roots are identical with free morphemes, such as *red*, *book*, and *moon*. They can stand alone as words. The roots that cannot stand alone as words are **bound roots**. All bound roots are bound morphemes. Many bound roots are derived from foreign sources, especially Greek and Latin, such as *-ceive* in *receive, deceive* or *conceive*, and *-tain* in *contain, detain* or *retain*. *-ceive* and *-tain* are both derived from Latin: *-ceive* means "to take" and *-tain* means "to hold." A bound root, like a free root, also carries the main component of meaning in a word. The difference is that a bound root is always in combination with at least one other root or affix.

Affixes are forms that are attached to words or word elements to modify meaning or function. All affixes are bound morphemes. According to the functions of affixes, we can divide them into **derivational affixes** and **inflectional affixes**, which are identical with derivational morphemes and inflectional morphemes.

Linguists classify affix into prefix and suffix, in view of the place where exactly an affix is attached to a word. **Prefixes** are attached at the onset of a free morpheme, while **suffixes** are attached to the end. While in English suffixes can be either derivational or inflectional (teach*er*, slow*ly* vs. apple*s*, kick*ed*), prefixes are always derivational (*untie*, *recover*, *defrost*).

The Root, the Stem and the Base

Finally, in order to make the segmentation of words into smaller parts a little clearer, we differentiate between the root, the stem and the base of a word in morphological terms.

A root, as mentioned earlier, is the basic unchangeable form of a word which carries the main component of meaning in a word. It defies further analysis. For example, in the word *reactions*, removing *re-*, *-ion*, and *-s* leaves the root *act*. In terms of derivational and inflectional morphology, a root is the part of a word form that remains when all derivational and inflectional affixes have been removed.

A stem may consist of a single root morpheme as in *book* or of two root morphemes as in *bookcase*. A stem is the part of the word form which remains when all inflectional affixes have been removed. For example, *act* is the stem of *acted*; *action* is the stem of *actions*; *reaction* is the stem of *reactions*.

A base is a form to which affixes of any kind, either derivational or inflectional, can be added. It can be a root or a stem. In the case of *reactions*, *act* is a base, *action* is a base, so are *react* and *reaction*.

After You Read

Knowledge Focus

1. Discuss the following questions with your partner.

1) What is a morpheme?
2) What is the relationship between a morpheme and an allomorph?
3) What are the differences between free morphemes and bound morphemes?
4) What kinds of morphemes are free lexical morphemes?
5) What kinds of morphemes are free grammatical morphemes?
6) How do morphemes differ from phonemes and syllables? Give an example to illustrate your point.
7) What is the main difference between derivational morphemes and inflectional morphemes?
8) What is a bound root?
9) What are affixes? How can affixes be divided?
10) How can we differentiate between the base, the stem and the root of a word in morphological terms?

2. Tell whether the following statements are true or false according to the knowledge you learned and why.

1) Structurally, a word is the smallest unit of a language which stands alone to convey meaning. (   )
2) Allomorphs usually occur at random because they are not phonetically conditioned and unpredictable. (   )
3) Free morphemes may constitute words by themselves. (   )
4) We might as well say free morphemes are free roots. (   )

5) Words made up of only bound morphemes are rare in English. (   )
6) In English, bound roots are either Latin or French. (   )
7) Affixes attached to the end of words to indicate grammatical relationships are known as derivational morphemes. (   )
8) Bound root is the part of the word that carries the fundamental meaning but has to be used in combination with other morphemes to make words. (   )
9) A stem may consist of a single root morpheme as in *iron* or of two root morphemes as in a compound like *handcuff*. (   )
10) Prefixes usually modify the part of speech of the original word, not the meaning of it. (   )

3. Mark the choice that can best complete the statement.

1) The morpheme *see* in the common word *sightseeing* is a(n) _____.
   A. bound morpheme   B. bound form
   C. inflectional morpheme   D. free morpheme

2) _____ are those that cannot be used independently but have to be combined with other morphemes, either free or bound, to form a word.
   A. Free morphemes   B. Bound morphemes
   C. Roots   D. Stems

3) _____ is a branch of grammar which studies the internal structure of words and the rules by which words are formed.
   A. Syntax   B. Grammar
   C. Morphology   D. Morpheme

4) The meaning carried by the inflectional morpheme is _____.
   A. lexical   B. morphemic
   C. grammatical   D. semantic

5) Bound morphemes are those that _____.
   A. have to be used independently
   B. can not be combined with other morphemes
   C. can either be free or bound
   D. have to be combined with other morphemes

6) _____ modify the meaning of the stem, but usually do not change the part of speech of the original word.
   A. Prefixes   B. Suffixes
   C. Roots   D. Affixes

7) _____ are often thought to be the smallest meaningful units of language by the linguists.
   A. Words   B. Morphemes
   C. Phonemes   D. Sentences

8) In the word *books*, -s is _____.
   A. a derivational affix   B. a stem
   C. an inflectional affix   D. a root

9) The variant forms of a morpheme as conditioned by position or adjoining sounds are termed as _____.
   A. phonemes   B. allomorphs   C. morphs   D. phones

10) In the words *recollection*, *idealistic*, and *ex-prisoner*, re-, -ion, -ist, -ic, ex-, and -er are _____.

A. prefixes
B. suffixes
C. free morphemes
D. bound morphemes

4. Please label the following that you think are roots in English.

Words	Yes	No
zebra		
boxes		
act		
practical		
nation		
does		
oxen		
black		
untie		
bigger		

5. Select five words with inflectional morphemes and five words with derivational morphemes from the following list of words.

- ☐ elements
- ☐ gain
- ☐ and
- ☐ unkind
- ☐ as
- ☐ some
- ☐ case
- ☐ example
- ☐ feature
- ☐ great
- ☐ have
- ☐ linked
- ☐ Indo-European
- ☐ speech
- ☐ egg
- ☐ off
- ☐ ordering
- ☐ one
- ☐ morphology
- ☐ Persians
- ☐ killed
- ☐ such
- ☐ cram
- ☐ tend
- ☐ arrival
- ☐ these
- ☐ thoughtful
- ☐ the

Language Focus

1. Fill in the blanks with the following words you have learned in the text. Change the forms where necessary.

differentiate	reversal	virtually	segmentation	demonstrate
component	defy	variant	predictable	exotic

1) _____ all students will be exempt from the tax.
2) Trust is a vital _____ in any relationship.
3) His sudden departure _____ that he's unreliable.
4) She travels to all kinds of _____ locations all over the world.

5) Some Internet firms have suffered a painful _____ of fortune.
6) In March and April, the weather is much less _____.
7) The door _____ all attempts to open it.
8) The _____ of social classes and gender discrimination once determined who should receive education and what kind of education one should take.
9) Can you _____ one variety from the other?
10) The story has many _____.

2. Proofreading & Error Correction.

A morpheme is the smallest unit of meaning in a word. The word *inexpensive* comprises two morphemes *in* and *expensive*. Each morpheme has its own meaning. The addition of *in* to *expensive*, for example, gives the sensation of *not*. Another example would be *laughed* which is made of two morphemes *laugh* and *ed*; with the addition of *ed* altered the tense of the first morpheme and thus the time of occurrence of the process it denotes.

Two observations can be made immediately. First, morphemes convey semantico-syntactic information. Secondly, there are two classes of morphemes: morphemes which occur independent as words and are co-terminous with specific word-forms, and morphemes which occur only as part of a word and which can not stand on its own. The first class, which are called free morphemes, would include *expensive* and *laugh*. The second class, that are called bound morphemes, would include *in* and *ed*. We should note, however, that some morphemes can have the same form but still are different morphemes, for example, the *s* in *cats*, *cat's* and *laughs* or the *er* in *smaller*, *winner*, *eraser*. These variants are usually termed allomorphs. We should also recognize that as the term *lexeme*, *morpheme* is an abstraction. To be strict, morphemes do not actually occur to words. Morphemes are realized by forms which are called *morphs*. But the term *morph* will be used only while the more specialized sense is required.

1) _____
2) _____
3) _____
4) _____
5) _____
6) _____
7) _____
8) _____
9) _____
10) _____

3. Translate the following paragraph into Chinese.

In all cases the derived word means something different than the parent and the word class may change with each derivation. As demonstrated in the examples above, sometimes derivation will not cause the world class to change, but in such a case the meaning will usually be significantly different from that of the parent word, often expressing opposition or reversal.

Comprehensive Work

1. **Discuss the following terms with your partner and put them in a tree diagram to show their logical relationships.**

   affix   morpheme
   derivational affix   bound morpheme
   free root   bound root
   inflectional affix   prefix
   suffix   free morpheme

2. **To Be a Morphologist**

   Step 1: Consider the following Modern Greek and English sentences (which have the same meaning).

[1] skilos efaye tin pondiki.	A. The dog ate the mouse.
[2] I pondiki efaye to skilo.	B. The mouse ate the dog.
[3] Oi skiloi efagan tis pondikes.	C. The dogs ate the mice.
[4] Oi pondikes efagan tous skilous.	D. The mice ate the dogs.
[5] To fayito tou skilou...	E. The dog's food...
[6] To fayito ton skilon...	F. The dogs' food...
[7] To fayito tis pondikis...	G. The mouse's food...
[8] To fayito ton pondikon...	H. The mice's food...

   Step 2: Identify all the morphemes in the written forms of the corresponding Greek and English words for dog and mouse. Some are done for you.

dog		mouse	
Greek	English	Greek	English
skil+os			
skil+o		pondik+i	
skil+ou		pondik+is	
skil+oi			
skil+ous		pondik+on	
	dog+s'		

3. Writing

In the following cartoon, one of the women says to the other, "They call it a relation*ship* because it so often sinks." Use the knowledge that you learned about morphology to illustrate what's wrong with the woman's understanding of the word *relationship*.

"They call it a relation'ship' because it so ofen sinks."

Read More

Text B Latin and Greek Roots and Affixes in English Vocabulary

English is a living language, and it is growing all the time. One way that new words come into the language is when words are borrowed from other languages. New words are also created when words or word elements, such as roots, prefixes, and suffixes, are combined in new ways.

Many English words and word elements can be traced back to Latin and Greek. A word root is a part of a word. It contains the core meaning of the word. A prefix is also a word part that cannot stand alone. It is placed at the beginning of a word to change its meaning. A suffix is a word part that is placed at the end of a word to change its meaning. Often we can guess the meaning of an unfamiliar word if you know the meaning of its parts; that is, the root and any prefixes or suffixes that are attached to it.

Latin Roots, Prefixes and Suffixes

Latin was the language spoken by the ancient Romans. As the Romans conquered most of Europe, the Latin language spread throughout the region. Over time, the Latin spoken in different areas developed into separate languages, including Italian, French, Spanish, and Portuguese. These languages are considered "sisters," as they all descended from Latin, their "mother" language.

In 1066 England was conquered by William, duke of Normandy, which is in northern France. For several hundred years after the Norman invasion, French was the language of court and polite society in England. It was during this period that many French words were borrowed into English. Linguists estimate that some 60% of our common everyday vocabulary today comes from French. Thus many Latin words came into English indirectly through French.

Many Latin words came into English directly, though, too. Monks from Rome brought religious vocabulary as well as Christianity to England beginning in the 6th century. From the Middle Ages onward many scientific, scholarly, and legal terms were borrowed from Latin.

During the 17th and 18th centuries, dictionary writers and grammarians generally felt that English was an imperfect language whereas Latin was perfect. In order to improve the language, they deliberately made up a lot of English words from Latin words. For example, *fraternity*, from Latin *fraternitas*, was thought to be better than the native English word *brotherhood*.

Many English words and word parts can be traced back to Latin and Greek. The following table lists some common Latin roots.

Latin Root	Basic Meaning	Example Words
-dict-	to say	contradict, dictate, diction, edict, predict
-duc-	to lead, bring, take	deduce, produce, reduce
-gress-	to walk	digress, progress, transgress
-ject-	to throw	eject, inject, interject, project, reject, subject
-pel-	to drive	compel, dispel, impel, repel
-pend-	to hang	append, depend, impend, pendant, pendulum
-port-	to carry	comport, deport, export, import, report, support
-scrib-, -script-	to write	describe, description, prescribe, prescription, subscribe, subscription, transcribe, transcription
-tract-	to pull, drag, draw	attract, contract, detract, extract, protract, retract, traction
-vert-	to turn	convert, divert, invert, revert

From the example words in the above table, it is easy to see how roots combine with prefixes to form new words. For example, the root *-tract-*, meaning "to pull," can combine with a number of prefixes, including *de-* and *re-*. *Detract* means literally "to pull away" (*de-*, "away, off") and *retract* means literally "to pull back" (*re-*, "again, back"). The following table gives a list of Latin prefixes and their basic meanings.

Latin Prefix	Basic Meaning	Example Words
co-	together	coauthor, coedit, coheir
de-	away, off; generally indicates reversal or removal in English	deactivate, debone, defrost, decompress, deplane
dis-	not, not any	disbelief, discomfort, discredit, disrepair, disrespect
inter-	between, among	international, interfaith, intertwine, intercellular, interject
non-	not	nonessential, nonmetallic, nonresident, nonviolence, nonskid, nonstop
post-	after	postdate, postwar, postnasal, postnatal
pre-	before	preconceive, preexist, premeditate, predispose, prepossess, prepay
re-	again; back, backward	rearrange, rebuild, recall, remake, rerun, rewrite
sub-	under	submarine, subsoil, subway, subhuman, substandard
trans-	across, beyond, through	transatlantic, transpolar

Words and word roots may also combine with suffixes. Here are examples of some important English suffixes that come from Latin:

Latin Suffix	Basic Meaning	Example Words
-able, -ible	forms adjectives and means "capable or worthy of"	likable, flexible
-ation	forms nouns from verbs	creation, civilization, automation, speculation, information
-fy, -ify	forms verbs and means "to make or cause to become"	purify, acidify, humidify
-ment	forms nouns from verbs	entertainment, amazement, statement, banishment
-ty, -ity	forms nouns from adjectives	subtlety, certainty, cruelty, frailty, loyalty, royalty; eccentricity, electricity, peculiarity, similarity, technicality

Greek Roots, Prefixes and Suffixes

The following table lists some common Greek roots.

Greek Root	Basic Meaning	Example Words
-anthrop-	human	misanthrope, philanthropy, anthropomorphic
-chron-	time	anachronism, chronic, chronicle, synchronize, chronometer
-dem-	people	democracy, demography, demagogue, endemic, pandemic
-morph-	form	amorphous, metamorphic, morphology
-path-	feeling, suffering	empathy, sympathy, apathy, apathetic, psychopathic
-pedo-, -ped-	child, children	pediatrician, pedagogue
-philo-, -phil-	having a strong affinity or love for	philanthropy, philharmonic, philosophy
-phon-	sound	polyphonic, cacophony, phonetics

The following table gives a list of Greek prefixes and their basic meanings.

Greek Prefix	Basic Meaning	Example Words
a-, an-	without	achromatic, amoral, atypical, anaerobic
anti-, ant-	opposite; opposing	anticrime, antipollution, antacid
auto-	self, same	autobiography, automatic, autopilot
bio-, bi-	life, living organism	biology, biophysics, biotechnology, biopsy

Greek Prefix	Basic Meaning	Example Words
geo-	Earth; geography	geography, geomagnetism, geophysics, geopolitics
hyper-	excessive, excessively	hyperactive, hypercritical, hypersensitive
micro-	small	microcosm, micronucleus, microscope
mono-	one, single, alone	monochrome, monosyllable, monoxide
neo-	new, recent	neonatal, neophyte, neoconservatism, neofascism, neodymium
pan-	all	panorama, panchromatic, pandemic, pantheism
thermo-, therm-	heat	thermal, thermometer, thermostat

Words and word roots may also combine with suffixes. Here are examples of some important English suffixes that come from Greek:

Greek Suffix	Basic Meaning	Example Words
-ism	forms nouns and means "the act, state, or theory of"	criticism, optimism, capitalism
-ist	forms agent nouns from verbs ending in -ize or nouns ending in -ism and is used like -er	conformist, copyist, cyclist
-ize	forms verbs from nouns and adjectives	formalize, jeopardize, legalize, modernize, emphasize, hospitalize, industrialize, computerize
-gram	something written or drawn, a record	cardiogram, telegram
-graph	something written or drawn; an instrument for writing, drawing, or recording	monograph, phonograph, seismograph
-logue, -log	speech, discourse; to speak	monologue, dialogue, travelogue
-logy	discourse, expression; science, theory, study	phraseology, biology, dermatology
-meter, -metry	measuring device; measure	spectrometer, geometry, kilometer, parameter, perimeter
-oid	forms adjectives and nouns and means "like, resembling" or "shape, form"	humanoid, spheroid, trapezoid
-phile	one that loves or has a strong affinity for; loving	audiophile, Francophile

Greek Suffix	Basic Meaning	Example Words
-phobe, -phobia	one that fears a specified thing; an intense fear of a specified thing	agoraphobe, agoraphobia, xenophobe, xenophobia
-phone	sound; device that receives or emits sound; speaker of a language	homophone, geophone, telephone, Francophone

Questions for Discussion or Reflection
1. How are new words created in English?
2. How can we guess the meaning of an unfamiliar word?
3. Why are such languages as Italian, French, Spanish and Portuguese considered "sisters"?
4. How did Latin words come into English?

Text C Roots and Stems

Morphologically complex word consists of a root and one or more affixes. A root is a lexical content morpheme that cannot be analyzed into smaller parts. Some examples of English roots are *paint* in *painter*, *read* in *reread*, and *ceive* in *conceive*. A root may or may not stand alone as a word (*paint* does; *ceive* doesn't). In languages that have circumfixes, the root is the form around which the circumfix attaches, for example, the Chickasaw root *chokm* in *ikchokmo* ("he isn't good"). In infixing languages the root is the form into which the infix is inserted, for example *fikas* in the Bontoc word *fumikas* ("to be strong").

Semitic languages like Hebrew and Arabic have a unique morphological system. Nouns and verbs are built on a foundation of three consonants, and one derives related words by varying the pattern of vowels and syllables. For example, the root for "write" in Egyptian Arabic is *ktb* from which the following words (among others) are formed:

katab	"he wrote"
kaatib	"writer"
kitáab	"book"
kútub	"books"

When a root morpheme is combined with an affix, it forms a stem, which may or may not be a word (*painter* is both a word and a stem; *-ceive + er* is only a stem). Other affixes can be added to a stem to form a more complex stem, as shown in the following:

root	*Chomsky*	(proper) noun
stem	*Chomsky + ite*	noun + suffix
word	*Chomsky + ite + s*	noun + suffix + suffix
root	*believe*	verb
stem	*believe + able*	verb + suffix
word	*un + believe + able*	prefix + verb + suffix
root	*system*	noun
stem	*system + atic*	noun + suffix
stem	*un + system + atic*	prefix + noun + suffix
stem	*un + system + atic + al*	prefix + noun + suffix + suffix

word   *un + system + atic + al + ly*   prefix + noun + suffix + suffix + suffix

As one adds each affix to a stem, a new stem and a new word are formed.

Questions for Discussion or Reflection

1. How do you define circumfix and infix?
2. How do we differentiate between a root and a stem?
3. Analyze the words *individualistic* and *undesirables* in terms of root and stem.

Notes

1. **Chickasaw language:** a Native American language of the Muskogean family. It is agglutinative and follows the pattern of Subject Object Verb. The language is closely related to, though perhaps not entirely mutually intelligible with, Choctaw. It is spoken by the Chickasaw tribe, now residing in Southeast Oklahoma, centered around Ada.
2. **Bontoc:** a native dialect of the indigenous people living in the capital town of Mountain Province, Philippines.

For Fun

Works to Read

1. ***Red Hot Root Words: Mastering Vocabulary with Prefixes, Suffixes and Root Words (Book 2)*** by Dianne Draze

   This book helps students acquire the keys for studying Greek and Latin prefixes, root words and suffixes. Each of the lessons includes: 2 to 4 prefixes, suffixes, or root words along with meanings and sample words, definitions and sample sentences for each new word, and a worksheet that presents a variety of ways to apply knowledge and expand understanding of the definitions and uses of the word parts.

   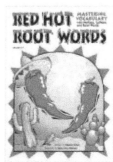

2. ***The Least You Should Know about Vocabulary Building: Word Roots*** by Carol Friend, Laura D. Knight, and Teresa Ferster Glazier

   This book uses words you already know to show how to develop your vocabulary. Plus, this edition has built-in study tips and an excellent index to help make papers and tests problem-free.

Websites to Visit

1. https://www.vocabtest.com/morphemes/
   The website has 15 units of morphemes practice tests. You can select a morpheme unit you want to learn and test your knowledge about those morphemes.
2. http://www.webenglishteacher.com/word-roots.html
   This website presents many reading materials and games, and is a good place to learn and practice word roots.
3. http://www.prefixsuffix.com
   The website gives access to over 2,000 root words and provides two teaching games that will test your knowledge and improve your vocabulary.

Unit 6
Major Word Formations in English

> A new word is like a fresh seed sown on the ground of the discussion.
> —— Ludwig Wittgenstein

Unit Goals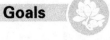

- To understand the definitions of compounding, derivation and conversion
- To grasp the process of forming new words by compounding, derivation and conversion
- To be familiar with the classification of compounds
- To comprehend the difference between prefixation and suffixation
- To be able to explain the meanings of converted words in sentences

 Before You Read

1. **Fill in the blanks with the right colors and figure out the meanings of the compounds.**
   1) Icy road is a hazard to all the drivers, especially the _____ hand.
      A. yellow   B. green   C. black   D. white
   2) My brother is the _____ sheep of the family. Instead of getting a job, he does nothing but hit the bars and clubs every night.
      A. white   B. brown   C. yellow   D. black
   3) The prince of the country will not marry any girl who has no _____ blood.
      A. red   B. black   C. blue   D. green
   4) The men and women who do the office work are called _____-collar workers.
      A. pink   B. blue   C. white   D. purple
   5) _____ meat contains the most easily absorbed form of iron.
      A. Red   B. White   C. Pink   D. Yellow

2. **Guess the meanings of the underlined derived words and discuss your understanding of derivation with your partner.**
   1) The tennis player announced her retirement on her <u>microblog</u>, bidding farewell to the sport.
   2) Sixty percent of those polled say that it is completely acceptable to <u>unfriend</u> an ex-boyfriend or ex-girlfriend.
   3) <u>Sub-health</u> is mainly caused by too much work pressure and the hurried pace of life.

4) <u>Lookism</u> is a rampant problem in the workplace and indeed everywhere we go.
5) —Why are you so sad?
   —I've just finished watching the TV drama *The Legend of Zhen Huan*, and am having <u>post-drama</u> depression.

Start to Read

Text A English Compound

Compound words are formed when two or more words are put together to form a new word with a new meaning. They can function as different parts of speech.

Characteristics of Compounds

Compounds have certain features that may distinguish themselves from noun phrases in the following aspects.

a. Orthographic Features

Since English is a mostly analytic language, unlike most other Germanic languages, it creates compounds by concatenating words without case markers. As in other Germanic languages, the compounds may be arbitrarily long. However, this is obscured by the fact that the written representation of long compounds always contains blanks. Short compounds may be written in three different ways, which do not correspond to different pronunciations, however.

```
AIR + PORT = AIRPORT
HOUSE + BOAT = HOUSEBOAT
FLOWER + POT = FLOWERPOT
HEAD + ROOM = HEADROOM
```

Closed/Solid compounds are formed when two unique words are joined together. These two words are usually moderately short words. They do not have a space between them and they are the type that generally comes to mind when we think of compound words. For example:

I love the *fireworks* on the fourth of July.

Make sure you hold hands when you come to the *crosswalk*.

The ocean was bathed in *moonlight*.

Did you hear about the terrible *earthquake*?

The *fireflies* buzzed in the night sky.

Other examples are *football, railroad, housewife, lawsuit, wallpaper*, etc.

Open compounds have a space between the words but when they are read together, a new meaning is formed. For example:

Ice cream is my favorite dessert.

The line at the *post office* snaked all the way out the door and around the corner.

Rhonda is my *half sister*.

There must be a *full moon* out tonight.

Other examples are *middle class, real estate, fire escape, express train, distance learning*, etc.

Hyphenated compounds are connected by a hyphen. To avoid confusion, some compounds are often hyphenated. For example:

My *mother-in-law* is coming for a visit.

The *merry-go-round* at the carnival thrilled Ella.

Some *over-the-counter* drugs can have serious side effects.

If you're concerned for your *well-being*, make sure you eat healthy foods and get plenty of exercise.

Other examples are *mass-produced, hand-picked, good-looking, tax-free*, etc.

Compounds that contain affixes, such as *house-builder* and *single-mindedness*, as well as adjective-adjective compounds and verb-verb compounds, such as *blue-green* and *freeze-dried*, are often hyphenated. Compounds that contain articles, prepositions or conjunctions, such as *rent-a-cop, mother-of-pearl* and *salt-and-pepper*, are also often hyphenated.

Usage in the U.S. and in the U.K. differs and often depends on the individual choice of the writer rather than on a hard-and-fast rule; therefore, closed, open, and hyphenated forms may be encountered for the same compound noun, such as the triplets *containership/ container ship/ container-ship* and *particleboard/ particle board/ particle-board*.

b. Phonological Features

Stress patterns may distinguish a compound word from a free phrase consisting of the same component words. For example, *a black board*, adjective plus noun, is any board that is black, and has equal stress on both elements. The compound *blackboard*, on the other hand, though it may have started out historically as *black board*, now is stressed on only the first element, *black*. Thus a compound such as *the White House* normally has a falling intonation which a phrase such as *a white house* does not.

c. Semantic Features

In some cases, the meaning of a compound can be determined by combining the meanings of the parts. In other cases, the meaning of a compound cannot be determined by combining the meanings of the parts. For example, a *blueberry* is a *berry* that is *blue*. However, a *breakup* is not a relationship that was severed into pieces in an upward direction.

Compound nouns should not be confused with nouns modified by adjectives, verbs and other nouns. For example, the adjective *black* of the noun phrase *black bird* functions as a noun phrase modifier, while the adjective *black* of the compound noun *blackbird* is an inseparable part of the noun. *A black bird* refers to any bird that is black in color, whereas *a blackbird* is a specific type of bird.

In some compounds, the semantic head is contained within the compound itself—*a blueberry* is a kind of berry, for example, and *a blackbird* is a kind of bird. However, in another common type of compound, the semantic head is not explicitly expressed. *A redhead*, for example, is not a kind of head, but is a person with red hair. Similarly, *a blockhead* is also not a head, but a person with a head that is as hard and unreceptive as a block (i.e., stupid).

Classification of Compounds

Compounds can be classified according to parts of speech of the compounds. Noun compounds, adjective compounds and verb compounds are three main categories.

a. Noun Compounds

A noun compound is a noun that is made with two or more words. It is usually [noun + noun] or [adjective + noun], but there are other combinations.

noun + noun	*football*	Shall we play *football* today?
adjective + noun	*software*	She installed the new *software*.
verb + noun	*swimming pool*	What a beautiful *swimming pool*!
noun + verb	*haircut*	You need a *haircut*.
verb + preposition	*check-out*	Please remember that *check-out* is at 12 noon.
noun + prepositional phrase	*mother-in-law*	My *mother-in-law* lives with us.
preposition + noun	*underworld*	Do you think the police accept money from the *underworld*?
preposition + verb	*output*	The average *output* of the factory is 20 cars a day.
noun + adjective	*handful*	She scooped up *handfuls* of loose earth.
adjective + verb	*dry cleaning*	I would definitely take it to *dry cleaning*.
verb + adverb	*sit-in*	Several thousand students staged *sit-ins*.
adverb + verb	*downfall*	Greed led to his *downfall*.

In general we make the plural form of a noun compound by adding *-s* to the base word (the most significant word). Here is a list of examples:

Singular Form	Plural Form
a *tennis shoe*	three *tennis shoes*
one *assistant headmaster*	five *assistant headmasters*
the *sergeant major*	some *sergeants major*
a *mother-in-law*	two *mothers-in-law*
an *assistant secretary of state*	three *assistant secretaries of state*
my *toothbrush*	our *toothbrushes*
a *doctor of philosophy*	two *doctors of philosophy*
a *passerby*, a *passer-by*	two *passersby*, two *passers-by*

b. Adjective Compounds

An adjective compound is an adjective that comprises more than one word. Usually, a hyphen (or hyphens) is used to link the words together to show that it is one adjective. For example:

It is a *6-page* document.
Claire worked as a *part-time* keeper at the safari park.
That is an *all-too-common* mistake.

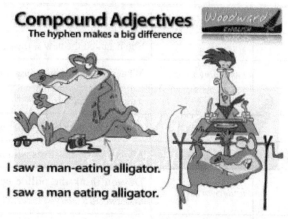

There are many types of adjective compounds. Here is a list of the most common types:

number + noun	I have a *three-week* vacation.
number + noun-ed	In the land of the blind, the *one-eyed* man is king.
adverb + past participle	She is a *well-known* actress.
noun + past participle	I love eating *sun-dried* raisins.
noun + present participle	That was a *record-breaking* jump.
noun + adjective	This is a *smoke-free* restaurant.
adjective + noun	It was a *last-minute* decision.
adjective + past participle	That is an *old-fashioned* dress.
adjective + present participle	She is a *good-looking* girl.

c. Verb Compounds

A verb compound is usually composed of a preposition and a verb, although other combinations also exist.

preposition + verb	*overrate, underline, outrun*
adverb + verb	*downsize, upgrade*
adjective + verb	*whitewash, blacklist*
noun + verb	*browbeat, sidestep, manhandle*
preposition + noun	*outfox*

From a morphological point of view, some verb compounds are difficult to analyze because several derivations are plausible. *Blacklist*, for instance, might be analyzed as an adjective + verb compound, or as an adjective + noun compound that becomes a verb through conversion or zero derivation. Such verb compounds are *outline, snowball,* and *nickname*. Other verb compounds are created through back-formation, *lip-read,* for instance. Other examples are *mass-produce, baby-sit,* and *proofread*.

There was a tendency in the 18th century to use hyphens excessively, that is, to hyphenate all previously established solid verb compounds. American English, however, has diminished the use of hyphens, while British English is more conservative.

After You Read

Knowledge Focus
1. **Discuss the following questions with your partner.**
   1) What is a compound word?
   2) In how many ways can short compounds be written?
   3) What kinds of compounds are often hyphenated?
   4) What are the phonological features of compounds?
   5) What are the semantic features of compounds?
   6) In what way are compounds usually classified?
   7) How is the plural form of noun compounds formed?
   8) Why are adjective compounds often hyphenated?
   9) What are the usual methods to form verb compounds?
   10) What are the differences between compounds and free phrases?

2. **Tell whether the following statements are true or false according to the knowledge you learned and why.**
   1) Compounding is a main type of word-formation process consisting of joining two or more words to form a new word. (   )
   2) Compounds are words formed by combining affixes and stems. (   )
   3) There is a fixed rule as to how to write a compound. (   )
   4) In compounds the word stress usually occurs on the first constituent. (   )
   5) A noun phrase has the primary stress on the first element and the secondary stress, if any, on the second. (   )
   6) The meaning of a compound is the combination of stems. (   )
   7) Compounding can occur only in the three major word classes, nouns and, to lesser extent, adjectives, and, to least extent, verbs. (   )
   8) The plural form of all noun compounds is formed by adding -*s* to the end of the word. (   )
   9) An adjective compound is often hyphenated to avoid misunderstanding. (   )
   10) Nowadays, all the verb compounds are hyphenated. (   )

3. Label the following words that you think are compounds.

Words	Yes	No
Shakespearian		
downtown		
environmentalist		
mother-of-pearl		
skywards		
distance learning		
washable		
childhood		
dreamlike		
bookworm		

4. List 10 compound words related to food.

Compound Word	Meaning	Compound Word	Meaning

5. Can you shorten the following phrases by using compounds?
   1) a room for stores
   2) a tape for measuring up to 300 cms
   3) the assistant manager of the restaurant
   4) a station for express trains
   5) size of cable
   6) reduction in cost
   7) two periods of three months

8) plugs with 3 pins
9) two steel boxes for tools
10) the husband of my daughter

Language Focus

1. **Fill in the blanks with the following words you have learned in the text. Change the forms where necessary.**

| analytic | arbitrarily | obscure | correspond | moderately |
| triplet | sever | explicitly | unreceptive | plausible |

1) He did _____ well in the exams.
2) My cousin gave birth to _____.
3) Latin is a synthetic language, while English is _____.
4) She was so _____ she would have deceived anyone.
5) We mustn't let these minor details _____ the main issue.
6) She has _____ her connection with the firm.
7) It is unjust if one party should treat a contract _____ at the expense of the other.
8) Large firms are generally _____ to new ideas.
9) Much of it has been clearly determined and _____ directed to this high aim.
10) Your account of events does not _____ with hers.

2. **Proofreading & Error Correction.**

In English very often lexical items are created not by affixation yet by conversion or zero derivation, i.e., without any alteration being made to the shape of the input base. The word-form remains the same, but it realizes a different lexical item.

Conversion of verbs into nouns and nouns into verbs is extreme productive in English. Usually the same word-form can be used as a verb and a noun, with only the grammatical context enables us to know which category it belongs. Thus, *jump* in the two sentences below are exactly the same in form but it belongs to two different lexemes. In [a] *jump* is the non-finite form of the verb "jump" when in [b] it is the singular form of the noun *jump*.

    a. The pig will jump over the stile!
    b. What a jump!

In *What a jump!* the verb converted into a noun by "zero derivation," i.e., without using any affix. What enables us to know if the word is a noun or a verb is the position that it

1) _____
2) _____
3) _____
4) _____
5) _____
6) _____
7) _____
8) _____
9) _____

occupies in the sentence. If we see the subject *the pig* and the auxiliary verb *will* before the word *jump*, we know it must be a verb. But when *jump* occurs after the definite article *a* we know it must be a noun.

10) _____

3. Translate the following paragraph into Chinese.

Since English is a mostly analytic language, unlike most other Germanic languages, it creates compounds by concatenating words without case markers. As in other Germanic languages, the compounds may be arbitrarily long. However, this is obscured by the fact that the written representation of long compounds always contains blanks. Short compounds may be written in three different ways, which do not correspond to different pronunciations, however.

Comprehensive Work

1. Match the parts of the following compound nouns and then match them with the pictures.

2. Writing

Just a few days after Apple launched the iPhone 6 Plus in September 2014, the company already received customer complaints that the handsets bent after being placed in their pockets. As a way to properly identify the issue, some people began to use the term *Bendgate* to refer to the warping of the iPhone 6 Plus inside pockets.

Is the term *Bendgate* a compound or a derived word? Support your point of view with details.

Read More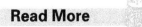

Text B Derived Words

Derivation is the process of forming a new word on the basis of an existing word by adding prefixes, particles added to the beginning of words, or suffixes, particles added to the end. For example, the English suffix *-er* creates a noun meaning "someone who does X" from a verb, where "X" is the meaning of the verb the noun is created from. So, from the verb *run* we can create *runner* (someone who runs), from *work* we can create *worker* (someone who works) and so on.

The suffix *-ing* has many functions in English but one of them is to create nouns from verbs meaning "the thing created by X-ing." Examples are *carving* (the thing carved), *cutting* (the thing cut), *painting* (the thing painted), and so forth. Of course, this suffix is more often used to create a noun meaning the action of the verb itself, as in *running, cooking, drinking,* and *acting*. Here is a list of the most common endings and prefixes used to derive words in English.

```
PORT
IMPORT
EXPORT
TRANSPORT
PORTABLE
DEPORTING
TRANSPORTATION
IMPORTANT
```

	Some English Derivational Affixes		
Base	**Derived Word**	**Derivation**	**Derivational Meaning**
carve	*carv**er***	verb to noun	someone who v-s
carve	*carv**ing***	verb to noun	the result of v-ing
decide	*deci**sion***	verb to noun	the result of v-ing
state	*state**ment***	verb to noun	the result of v-ing
train	*train**ing***	verb to noun	the process of v-ing
train	*train**ee***	verb to noun	someone who is v-ed
excite	*exci**table***	verb to adj.	that can be v-ed
excite	*exci**ting***	verb to adj.	that v-s
domestic	*domestic**ate***	adj. to verb	make adj.
quick	*quick**en***	adj. to verb	make adj.
solid	*solid**ify***	adj. to verb	make adj.
write	***re**write*	verb to verb	v again
write	***under**write*	verb to verb	not v enough
write	***over**write*	verb to verb	v too much
tender	*tender**ness***	adj. to noun	quality expressed by the adj.
legible	*legi**bility***	adj. to noun	quality expressed by the adj.

Some English Derivational Affixes			
Base	Derived Word	Derivation	Derivational Meaning
important	*importance*	adj. to noun	quality expressed by the adj.

The ability to add affixes, whether prefixes or suffixes, makes English extremely flexible. There are very few rules in the addition of affixes in English, and Anglo-Saxon affixes can be attached to Latin or Greek roots, or vice versa. An extreme example is the word *incomprehensibility*, which is based on the simple root *-hen-* (original from Indo-European root word *ghend*, meaning "to grasp or seize") with no less than 5 affixes: *in-* (not), *com-* (with), *pre-* (before), *-ible* (capable) and *-ity* (being).

"I believe in the incomprehensibility of God."

However, the sheer variety and number of possible affixes in English can lead to some confusion. For instance, there is no single standard method for something as basic as making a noun into an adjective (*-able*, *-al*, *-ous* and *-y* are just some of the possibilities). There are at least nine different negation prefixes (*a-*, *anti-*, *dis-*, *il-*, *im-*, *in-*, *ir-*, *non-* and *un-*), and it is almost impossible for a non-native speaker to predict which is to be used with which root word. To make matters worse, some apparently negative forms do not even negate the meanings of their roots (e.g. *flammable* and *inflammable*, *habitable* and *inhabitable*, *ravel* and *unravel*).

Some affix additions are surprisingly recent. *Officialdom* and *boredom* joined the ancient word *kingdom* as recently as the 20th century, and *apolitical* as the negation of *political* did not appear until 1952. Adding affixes remains the simplest and perhaps the commonest method of creating new words.

Exercises

1. What is an equivalent of "derivation"?
- ☐ compounding
- ☐ conversion
- ☐ affixation
- ☐ prefixation
- ☐ suffixation

2. Form antonyms of the following with negative prefixes.

1) mortal
2) fortune
3) tolerable
4) forgettable
5) code
6) loyal
7) regular
8) alcoholic
9) literate
10) theism

3. **Fill in the blanks with the proper form of the words in the brackets and study the famous quotations.**
   1) All good poetry is the spontaneous overflow of powerful feelings: it takes its origin from emotion recollected in _____ (tranquil). —William Wordsworth
   2) Leadership and learning are _____ (dispensable) to each other. —John F. Kennedy
   3) Always bear in mind that your own _____ (resolve) to succeed is more important than any other. —Abraham Lincoln
   4) Machines have altered our way of life, but not our instincts. Consequently, there is _____ (adjustment). —Bertrand Russell
   5) In the end, we will remember not the words of our enemies, but the _____ (silent) of our friends. —Martin Luther King

Text C Conversion

Conversion is the word formation process in which a word of one grammatical form becomes a word of another grammatical form without the addition of an affix. For example, the noun *email* appeared in English before the verb. A decade ago, one said, "You can send me an *email* (noun)", whereas now one can simply say, "You can *email* (verb) me". The original noun *email* experienced conversion, thus resulting in the new verb *email*. Conversion is also referred to as **zero derivation** or **null derivation** with the assumption that the formal change between words results in the addition of an invisible morpheme. However, many linguists argue for a clear distinction between the word formation processes of derivation and conversion.

There are various types of conversion: noun to verb, verb to noun, adjective to verb, and so on.

Noun to Verb Conversion

The most productive form of conversion in English is noun to verb conversion. Noun to verb conversion is also referred to as verbification or verbing. The following list provides examples of verbs converted from nouns:

Noun – Verb
access – to access
bottle – to bottle
can – to can
divorce – to divorce
dress – to dress
drink – to drink
eye – to eye
fool – to fool
Google – to google
host – to host
knife – to knife
microwave – to microwave
name – to name
pocket – to pocket

Noun – Verb
radio – to radio
salt – to salt
ship – to ship
talk – to talk
tape – to tape
x-ray – to x-ray

For Example:
a. My grandmother put the juice in a *bottle* (noun) and the pickles in a *can* (noun).
   My grandmother *bottled* (verb) the juice and *canned* (verb) the pickles.
b. She heated her lunch in the *microwave* (noun).
   She *microwaved* (verb) her lunch.
c. The doctor *eyed* (verb) my swollen *eye* (noun).

Verb to Noun Conversion

Another productive form of conversion in English is verb to noun conversion. Verb to noun conversion is also referred to as nominalization. The following list provides examples of nouns converted from verbs:

Verb – Noun
to alert – alert
to attack – attack
to call – call
to clone – clone
to command – command
to cover – cover
to cry – cry
to experience – experience
to fear – fear

Verb – Noun
to feel – feel
to hope – hope
to increase – increase
to judge – judge
to laugh – laugh
to rise – rise
to run – run
to sleep – sleep
to start – start
to turn – turn
to visit – visit

For Example:
  a. The guard *alerted* (verb) the general to the *attack* (noun).
     The enemy *attacked* (verb) before an *alert* (noun) could be sounded.
  b. The baby *cried* (verb) all night.
     Sometimes one just needs a good *cry* (noun).
  c. It was great to finally get to *experience* (verb) their *experience* (noun).

Adjective to Verb Conversion

Adjectives can also go through the process of conversion. The following list provides examples of verbs converted from adjectives:

Adjective – Verb
bare – to bare
blunt – to blunt
busy – to busy (oneself)
calm – to calm (down)
clear – to clear
cool – to cool
dim – to dim (out)
dry – to dry
dirty – to dirty
empty – to empty
free – to free
idle – to idle (away)
narrow – to narrow

Adjective – Verb
right – to right
slim – to slim
slow – to slow (down)
smooth – to smooth (out)
sober – to sober (up)
tame – to tame
warm – to warm

For Example:
  a. Kate is *busy* (adjective) with the preparations for the party.
     She *busied* (verb) herself with the preparations for the party.
  b. They spent many *idle* (adjective) hours just talking and watching television.
     They *idled* (verb) the days away, talking and watching television.
  c. There is only a *slim* (adjective) chance that she can *slim* (verb) down to 50 kilos before her wedding.

Other Conversions
  Conversion also occurs, although less frequently, to and from other grammatical forms. For example:
  She is a *natural* for the job. (adjective to noun)
  He's been here for years; he should know the *ins* and *outs* of the job by now. (adverb to noun)
  Life is full of *ups* and *downs*. (preposition to noun)
  If they catch you stealing, you're fired on the spot—no *ifs*, *ands*, or *buts* about it. (conjunction to noun)
  I love the *ho ho hos* of Christmas time. (interjection to noun)
  Workers at the factory *downed* tools in protest last night. (adverb to verb)
  They kept *upping* the price. (preposition to verb)

Shakespeare was the conversion expert.

"I eared her language." (from *The Two Noble Kinsmen*)

"He words me." (from *Antony and Cleopatra*)

In some cases, conversion is accompanied by slight changes which affect pronunciation or stress distribution.
  With respect to pronunciation, there are some nouns ending in voiceless fricative consonants /-s/, /-f/ and /-θ/ which are converted into verbs with the voicing of the final consonant into /-z/, /-v/ and

/-ð/, respectively. For example, the noun *use* /-s/ shifts to the verb *to use* /-z/ without any change but the voicing of the final consonant.

With respect to stress pattern, there are some two-syllable verbs which shift to nouns or adjectives with a change in word stress from the verb distribution /-ʹ-/ to the noun and adjective pattern /ʹ—/ (this stress shift also affects the phonetic pattern, especially the length of the vowels involved). These are the cases of the verb *conduct* to the noun *conduct*, from the verb *protest* to the noun *protest*, and from the verb *increase* to the noun *increase*.

Exercises

1. Read aloud the following sentences and translate them into Chinese. Pay attention to the shift of stress.
   1) The country *imports* most of its raw materials.
      Cheap foreign *imports* should be restricted.
   2) Historians *record* how Rome fell.
      The airline has a bad safety *record*.
   3) What made you *suspect* her of having taken the money?
      He's a prime *suspect* in the murder case.
   4) The council will not *permit* you to build here.
      You cannot enter a military base without a *permit*.
   5) She's being *transferred* to our Paris branch.
      The club's goalkeeper has asked for a *transfer* to another club.

2. Change the construction of the following sentences by converting the verbs into nouns.
   1) She was *crippled* in a car accident.
   2) Mr. Johnson *coaches* swimmers.
   3) Jack *nailed* a lid on a box.
   4) David will *referee* the basketball match.
   5) Will you please *label* your luggage?

3. Pick out the converted words in the following sentences and explain the meanings.
   1) The deceased's ashes were scattered over the mountain.
   2) There is a through train to Paris.
   3) The paper had yellowed with age.
   4) We took some uppers for the show, and then after our performance we all hit the sack, exhausted.
   5) He and the manager were closeted together for three hours.

Text D Deriving Nouns from Verbs: Names for People

In linguistics, an agent noun is a word that is derived from another word denoting an action, and that identifies an entity that does that action. For example, *driver* is an agent noun formed from the verb *drive*. Agent nouns can be formed by adding the suffixes *-er*, *-or*, and *-ar* to the base forms of verbs.

Verb-Noun Derivation

Derivation is the process whereby the addition of affixes, chiefly prefixes and suffixes in English, to base forms results in the creation of new words. In English, the affixation of the suffixes *-er, -or,* and *ar* to verbs creates nouns. The *-er, -or,* and *ar* are referred to as agentive suffixes because their affixation to action verbs produces agent nouns, or nouns that identify the person or other entity performing the action. In other words, agent nouns are usually names for people. For example, affixing *-er* to the base form of the verb *learn* results in the noun *learner*, meaning someone who learns, and affixing *-or* to the base form of the verb *interrogate* results in the noun *interrogator*, meaning someone who interrogates.

Some Agent Nouns

The following three lists provide examples of some common agent nouns in English organized by *-er, -or,* and *ar* suffix.

Verb – Noun (-er)	Verb – Noun (-or)
bake – baker	act – actor
clean – cleaner	administrate – administrator
dance – dancer	advise – advisor
employ – employer	animate – animator
farm – farmer	audit – auditor
garden – gardener	conduct – conductor
lead – leader	decorate – decorator
listen – listener	direct – director
manage – manager	edit – editor
mourn – mourner	educate – educator
observe – observer	govern – governor
paint – painter	instruct – instructor
publish – publisher	invent – inventor
read – reader	investigate – investigator
research – researcher	negotiate – negotiator
sell – seller	operate – operator
teach – teacher	possess – possessor
travel – traveler	sail – sailor
use – user	supervise – supervisor
write – writer	visit – visitor
Verb – Noun (-ar)	
beg – beggar	
lie – liar	

Spelling Rules for Agent Nouns

For verbs spelled with a final consonant preceded by either two vowels or additional consonants or with a vowel preceded by a consonant, simply add the agent suffix:

act – actor

design – designer
ski – skier
teach – teacher

For verbs spelled with a final *w*, *x*, or *y* preceded by a vowel, simply add the agent suffix:

box – boxer
brew – brewer
play – player
survey – surveyor

For verbs spelled with a final "silent" *e* preceded by a consonant, remove the *e* and then add the agent suffix:

drive – driver
love – lover
observe – observer
supervise – supervisor

For verbs spelled with a final *y* preceded by a consonant, change the *y* to *i* and then add the agent suffix:

cry – crier
fly – flier
supply – supplier
worry – worrier

For two-syllable verbs spelled with a final *le*, remove the *e* and then add the agent suffix:

cobble – cobbler
handle – handler
meddle – meddler
tumble – tumbler

For two-syllable verbs spelled with a final *er*, simply add the agent suffix:

discover – discoverer
gather – gatherer
murder – murderer
suffer – sufferer

For one-syllable verbs that end in a single vowel followed by a single consonant other than *w*, *x*, or *y*, double the final consonant and then add the agent suffix:

beg – beggar
drum – drummer
jog – jogger
plan – planner

For two-syllable verbs that end in a single vowel followed by a single consonant other than *w*, *x*, or *y*, double the final consonant and then add the agent suffix:

begin – beginner
format – formatter

For verbs that end with the letter *c*, add the letter *k* after the *c* and then add the agent suffix:

frolic – frolicker

mimic – mimicker
picnic – picnicker
traffic – trafficker

Exercises

1. What suffixes are referred to as agentive suffixes? Why?
2. What are the spelling rules for agent nouns?
3. Are there other suffixes besides -er, -or, and ar that can be added to verbs to form agent nouns?
4. Each of the following sentences contains a word printed in italics. Complete the sentence by using the word to form a noun that refers to a person, and distinguish agent nouns from others.

   1) A woman who *waits* on tables in a restaurant is a _____.
   2) If someone *interviews* you, you are the _____ and he or she is the _____.
   3) The great _____ Charles Dickens wrote many famous *novels*.
   4) The _____ are the people who *immigrate* to a foreign country.
   5) A _____ is someone who makes *music* by playing or conducting.

For Fun

Works to Read

1. ***Word-Formation in English*** by Ingo Plag

   This book is an introduction to the study of word-formation, focusing on English. The book's didactic aim is to enable students with little or no prior linguistic knowledge to do their own practical analyses of complex words. It is a textbook directed towards university students of English and Linguistics at all levels.

2. ***The Oxford Handbook of Compounding*** by Rochelle Lieber and Pavol Stekauer

   This book presents a comprehensive review of theoretical work on the linguistics and psycholinguistics of compound words and combines it with a series of surveys of compounding in a variety of languages from a wide range of language families.

Websites to Visit

1. http://www.nonstopenglish.com/allexercises/vocabulary/vocabulary-wordformation-006.asp
   The website has interesting vocabulary exercises on word formation.
2. http://www.esl-galaxy.com/prefixsuffix.html
   The website provides exercises and quizzes on prefixes and suffixes.
3. http://rbeaudoin333.homestead.com/compoundwords1.html
   The website is the place where you can practice compound words for fun.

Unit 7

Minor Word Formations in English

> The most valuable of all talents is that of never using two words when one will do.
>
> —— Thomas Jefferson

Unit Goals

- To understand the definitions of blending, clipping, back-formation, acronymy, reduplication and eponyms
- To grasp the minor processes of word formation in English
- To learn the different types of blending and clipping
- To comprehend the difference between acronyms and initialisms

Before You Read

1. Guess the meanings of the following blends based on the pictures. Try to figure out what a blend is and how these blends are formed.

①
②
③
④

① bromeo = _____ + _____

② shopaholic = _____ + _____
③ phubbing = _____ + _____
④ bromance = _____ + _____

2. **What do the following abbreviations stand for? Discuss how these abbreviations are formed with your partner.**

1) *CD* stands for _____.
   A. current delirium   B. compost disc
   C. compass disc   D. compact disc

2) *Dorm* stands for _____.
   A. dormitory   B. dormouse
   C. dormer   D. dormant

3) *Prof* stands for _____.
   A. profile   B. profane
   C. professor   D. proficiency

4) *AIDS* stands for _____.
   A. American Investigation Data System
   B. Acquired Immune Deficiency Syndrome
   C. Always In Dead Silence

5) *MBA* stands for _____.
   A. More Bad Advice
   B. Married But Available
   C. Master of Business Administration

Start to Read

Text A   Minor Process of Word Formation

Apart from the major types of word formation, there are also minor types of word formation, such as blending, clipping and back-formation.

Blending

A blend is a word formed from parts of two other words. These parts are sometimes, but not always, morphemes.

In everyday life, blends are actually a common type of speech error. When we search our mental lexicons for words, we often come upon two words with the same meaning that are pronounced similarly. Because human beings are so quick at speaking, sometimes we have to use one of these words before we are finished choosing which one to use. For example, the adverbs *mainly* and *mostly* are almost interchangeable, for their structure and meanings are very similar as are their pronunciations. Someone wanting to say "It was *mainly/mostly* his own doing" might find both these words simultaneously in his or her mental lexicon while uttering this sentence and end up saying "It was *maistly* his own doing." Here are some more blends that have occurred as actual speech errors.

English Speech Error Blends	
Utterance	**Blended**
My *stummy* hurts.	stomach/tummy
There's a *dreeze* blowing through the room.	draft/breeze
That's the end of today's *lection*.	lecture/lesson

Indeed, there is a natural tendency caused by the nature of lexical selection during speech to create blends, but we also do it consciously. When English-speakers began driving their cars everywhere rather than taking the train, someone came up with the idea of a hotel where they could park their motor cars right by the door to their room. This hotel differed from others in that it accommodated what were called then "motor cars." To distinguish this type of hotel from others, someone blended *motor* and *hotel* together, giving us *motel*.

Most blends are formed by one of the following methods:

a. head + tail

The beginning of one word is added to the end of the other. For example, *brunch* is a blend of *breakfast* and *lunch*. This is the most common method of blending.

b. head + head

The beginnings of two words are combined. For example, *sci-fi* is a blend of *science* and *fiction*.

c. head + word

The beginning of one word is combined with the whole form of the other. For example, *medicare* is a blend of *medical* and *care*.

d. word + tail

The whole form of one word is combined with the end of the other. For example, *guesstimate* is a blend of *guess* and *estimate*.

e. Two words are blended around a common sequence of sounds. For example, the word *Californication*, from a song by the Red Hot Chili Peppers and also the title of an American comedy-drama TV series, is a blend of *California* and *fornication*.

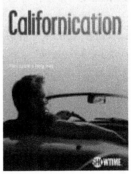

f. Multiple sounds from two component words are blended, while mostly preserving the sounds' order. Poet Lewis Carroll was well-known for these kinds of blends. An example of this is the word *slithy*, a blend of *lithe* and *slimy*. This method is difficult to achieve and is considered a sign of Carroll's verbal wit.

We should note that when two words are blended, at least one of them is not in its complete form. When two words are combined in their entirety, the result is considered a compound word rather than a blend. For example, *watermelon* is a compound, not a blend.

Clipping

Clipping is the word formation process which consists in the reduction of a word to one of its parts. It is an even more wide-spread way of creating new words. Clippings are also known as "shortenings."

An interesting thing about clipping is that the newly clipped word usually continues to exist alongside the original, so *doc* and *doctor* coexist; *phone* and *telephone* don't seem to get in each other's way. The same applies to *bio* and *biology*, *math* and *mathematics*, and so on. Another interesting thing about clipping is that we do not seem to care much which end of a word we clip. We clip the end of *prof(essor)*, *sub(marine)* and *prep(are)*, but the beginning of *(tele)phone*, *(cara)van* and *(ham)burger*. Sometimes we clip both ends. As a result, we get *(in)flu(enza)*.

Clipping mainly consists of the following types:

a. Back clipping

Back clipping is the most common type, in which the beginning is retained. Examples are: *ad* (advertisement), *exam* (examination), *fan* (fanatic), *gas* (gasoline), *memo* (memorandum) and *gym* (gymnasium, gymnastics).

b. Front clipping

Front clipping retains the final part. Examples are: *bus* (omnibus), *plane* (airplane), *quake* (earthquake), *chute* (parachute), *coon* (raccoon) and *gator* (alligator).

c. Front and back clipping

In front and back clipping, the middle of the word is retained. Examples are: *tec* (detective), *jams* (pajamas) and *fridge* (refrigerator).

d. Phrase clipping

Phrase clipping involves the shortening of a phrase. Examples are: *pub* (public house), *zoo* (zoological garden), *pop* (popular music) and *perm* (permanent waves).

In some cases, clipping alters spelling as indicated by *fridge* (refrigerator). More examples are: *bike* (bicycle), *coke* (coca cola), *hanky* (handkerchief) and *biz* (business).

Back-formation

Back-formation refers to the process of creating a new word by removing actual or supposed affixes. Back-formations are shortened words created from longer words, thus back-formations may be viewed as a sub-type of clipping.

It is a historical fact about English that the nouns *peddler*, *beggar*, *hawker*, *stoker*, *scavenger*, *swindler*, *editor*, *burglar* and *sculptor* all existed in the language before the corresponding verbs *peddle*, *beg*, *hawk*, *stoke*, *scavenge*, *swindle*, *edit*, *burgle* and *sculpt*. Each of these nouns denoted a general profession or activity, and speakers simply assumed that the sound at the end of each one was the suffix *-er*. Having made this assumption, speakers could then subtract the final *-er* and arrive at a new verb, just as we can subtract the *-er* affix on *writer* and arrive at the verb *write*. In short, back-formation is the process of using a word formation rule to analyze a morphologically simple word as if it were a complex word in order to arrive at a new, simpler form.

Many words came into English by this route. *Pease* was once a mass noun but was reinterpreted as a plural, leading to the back-formation *pea*. The noun *statistic* was likewise a back-formation from the field of study *statistics*.

An interesting contemporary example of back-formation involves the suffix *-er*. *Lase*r (light amplification by stimulated emission of radiation) ends in *er* only because *e* stands for *emission* and *r* stands for *radiation*. Speakers quickly forget such origins, though, and before long physicists had invented the verb *lase*, used in sentences such as "This dye, under the appropriate laboratory conditions, will lase," where *lase* refers to emitting radiation of a certain sort. The *er* on *laser* accidentally resembles the suffix *-er*, and the word itself denotes an instrument; hence, physicists took this *er* sequence to be the suffix and subtracted it to form a new verb.

Another recent example involves the plural suffix *-s*. The word in question is *kudos*, which is a synonym for *praise*. The finals *-s* in this word is not a plural morpheme. However, some speakers now use the word *kudo*, having mistakenly analyzed the *s* as a plural morpheme and removed it to derive a singular. In other words, they use the originally singular noun *kudos* as a plural, *praises*, and their new back-formation *kudo* as a singular, *praise*. In the original pronunciation of *kudos*, the final *s* sounded like the *s* in *mouse*. Interestingly, the speakers who use both *kudos* and the back-formation *kudo* pronounce the *s* in *kudos* like *z*, as in *dogs*. It turns out that this is no accident. Once the *s* in *kudos* has been analyzed as being the plural *-s*, it must be pronounced like *z* in this word.

It is ironic that even the word *back-formation* is undergoing back-formation. The technical linguistic term *back-formation* existed in English first, and now one hears linguists saying "Speakers backformed word X from word Y," creating a new verb in English, *backform*. What is happening is possibly because English has many examples of words that has *verb* and *verb + -ion* pairs. In these pairs, the *-ion* suffix is added to verb forms in order to create nouns such as *insert/ insertion, project/ projection*, etc. Hence, the speakers assume that they can take *-ion* from any noun and arrive back at a verb.

More examples are as follows:

Existed Earlier	Formed Later by Back-formation
resurrection	*resurrect*
preemption	*preempt*
vivisection	*vivisect*
electrocution	*electrocute*
television	*televise*
emotion	*emote*
donation	*donate*

Even though many English words are formed this way, new coinages may sound strange and are often used for humorous effect. For example, *gruntled* or *pervious* (from *disgruntled* and *impervious*) would be considered mistakes today and used only in humorous contexts.

Frequently back-formations begin in colloquial use and only gradually become accepted. For example, *enthuse* (from *enthusiasm*) is gaining popularity, though it is still considered substandard by some today.

After You Read

Knowledge Focus

1. Discuss the following questions with your partner.
   1) How do you understand "Blends are actually a common type of speech error"?
   2) How many ways are there to form blends? Give examples.
   3) What is the most common method of blending?
   4) What is the difference between a blend and a compound?
   5) Do clippings coexist with the original words?
   6) How many types does clipping mainly consist of? Give examples.
   7) What is the most common type of clipping?
   8) What is the difference between back-formation and back clipping?
   9) How do you understand that back-formation is "the process of creating a new word by removing actual or supposed affixes"?
   10) How is the word *back-formation* undergoing back-formation?

2. Tell whether the following statements are true or false according to the knowledge you learned and why.
   1) Blending, compounding and clipping are all minor types of word formation in English. (   )
   2) Blending is the formation of new words by combining parts of two words or a word plus a part of another word. (   )
   3) There are many ways to form blends. One of them is to combine two words in their complete forms. (   )
   4) Clipping, a way of making a word, is to shorten a longer word by cutting a part off the original and adding a new part to the original. (   )
   5) Clipped words are those created by clipping part of a word, leaving only a piece of the old word. (   )
   6) Clipping never alters spelling. (   )
   7) Back-formation is the method of creating words by removing the supposed suffixes. (   )
   8) Back-formation is considered to be the opposite process of prefixation. (   )
   9) The process by which a word is shortened without changing its meaning and part of speech is called back-formation. (   )
   10) Any long word with multiple syllables can be backformed. (   )

3. Tell whether the following words are blends, clippings or back-formations. Put a tick (√) in the corresponding column.

Words	Blending	Clipping	Back-formation
brunch			
burger			
donate			
jams			

Words	Blending	Clipping	Back-formation
medicare			
memo			
plane			
resurrect			
sci-fi			
zoo			

Language Focus

1. Fill in the blanks with the following words you have learned in the text. Change the forms where necessary.

| retain | assumption | preserve | tendency | simultaneously |
| emit | consciously | accommodate | stimulate | utterance |

1) The opera will be broadcast _____ on television and radio.
2) She was probably not _____ aware of the true nature of her feelings.
3) I have a _____ to talk too much when I'm nervous.
4) This hotel can _____ up to 500 guests.
5) Efforts to _____ the peace have failed.
6) Praise always _____ him to make greater efforts.
7) We _____ the original fireplace when we decorated the room.
8) The cheese is _____ a strong smell.
9) The theory is based on a series of wrong _____.
10) Politicians are judged by their public _____.

2. Proofreading & Error Correction.

As an alternative to using native elements to produce a new label, one can, of course, turn into other languages for material.

A language can form new compounds using elements taken for the classical languages. The word *television* is composed from a Greek element indicating distance and a Latin element indicating sight. In field of medicine, terminology is generally based on classical elements; *hepatitis*, for example, is based on the Greek equivalence of *liver*. Such words are called neo-classical compounds. Like blend words, they are composed with elements that cannot exist by themselves.

One case where we do find a widespread correlation is among the concept of mother and the

1) _____

2) _____

3) _____

4) _____

5) _____

6) _____

sound [m]: Arabic uses the word (in transliteration) *umm*, Chinese uses the word *ma*. An Inca goddess of agriculture was called *Pachamama*, Mother Earth. It has suggested that [m], one of the first consonant sounds that a child makes, has been widely associated to the mother because that is the sound that the child makes when its lips are seeking out the breast. Indeed, the Latin word for a breast is *mamma*, that being the source of such English words like *mammal* and *mammary*.

7) _____

8) _____

9) _____

10) _____

3. Translate the following paragraph into Chinese.

In everyday life, blends are actually a common type of speech error. When we search our mental lexicons for words, we often come upon two words with the same meaning that are pronounced similarly. Because human beings are so quick at speaking, sometimes we have to use one of these words before we are finished choosing which one to use.

Comprehensive Work

1. Use the clipped forms of the following words to complete the dialogues with your partner.

| sergeant | gymnasium | gasoline | dormitory | handkerchief |
| influenza | comfortable | bicycle | refrigerator | mathematics |

1) Mary: Where did Alice go?
   Classmate: _____
2) Teacher: What's your favorite subject?
   Student: _____
3) Jerry: Where did you put the ice cream?
   Sister: _____
4) Ann: How did you get here?
   Tom: _____
5) Teacher: Why were you absent yesterday?
   Student: _____
6) Sergeant: Get these windows cleaned, soldier.
   Private: _____
7) Mother: Did you wipe your nose on your sleeve?
   Child: _____
8) Wife: What's wrong with our car?
   Husband: _____
9) John: Where is the basketball match?
   Will: _____
10) Mother: How do you like your new bed?
    Child: _____

2. Work in a group of three. Use one of the images below to illustrate a minor type of word formation, and share with your group members.

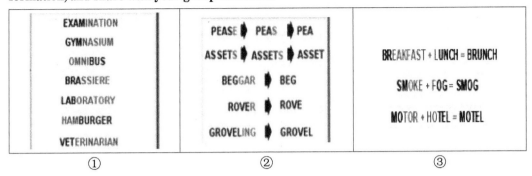

3. Writing

The build-up to the Copenhagen Climate Change Conference (2009) was full of optimism and hope. Unfortunately, instead of a positive outcome, most commentators saw it as a failure. *The New Indian Express* commented: It was billed by its Danish hosts as *Hopenhagen*, but long before it wound its way to a damning and disappointing conclusion; it was attracting new appellations in the media like *Nopenhagen* and *Flopenhagen*.

What type of word formation is used in the above comments? What message does it convey?

Read More

Text B Acronymy

Acronymy is a word-formation process by joining the initial letters of words or word parts in a phrase or name, resulting in acronyms and initialisms. Both acronyms and initialisms are abbreviations, but there is a key difference between the two.

Acronyms

An acronym is a pronounceable word that is formed using the first letters of the words or word parts in a phrase or name. The part of the definition of acronym that many people miss is that the resulting abbreviation needs to be pronounceable as a word. For example, we say "nay-to" for *NATO* (the North Atlantic Treaty Organization), which means that we are saying a word, as opposed to saying each letter "ehn-ay-tee-oh." Other examples of acronyms are *RAM* (Random Access  Memory), *LASER* (Light Amplification by Stimulated Emission of Radiation), *NASA* (National Aeronautics and Space Administration), and *OPEC* (Organization of Petroleum Exporting Countries). Occasionally, not just letters but a whole or part syllable can be used in the formation of an acronym. A case in point is *RADAR* (Radio Detection and Ranging).

Initialisms

Initialisms are very similar to acronyms in that they are made up of letters of some name or

phrase, usually the initial letter of each word as is common with acronyms. The difference between an acronym and initialism is that the abbreviation formed with initialisms is not pronounced as a word, rather we say the individual letters, such as *FBI* (Federal Bureau of Investigation), *CIA* (Central Intelligence Agency), UFO (Unidentified Flying Object) and *DVD* (Digital Video Disk or Digital Versatile Disk).

Exercises

1. Is the statement "Acronyms are words formed from the initial letters of words and pronounced as letters" true or false? why?
2. Is the statement "*TOEFL, IELTS* and *GRE* are all acronyms" true or false? why?
3. What is the difference between acronyms and initialisms?
4. Initialisms are being added to the daily vocabulary with the proliferation of computers and widespread use of the Internet. Do you recognize the following initialisms—*BTW, FYI, LOL, ICQ* and *BRB*? What other initialisms that are used in memos, email or text messaging can you think of?

Text C Reduplication

The coinage of new words and phrases into English has been greatly enhanced by the pleasure we get from playing with words. There are numerous alliterative and rhyming idioms, which are a significant feature of the language. These are not restricted to poets and Cockneys; everyone uses them. We start in the nursery with *choo-choos*, move on in adult life to *hanky-panky* and end up in the nursing home having a *sing-song*.

The repeating of parts of words to make new forms is called reduplication. There are various categories of this: rhyming, exact and ablaut (vowel substitution). Examples are, respectively, *okey-dokey*, *wee-wee* and *zig-zag*. The impetus for the coining of these seems to be nothing more than the enjoyment of wordplay. The words that make up these reduplicated idioms often have little meaning in themselves and only appear as part of a pair. In other cases, one word will allude to some existing meaning and the other half of the pair is added for effect or emphasis.

New coinages have often appeared at times of national confidence when an outgoing and playful nature is expressed in language. For example, during the 1920s, following the First World War, many nonsense word pairs were coined—the *bee's knees, heebie-jeebies*, etc.

The introduction of such terms began with Old English and continues today. *Willy-nilly* is over a thousand years old. *Riff-raff* dates from the 1400s and *helter-skelter, arsy-versy* (a form of *vice-versa*), and *hocus-pocus* all date from the 16th century. Coming up to date we have *bling-bling, boob-tube* and *hip-hop*.

Exercises

1. Use the reduplicatives mentioned in the text to complete the sentences.

1) He found himself drawn, _____, into the argument.
2) She thinks she's the _____.
3) Don't bring any _____ into my house!
4) Being alone in the dark gives me the _____.
5) I still think that horoscopes are a load of _____.

2. How many main categories can reduplicatives be divided into? Can you think of some examples other than the given ones for each category?

Text D Eponyms

Eponyms are words derived from proper names and are another of the many creative ways that the vocabulary of a language expands.

Some eponyms are fairly well-known. Examples are *sandwich*, famously consumed (if not invented) by John Montagu, Fourth Earl of Sandwich, *pasteurization*, from the name of the fearless French chemist who invented the process, *valentine*, from the saintly name of not one but two early Christian martyrs, and *quixotic*, from the windmill-tilting hero of Cervantes' great romance, *Don Quixote*.

But there are hundreds of other eponyms whose etymologies are less familiar. Here are nine of them.

- *Amp and Ampere* (from André Marie Ampère, 1775-1836) The term for a unit of electric current was named after the French mathematician who is credited with the discovery of electromagnetism.
- *Diesel* (from Rudolf Diesel, 1858-1913) After surviving the explosion of his first internal combustion engine, German engineer Rudolf Diesel went on to achieve wealth and fame until drowning when he went overboard while crossing the English Channel by steamer.
- *Draconian* (from Draco, 7th century BC) The first chief magistrate of ancient Athens, Draco composed a memorably harsh legal code, one that liberally applied the death penalty.
- *Dunce* (from John Duns Scotus, 1265-1308) Though Scotus himself was a highly regarded theologian and philosopher, his quarreling followers brought the master's name into disrepute. By the 16th century, *dunce* had become a derogatory term for a slow-witted or ignorant person.
- *Guppy* (from R.J. Lechmere Guppy, 1836-1916) This small freshwater fish bears the name of the British-born naturalist who discovered it while he was living in Trinidad.
- *Leotard* (from Jules Leotard, 1830-1870) French aerialist Jules Leotard not only had a tight-fitting garment named after him but also had a popular song written about him, "The Daring Young Man on the Flying Trapeze."
- *Mausoleum* (from Mausolus, ruler of the ancient Asian country of Caria, 377–353 BC) Over 100 feet high, the tomb of King Mausolus survived into the 12th century and was considered

one of the Seven Wonders of the Ancient World. Since then, the word *mausoleum* has come to be used for any large, above-ground tomb.
- *Salisbury steak* (from James H. Salisbury, 1823–1905) American physician James Salisbury invented this cafeteria staple as part of his highly questionable all-meat diet.
- *Sequoia* (from Sequoyah, also known as George Guess, 1770–1843) A Cherokee silversmith, Sequoyah devised a practical writing system for the Cherokee language, thus enabling his tribe to read and write. Shortly after his death, the huge California cypress tree was named in his honor.

For Fun

Works to Read

1. ***The Eponym Dictionary of Birds*** by Bo Beolens, Michael Watkins and Michael Grayson

    This extraordinary work lists more than 4,000 eponymous names covering 10,000 genera, species and subspecies of birds. Every taxon with an eponymous vernacular or scientific name is listed, followed by a concise biography of the person concerned. The text is punctuated with intriguing or little-known facts, unearthed in the course of the authors' extensive research.

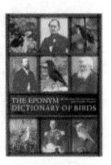

2. ***A Year of New Words*** by Edwin Battistella

    In 2012, linguist Edwin Battistella made up and tweeted a word a day. This book tells the story of those words—the blends, clippings, prefixes, suffixes, malapropisms and more that formed the basis for 366 made-up words. It is an entertaining story of words with some serious linguistics underneath.

Websites to Visit

1. http://www.acronymfinder.com/

    Acronym Finder is the world's largest and most comprehensive dictionary of acronyms, initialisms and abbreviations. On this website, you can find out what any acronym, initialism or abbreviation stands for.

2. http://www.learn-english-today.com/new-words/new-words-in-english.html

    The website provides a collection of recently-coined words, terms and expressions with their meaning.

3. http://www.englishexercises.org/

    On this website, you will find hundreds of exercises to learn English online: vocabulary, grammar, listening, songs, etc. These exercises have been made by English language teachers from all over the world.

Unit 8

Word Meaning and Motivation

> Words are things, and a small drop of ink
> Falling like dew, upon a thought, produces
> That which makes thousands, perhaps millions, think
> —— George Gordon Byron

Unit Goals

- To understand the definitions of grammatical meaning and lexical meaning
- To grasp the classification of word meaning and the subdivision of lexical meaning
- To be familiar with the main types of word motivation
- To comprehend the relationship between the sound and meaning of most words

 ### Before You Read

1. What is the meaning of the word *mean*? Choose the best explanation for each sentence.

1) I'm sorry I hurt you: I didn't *mean* to.
   A. show   B. intend
2) You're more of an expert than me. I *mean*, you've got all that experience.
   A. suggest   B. that is to say
3) The flashing lights *mean* that the road is blocked.
   A. signify   B. imply
4) Her children *mean* the world to her.
   A. stand for   B. indicate
5) She is too *mean* to make a donation.
   A. unkind   B. ungenerous

2. Sound and Meaning

1) In how many languages can you say the name of the animal in the picture? Is there a logical relationship between the sound and the meaning?

2) Read the following lines from *Romeo and Juliet*. What is Juliet trying to say here? Can you invent some names for a rose? Imagine yourself using the new name(s) just invented, would you have difficulty making yourself understood?

Shakespeare – *Romeo and Juliet*

" What's in a name? That which we call a rose By any other word would smell as sweet; So Romeo would, were he not Romeo call'd, ..."

(II.ii.43-45)

"What does a name mean? The thing we call a rose would smell just as sweet if we called it by any other name. Romeo would be just as perfect even if he wasn't called Romeo."

3) What does the table of words below tell you about the relationship between sound and meaning?

1.	write	rite	right	wright
2.	pause	pores	pours	paws
3.	two	to	too	——

Start to Read

Text A Word Meaning in the English Language

Word meaning is the meaning of a lexeme—any unit of the vocabulary of a language, listed, defined in a dictionary and realized by their word-forms. There are two types of meaning: grammatical and lexical meaning. These two types also lie in English lexemes. The lexemes belonging to the open-classes of the major parts of speech such as nouns, adjectives, verbs and adverbs have full word-forms with both grammatical and lexical meaning. As those belonging to the closed-classes of articles, conjunctions, interjections, prepositions and certain pronouns and adverbs have empty word-forms, they are not dealt with here.

Grammatical Meaning

A lexeme may have different word-forms and these word-forms will generally differ in their grammatical meaning—the meaning in terms of grammar. For example, the forms of *student* and *students* differ in respect of their grammatical meaning, in that one is the singular form and the other is plural form; and the difference between singular forms and plural forms is semantically relevant: it affects sentence-meaning. The meaning of a sentence is determined partly by the meaning of the words (i.e., lexemes) of which it consists and partly by its grammatical meaning.

The term "categorical meaning" is part of grammatical meaning: it is that part of the meaning of lexemes which derives from their being members of one category of major parts of speech rather than another (nouns rather than verbs, verbs rather than adjectives, and so on). Thus, all lexemes with full word-forms have a categorical meaning.

For example, the lexemes *easy* and *difficult* have the same categorical meaning: they are both adjectives. Each lexeme, however, has certain semantically relevant grammatical properties. The two word-forms *easy* and *easier* of the lexeme *easy*, though sharing some part of their categorical meaning, differ grammatically in that: one is the absolute form and the other the comparative form. This difference does not occur to the lexeme *difficult*, for this lexeme has only one form *difficult*, which does not accept any inflection.

Though *easy* and *difficult* belong to the same category of adjectives, having the same categorical meaning, they do not share all the grammatical features in terms of morphology and syntax. Likewise, all the lexemes sharing categorical meaning do not have all the grammatical meanings in common.

Lexical Meaning

Lexical meaning makes a word different from any other word. The lexical meaning of a word may be thought of as the specific value it has in a particular language system, and the "personality" it acquires through usage within that system. It may be analyzed into descriptive and non-descriptive meaning.

The descriptive meaning of a lexeme is widely assumed to be the central factor in linguistic communication. The non-descriptive meaning of a lexeme, by contrast provides additional effects to its central meaning. The following is dealing with denotation as descriptive meaning, and connotation as non-descriptive meaning.

Denotation

Denotative meaning (sometimes called conceptual or cognitive meaning) is the direct or dictionary meaning of a word. It may be defined as the meaning used to convey ideas in order to describe the world. The denotation of a lexeme refers to the relationship that holds between that lexeme and persons, things, places, properties, processes and activities external to the language system. A lexeme, in general, denoted a class of entities in the world. For example, the lexeme *shirt* denotes a class of pieces of clothing worn on the upper part of the body; the lexeme *student* denotes all the students in the world; and the lexeme *happy* denotes the property of being happy. Denotation, thus, is invariant and context-independent. To put it in a nutshell, the denotation of a lexeme is of important value in making up of its descriptive meaning.

Connotation

The term "connotation" is particularly rich in technical senses. It is used in opposition with denotation. Connotation is, in fact, largely dependent on the context of usage of the word. There is no clear-cut classification of connotative meaning of a lexeme. It can be classified into expressive, presupposed and evoked meaning. It can refer to emotive, stylistic, discursive and evocative meaning.

Part of the connotation of a lexeme is its expressive meaning (sometimes called emotive, attitudinal or affective meaning), which communicates the speakers' evaluation or their attitudes. For example, *complain* and *whine* have the same descriptive meaning, but the latter communicates the speaker's annoyance when complaining while the former does not.

The connotation of a lexeme is its evoked meaning, which is a consequence of the existence of different dialects and registers within a language. Dialects are varieties of language associated with different characteristics of users (e.g. age, class and regional affiliation), and registers are varieties of language that a single speaker considers appropriate to a specific situation which may be formal or informal. *Bicycle* and *bike*, for instance, have the same descriptive meaning, but the former is a neutral word while the latter is an informal one, thus being used in less formal circumstances than the former. Other examples are *chat*, *talk*, and *converse*, which are used depending on different situations: informal, neutral, and formal, respectively.

Apart from this, part of the connotation of the lexeme is evocative meaning, which is different from the evoked meaning. It is the associations connected with a word. For example, a word such as *Christmas* could call up images of Christmas trees, family gatherings, presents and so on.

The Difference between Denotation and Connotation

The denotation of a word is its primary signification or reference, whereas its connotation is the range of secondary or associated significations and feelings which it commonly suggests or implies. For example, *home* denotes the house where one lives, but connotes privacy, intimacy, and coziness.

That is the reason real estate agents like to use *home* instead of *house* in their advertisements.

In short, the denotation of a word is its exact and literal meaning. The connotation of a word, on the other hand, consists of its emotive value. It is the subjective, personal, even poetic interpretation of a word.

Text B Motivation of Words

The term "motivation" is used to denote the relationship existing between the phonemic or morphemic composition and structural pattern of the word on the one hand, and its meaning on the other. There are three main types of motivation: phonetic motivation, morphological motivation, and semantic motivation.

Phonetic Motivation

When there is a certain similarity between the sounds that make up the word and those referred to by the sense, the motivation is phonetic. Examples are: *bang, buzz, cuckoo, giggle, gurgle, hiss, purr, whistle*, etc. Here the sounds of a word are imitative of sounds in nature because what is referred to is a sound or at least produces a characteristic sound. Although there exists a certain arbitrary element in the resulting phonemic shape of the word, one can see that this type of motivation is determined by the phonological system of each language as shown by the difference of echo-words for the same concept in different languages. Phonetic motivation is not a perfect replica of any acoustic structure but only a rough approximation. This accounts for the variability of echo-words within one language and between different languages, such as *cuckoo* (English), *Kuckuck* (German), and *coucou* (French).

Within the English vocabulary there are different words, all sound imitative, meaning "quick, foolish, indistinct talk": *babble, chatter, gabble, prattle*. In this last group echoic creations combine phonological and morphological motivation because they contain verbal suffixes *-le* and *-er* forming frequentative verbs. We see therefore that one word may combine different types of motivation.

Morphological Motivation

The morphological motivation may be quite regular. Thus, the prefix *ex-* means "former" when added to human nouns: *ex-serviceman, ex-wife*. Alongside with these cases there is a more general use of *ex-*: in borrowed words it is unstressed and motivation is faded (e.g. *expect*). The derived word *rethink* is motivated in as much as its morphological structure suggests the idea of thinking again. *Re-* is one of the most common prefixes of the English language. It means "again" and "back" and is added to verbal stems or abstract deverbal noun stems, as in *rebuild, reclaim, resell*, and *resettlement*. Here again these newer formations should be compared with older borrowings from Latin and French where *re-* is now unstressed, and the motivation is faded. Compare *re-cover* "cover again" and *recover* "get better." In short, morphological motivation is especially obvious in newly coined words, or at least words created in the present century.

In deciding whether a word of long standing in the language is morphologically motivated according to present-day patterns or not, one should be very careful. Similarity in sound form does not always correspond to similarity in morphological pattern. Agential suffix *-er* is affixable to any verb, so that V+*-er* means "one who V-s" or "something that V-s": *writer, receiver, bomber, rocker, knocker*. Yet, although the verb *numb* exists in English, *number* is not "one who numbs" but is derived from Old French *nombre* borrowed into English and completely assimilated. The cases of regular morphological motivation outnumber irregularities, and yet one must remember the principle of "fuzzy sets" in coming across the word *smoker* with its variants: "one who smokes tobacco" and "a railway car in which passengers may smoke." Many writers nowadays introduce the term "word-building meaning" instead of the term "morphological motivation."

Semantic Motivation

The third type of motivation is called semantic motivation. It is based on the co-existence of direct and figurative meanings of the same word within the same synchronous system. *Mouth* continues to denote a part of the human face, and at the same time it can metaphorically apply to any opening or outlet: *the mouth of a river, of a cave, of a furnace*. *Jacket* is a short coat and also a protective cover for a book, a phonograph record or an electric wire. *Ermine* is not only the name of a small animal, but also of its fur, and the office and rank of an English judge because in England ermine was worn by judges in court. In their direct meaning neither *mouth* nor *ermine* is motivated.

As to compounds, their motivation is morphological if the meaning of the whole is based on the direct meaning of the components, and semantic if the combination of components is used figuratively. Thus, *eyewash* "a lotion for the eyes" or *headache* "pain in the head," or *watchdog* "a dog kept for watching property" are all morphologically motivated. If, on the other hand, they are used metaphorically as "something said or done to deceive a person so that he thinks that what he sees is good, though in fact it is not," "anything or anyone very annoying" and "a watchful human guardian," respectively, then the motivation is semantic.

An interesting example of complex morpho-semantic motivation passing through several stages in its history is the word *teenager* "a person in his or her teens." The motivation may be historically traced as follows: the inflected form of the numeral *ten* produced the suffix *-teen*. The suffix later produces a stem with a metonymical meaning (semantic motivation), receives the plural ending *-s*, and then produces a new noun *teens* "the years of a person's life of which the numbers end in *-teen*,

namely from 13 to 19." In combination with *age* or *aged* the adjectives *teen-age* and *teen-aged* are coined, as in *teen-age boy*, *teen-age fashions*. A morphologically motivated noun *teenager* is then formed with the help of the suffix *-er* which is often added to compounds or noun phrases producing personal names according to the pattern "one connected with...". The pattern is frequent enough. One must keep in mind, however, that not all words with a similar morphemic composition will have the same derivational history and denote human beings. For example, *first-nighter* and *honeymooner* are personal nouns, but *two-seater* is "a car or an airplane seating two persons", *back-hander* is "a back-hand stroke in tennis" and *three-decker* "a sandwich made of three pieces of bread with two layers of filling."

When the connection between the meaning of the word and its form is conventional, that is, there is no perceptible reason for the word having this particular phonemic and morphemic composition, the word is said to be non-motivated for the present stage of language development. Every vocabulary is in a state of constant development. Words that seem non-motivated at present may have lost their motivation. The verb *earn* does not suggest at present any necessary connection with agriculture. The connection of form and meaning seems purely conventional. Historical analysis shows, however, that it is derived from Old English *(ze-)earnian* "to harvest." In Modern English, this connection no longer exists, and *earn* is now a non-motivated word. Complex morphological structures tend to unite and become indivisible units.

After You Read

Knowledge Focus

1. Discuss the following questions with your partner.
   1) How do you define grammatical meaning?
   2) What is the difference between grammatical meaning and lexical meaning?
   3) How do you understand categorical meaning?
   4) How can lexical meaning be subdivided?
   5) Is there a clear-cut classification of connotative meaning of a lexeme?
   6) What is the difference between denotation and connotation?
   7) How many main types of word motivation are there? What are they?
   8) Can one word combine different types of motivation? Give examples.
   9) Why should one be careful when deciding whether a word is morphologically motivated or not?
   10) Why do some English words seem to be non-motivated?

2. Tell whether the following statements are true or false according to the knowledge you learned and why.
   1) Categorical meaning is part of grammatical meaning. (   )
   2) Lexical meaning refers to the part of speech, tenses of verbs and stylistic features of words. (   )
   3) The conceptual meaning of a word is often unstable and hard to determine. (   )
   4) Lexical meaning is not only descriptive but also affective and social. (   )

5) The meaning of a sentence is the sum of the meanings of all its words and phrases putting together. (   )
6) Connotation is rarely dependent on the context of usage of the word. (   )
7) Affective meaning is concerned with the expression of feelings and attitudes of the speaker or writer. (   )
8) If the two words have the same conceptual meaning, they must have the same connotative meaning. (   )
9) One word may combine different types of motivation. (   )
10) Words are in a state of constant development. In Modern English, all the words are motivated. (   )

3. **What is an equivalent of "conceptual meaning"?**
   ☐ grammatical meaning
   ☐ lexical meaning
   ☐ stylistic meaning
   ☐ connotative meaning
   ☐ denotative meaning
   ☐ affective meaning

Language Focus

1. **Fill in the blanks with the following words you have learned in the text. Change the forms where necessary.**

| imitative | emotive | attitudinal | nutshell | discursive |
| perceptible | replica | intimacy | evocative | assimilate |

1) His talk was _____ of the bygone days.
2) To put it in a _____, we're bankrupt.
3) Everyone has _____ issues during his puberty.
4) Capital punishment is a highly _____ issue.
5) Amy was a younger _____ of her mother.
6) The price increase has had no _____ effect on sales.
7) The old _____ between them had gone for ever.
8) The U.S.A. has _____ people from many different countries.
9) His own toast was _____ and overlong, though rather touching.
10) His style of public speaking is _____ of the prime minister.

2. Proofreading & Error Correction.

Word meanings are what are sought and what should be provided with comprehensive dictionaries of a language. For much the history of semantic studies, and still to a considerably extent today, the investigation of word meaning has been based on the relationships of reference and denotation. Certainly meaning includes the relations between utterances and parts of utterances (e.g. words) and the world outside; and the reference and denotation are among such relations. But the purposes of linguistics it is desirable dealing with meaning by a more comprehensive treatment.

Sentences have meaning, and are meaningful; and a child learns the meaning of many words by hearing them in other people's uttering sentences and practicing such utterances themselves subject to the correction of others and the test of being understood by those to whom he is talking. The process goes on all our lives, and we learn new words and extend and increase our knowledge of the words we already know, as we hear and see them in fresh utterances and used slightly different from the ways which we are accustomed. The meaning of a word, therefore, may be considered as the way it is used and understood as a part of different sentences; what the dictionary does is to try and summarize for each word the way or ways it is used in the sort of sentences which it is found in the language.

1) _____
2) _____
3) _____

4) _____
5) _____

6) _____
7) _____

8) _____
9) _____

10) _____

3. Translate the following paragraph into Chinese.

The denotation of a word is its primary signification or reference, whereas its connotation is the range of secondary or associated significations and feelings which it commonly suggests or implies. For example, *home* denotes the house where one lives, but connotes privacy, intimacy, and coziness. That is the reason real estate agents like to use *home* instead of *house* in their advertisements.

Comprehensive Work

1. **In the following poem by William Wordsworth, distinguish between the denotative and connotative meanings of the last line.**

A slumber did my spirit seal;
I had no human fears:
She seemed a thing that could not feel
The touch of earthly years.

No motion has she now, no force:
She neither hears nor sees,
Rolled round in earth's diurnal course
With rocks and stones and trees.

2. **Writing**

Samuel Taylor Coleridge says, "There are three classes into which all the women past seventy that ever I knew were to be divided: 1) That dear old soul; 2) That old woman; 3) That old witch." Write about the different feelings the three phrases convey to you and relate it with the connotation of words.

Read More

Text C Aspects of Meaning

Geoffrey Leech presents a simpler breakdown of meaning into seven aspects. The first is the fundamental **denotative**—or, as Leech refers to it, the **conceptual**—meaning, that which defines the meaning of a lexeme in terms of its constituent features. Thus, to use the componential analysis, the conceptual meaning of the lexeme *woman* can be defined in terms of such properties as +human, −male and +adult. Here, then, we are dealing with a direct link between word and thing. But, the intermediary of the human mind often affects the nature of the semantic range of a lexeme. Different people, having been subjected to different experiences in life, have different mental images when they hear a lexeme. When different people hear the lexeme *woman* such qualities as beauty, compassion, practicality and emotion will feature with differing relative significance. Moreover, the relative significance of features will change as society changes; the association of housewife is much less prevalent in our society than it was fifty years ago. Such association is called **connotative** meaning by Leech. A lexeme may be more appropriate in a particular style. To draw from Leech's examples again, *cast* is associated with literary style while *chuck* is colloquial. This is **stylistic** meaning. *Shut up* in the sense of being quiet similarly has stylistic meaning, being colloquial, but in so far as it is indicative of a disrespectful attitude on the part of the speaker it also has **affective** meaning. Our response to one sense of a lexeme may be affected by another sense of that lexeme. We can, for example, scarcely use the word *gay* in its older sense of "merry" as it now invokes "homosexuality." This is **reflected** meaning. Lexemes may have a **collocative** meaning, requiring that they are used together with certain other lexemes but not with others. Collocation may be so restrictive that we can guess which word will follow a given word, an example being *blond*. Finally Leech refers to **thematic** meaning, to the emphasis that attaches to a lexeme as the result of the speaker's choice of grammatical structure or his use of stress; if in saying the sentence "John broke the vase" the speaker stresses the name *John* we understand that the question to be resolved was who broke the vase, whereas if he stresses the word *vase* we understand that the question was what it was that John broke.

Exercises

1. **Tell whether the italicized words in each of the following sentences are favorable or unfavorable.**

   1) Nothing does more hurt in a state than that *cunning* men pass for *wise*.
      A. unfavorable, favorable　　　　　　　B. favorable, unfavorable
   2) On the surface, he tried to *promote* peace, friendship and unity. His real object was to *instigate* a little rebellion.
      A. unfavorable, favorable　　　　　　　B. favorable, unfavorable
   3) It began as a *fad* but now there is a whole new *trend* toward smaller sunglasses.
      A. unfavorable, favorable　　　　　　　B. favorable, unfavorable
   4) Our *dog* always starts barking when that *cur* from down the street comes around.
      A. unfavorable, favorable　　　　　　　B. favorable, unfavorable
   5) We need to vote out the *politicians* and elect real *statesmen*.
      A. unfavorable, favorable　　　　　　　B. favorable, unfavorable

2. **The words *articulate*, *gossip*, *rambling*, *fluent*, and *mouthy* can all describe a person's ability of speech. What impression do you obtain of the person with the use of each of the words?**

Text D　Onomatopoeia

Onomatopoeia is not so unusual a term among those who write about words—though linguists today often prefer others, like *echoism* or *imitation*. The Greeks had a word for it, and we have borrowed it through Latin: *onomatopoiia*, the process of making words, which derives from *onoma*, a name, and *poiein*, to make. But we have extended the meaning beyond just making words to making words in a specific way—by echoing a sound that is linked to the thing we want to name.

English is full of such terms. Among them are repetitive childish imitations like *boo-hoo*, *choo-choo* and *bow-wow*, and exclamations such as *argh* and *ouch*. But there is also a whole medley of nouns and verbs, some of which created in other languages and borrowed into English: *bang, bash, bawl, beep, belch, blab, blare, bleat, blurt, bonk, bump, burble, buzz, clang, cheep, clank, clap, clatter, cuckoo*, etc.

It is not only single words that can be onomatopoeic. The effect is common in poetry, as in "The moan of doves in immemorial elms / And murmuring of innumerable bees" and

"I heard the ripple washing in the reeds / And the wild water lapping on the crag," both of which are from poems by Alfred, Lord Tennyson.

Exercises

1. Pick out the onomatopoeic words in the sentences below and translate the sentences into Chinese.

1) I banged the box down on the floor.
2) Stop jingling your keys like that!
3) The office is buzzing with rumors.
4) The windows were rattling in the wind.
5) Smoke puffed from the chimney.

2. Find the English words for the sound or cry of the following animals, and compare them with those in other languages.

3. Read the following excerpt and finish the task.

Onomatopoeia can be used as a rhetorical device to create the illusion of sound in a text, as in the following example:

> And ere three shrill notes the pipe he uttered, / You heard as if an army *muttered*; / The *muttering* grew to a *grumbling*; / And the *grumbling* grew to mighty *rumbling*; / And out of the house the rats came tumbling. (Browning 1888)

Find at least three examples of onomatopoeia in poetry or prose. You might find examples in unlikely places such as the newspaper and e-mails.

For Fun

Works to Read

1. ***The Language of Word Meaning*** by Federica Busa and Pierrette Bouillon

   This volume is a collection of original contribution from outstanding scholars exploring the relation between word meaning and human linguistic creativity. The chapters present different aspects surrounding the question of what is word meaning. The aim of the volume is to provide answers based on empirical linguistics methods that are relevant across all the disciplines and to provide a bridge among researchers looking at word meaning from different angles.

2. ***Words Words Words*** by David Crystal

   This book takes readers on a fascinating linguistic adventure, exploring the English language in all its oddity, complexity, and ever-changing beauty. Crystal celebrates new words, old words, words that "snarl" and words that "purr," elegant words and taboo words, plain English words and antonyms, spoonerisms and malapropisms, and a host of other written and spoken forms and variations.

Websites to Visit

1. http://www.lexipedia.com

   The website will show you a vivid chart of every word you submit with its meanings, attributes and relatives.

2. http://dictionary.reference.com/

   This is the world's most popular dictionary and thesaurus with definitions, synonyms, antonyms, idioms, word origins, quotes, audio pronunciations, example sentences and Word of the Day!

3. http://www.examples-of-onomatopoeia.com

   The website is a collection of the English onomatopoeic words. You can also play word games on it.

Unit 9

Sense Relations Between Words

> A synonym is a word you use when you can't spell the word you first thought of.
>
> —— Burt Bacharach

Unit Goals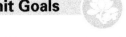

- To understand the definitions of synonymy and antonymy
- To be able to tell absolute synonyms from relative synonyms
- To identify the three types of antonyms
- To know the definitions of hyponymy and oxymoron

 Before You Read

1. How many pairs of antonyms can you find in the opening lines of *A Tale of Two Cities*? What is the effect of these antonyms?

    It was the best of times, it was the worst of times, it was the age of wisdom, it was the age of foolishness, it was the epoch of belief, it was the epoch of incredulity, it was the season of Light, it was the season of Darkness, it was the spring of hope, it was the winter of despair, we had everything before us, we had nothing before us…

2. Give words similar and opposite in meaning to the words below.

Words	Similar	Opposite
conceal		
fasten		
heroic		
loathe		
jealous		
jeopardy		
permanent		
reject		
vacant		

3. Please label the following pairs of words in which one item includes the other in meaning.

Words	Yes	No
bird/ hawk		
hawk/ kestrel		
ship/ fleet		
tool/ saw		
forest/ tree		
saw/ hacksaw		
woman/ mother		
animal/ dog		
tree/ pine tree		
car/ engine		

Start to Read

Text A Synonymy

Synonymy is a kind of semantic relation that means sameness of meaning. Technically, it occurs when two or more linguistic forms are used to substitute one another in any context in which their common meaning is not affected denotatively or connotatively. For example, words such as *sick* and *ill*, *quickly* and *speedily* may be viewed as examples of synonymy, simply because they share most of the characteristics with one another. Synonyms are traditionally defined as words different in sound and spelling, but identical or similar in meaning. Examples of some English synonyms are:

car and *automobile*   *smart* and *intelligent*
baby and *infant*   *student* and *pupil*
pretty and *attractive*   *sick* and *ill*
funny and *humorous*   *died* and *expired*

Synonyms can be nouns, adverbs or adjectives, as long as both members of the pair are of the same part of speech. Traditionally, synonymy can only hold between words, and, more precisely, between words belonging to the same part of speech; for example: *enormous* = *huge*; *gaze* = *stare*. This is the classic form of synonymy, covered by, for instance, synonym dictionaries.

Synonyms and Antonyms

It is noticeable that lexemes rarely have exactly the same meaning. There are usually stylistic, regional, emotional, or other differences to consider. Two lexemes might be synonymous in one sentence but different in another: *range* and *selection* are synonyms in *What a nice range/selection of furnishings*, but not in *There's the mountain range*.

In its strict sense, a synonym is a word with a meaning identical or very similar to that of another word. In fact, it is often said that there is no such thing as an absolute synonym for any word, that is, a form that is identical in every aspect of meaning so that the two can be applied interchangeably. According to this extreme view, the only true synonyms are terms having precisely the same denotation, connotation, and range of applicability. As it turns out, these so-called true synonyms are usually named **absolute synonyms**, which are frequently technical terms and almost always concrete words coming from linguistically disparate sources. Good examples of such pairs are *celiac* (from Greek) and *abdominal* (from Latin); and *car* (from Latin) and *automobile* (from French). These meet the criteria for true synonymy: they have precisely the same denotation, connotation, and range of applicability, and they are used in identical contexts.

As opposed to the absolute synonyms, **relative synonyms** are similar or nearly the same in denotation, however, relative synonyms may differ in shades of meaning, in affective meaning, in level of formality, in collocation, and in distribution.

Synonyms are derived from a variety of sources.

One source of synonyms is dialectal variation. In some dialects of North American English, a long, upholstered seat is called a *couch*, but speakers of another dialect call the same piece of furniture a *sofa*. Canadian English speaker might call this item a *chesterfield*, and still other speakers might call it a *divan*. Though these words all mean the same thing and are therefore synonyms, they tend to be dialect specific and may not be shared across dialect boundaries.

Other synonyms arise as a result of language change over time. Your grandparents might use a particular term that seems old-fashioned to you, and you might use a more modern term. For example, what might be a *pocketbook* for your grandmother is called in current fashion circles a *handbag* or a *purse*. An older term for *dress* is *frock*, and what used to be called a *baby carriage* or *perambulator* is now a *stroller* or *jogger*. We are less likely now to refer to *women* as *gals*.

Another possible source for synonyms is style and register. In casual speech, a speaker might say, "That's a nice ride," but in more formal speech, "That's a nice car." There are many words which refer to the same thing but belong to different stylistic layers: neutral, colloquial, literary, slang, vulgar, scientific and technical, and so on. The following is a group of synonyms with nearly the same denotative meaning but with different stylistic references: *to chide* (literary), *to berate* (neutral), *to scold* (neutral), *to blame* (neutral), *to carpet* (colloquial), *to tell off* (colloquial), *to bawl out* (slang).

Text B Antonymy

The term antonymy is used for "oppositeness of meaning"; words that are opposite in meaning are called antonyms. Antonymy is often thought of as the opposite of synonymy, but the status of the two are very different. For languages have no real need of true synonyms, and as we have seen, it is doubtful whether any true synonyms exist. But antonymy is a regular and very natural feature of language and can be defined fairly precisely.

The meaning of a word may be partially defined by saying what it is not. *Male* means "not female." *Dead* means "not alive." But ironically, the basic property of two words that are antonyms is that they share all but one semantic property. *Beautiful* and *tall* are not antonyms: *beautiful* and *ugly*, or *tall* and *short* are. The property they do not share is present in one and absent

Same meaning	are opposites
Yell, shout	Naughty, polite
Nasty, horrible	Take, give
Old, ancient	Opposite, same
Nice, generous	Nasty, clean
Yelp, bark	Young, ancient
means the same	means opposite

in the other. Thus, in order to be opposites, two words must be semantically similar or in the same semantic category, such as "gender" or "height."

The two words in each antonymic pair differ in only one aspect. They have a lot of semantic properties in common. Take the following pairs for example:

> *long—short* (length)
> *young—old* (age)
> *big—small* (size)
> *high—low* (height)

Some words are antonymous in some contexts but not others: *straight* is generally the opposite of *bent* or *curved*, but is the antonym of *gay* in the context of homosexuality.

While antonymy is typically found among adjectives, it is not restricted to this word class: *bring* and *take* (verbs), *death* and *life* (nouns), *noisily* and *quietly* (adverbs), *above* and *below* (prepositions), *after* and *before* (conjunctions or prepositions).

Antonyms are broadly divided into three categories: gradable antonyms, complementary antonyms, and relational antonyms (or converses).

Gradable Antonyms

These describe something which can be measured and compared with something else. For example, if one car is travelling at 75 miles per hour and one at 37 miles per hour, one is *fast* and the other is *slow*. *Good* and *bad* are antonyms, too. However, if an essay, is not good, that does not mean it is bad. There is a whole scale including *appalling, terrible, bad, poor, satisfactory, fair, good, excellent, incredible*, etc. Gradable antonyms include pairs like the following:

> *beautiful—ugly*
> *expensive—cheap*
> *deep—shallow*

These pairs are called gradable antonyms because they do not represent an either/or relation but rather a more/less relation. The words can be viewed as terms at the end-points of a continuum or gradient. Such pairs often occur in binomial phrases with *and*: (*blow*) *hot and cold*, (*search*) *high and low*.

Complementary Antonyms

Pairs of complementary antonyms represent the two opposite possibilities. There is no continuum, or middle-ground. For example, one is either *married* or *single*. Here there is no comparison or scale; it is a matter of being either one thing or another. Examples are *alive* and *dead*: you are either *alive* or *dead*, not somewhere in-between. Other examples are *male* and *female*, *asleep* and *awake*, *on* and *off*.

Relational Antonyms

In this type of antonymy, there is a relationship in which the two opposites must both exist. Relational antonyms express reciprocity. For example, if someone is *selling*, there must be someone *buying*. These antonyms depend on each other. You cannot buy something without someone else selling it to you. Other examples are *borrow* and *lend*, *wife* and *husband*.

Besides having morphologically unrelated antonyms, as in the examples above, English can also derive antonyms by means of prefixes and suffixes. Negative prefixes such as *dis-*, *un-* or *in-* may derive an antonym from the positive root, e.g. *dishonest, unsympathetic, infertile*. Compare also: *encourage—discourage*, but *entangle—disentangle, increase—decrease* and *include—exclude*. Similarly, the suffixes *-ful*, *-less* may derive pairs of antonyms, e.g. *useful—useless, thoughtful—thoughtless*.

After You Read

Knowledge Focus

1. **Tell whether the following statements are true or false according to the knowledge you learned and why.**
   1) Synonyms are traditionally defined as words different in sound and spelling, but identical in meaning. (   )
   2) In fact, most synonyms in English are interchangeable in all contexts. (   )
   3) Synonyms can be nouns, adverbs or adjectives, but cannot be of other parts of speech. (   )
   4) In ordinary language there are a lot of absolute synonyms. (   )
   5) One source of synonyms is dialectal variation. Another source of synonyms is language change over time. Still another source for synonyms is style and register. (   )
   6) For two words to be antonyms, they must not share any semantic property. (   )
   7) The meaning of a word may be partially defined by saying what it is not. (   )
   8) With gradable pairs the negative of one word is not synonymous with the other. (   )
   9) Complementary antonyms do not represent an either/or relation but rather a more/less relation. (   )
   10) Relational antonyms express reciprocity. (   )

2. **Match synonyms in Column A and Column B.**

Column A	Column B
acute	support
peaceful	ability
abrupt	sharp
interaction	transfer
convention	value
assess	communication
competence	offensive
fulfill	quiet
sponsor	custom
remove	satisfy

3. Identify what type of antonyms each pair falls into.

Antonyms		Type of Antonyms
absent	present	
husband	wife	
abundant	scarce	
buy	sell	
sadism	masochism	
doctor	patient	
forget	remember	
servant	master	
lazy	industrious	
joy	grief	

4. Pick out five pairs of antonyms and five pairs of synonyms from the following words.

> idealistic, intelligence, proceed, exhaustive, private, favorable, enormous, equal, agreement, public, appreciate, supportive, realistic, fair, reason, suspend, understand, huge, contradiction, energetic

Language Focus

1. Fill in the blanks with the following words or expressions you have learned in the text. Change the forms where necessary.

> identical   gradient   synonymous   converse   reciprocity
> criterion   upholster   continuum   berate   complementary

1) He feared she would _____ him for his forgetfulness.
2) What _____ are used for assessing a student's ability?
3) It is a mutual relationship, a true _____ we are now engaged in building.
4) The school's approach must be _____ to that of the parents.
5) The young couple plan to _____ their bedroom with velvet.
6) He says she is satisfied, but I believe the _____ to be true: she is very dissatisfied.
7) Nixon's name has become _____ with political scandal.
8) Nutritionally, infant formulas are almost _____ to breast milk.
9) The Creole language is really various dialects arranged on a _____.
10) The path goes up at a pretty steep _____ before leveling off.

2. Proofreading & Error Correction.

Synonyms tend to occur in clusters rather than being evenly spread throughout the vocabulary. Generally speaking, synonym clustering is much frequent in verbs or adjectives than in nouns; this contrasts to the fact that hyponymous relations are markedly more frequent in nouns.

There is an interesting question whether there are content areas which are more prone with the proliferation of synonyms than others. This is a difficult question, and it seems that synonyms are particularly frequent in areas which are in some way emotionally or socially sensible for human beings, and where is hence a special need to tailor language precise to context, especially in its non-propositional aspects. Hence, taboo areas of discourse are particularly rich in synonyms: it claimed, for instance, that English has over 120 terms for sexual intercourse; there is also a rich treasury of words for the sex organs, for urination and defecation, and so on. Other typical emotionally sensitive areas are death and money.

1) _____
2) _____
3) _____

4) _____
5) _____

6) _____

7) _____
8) _____
9) _____

10) _____

3. Translate the following paragraph into Chinese.

In its strict sense, a synonym is a word with a meaning identical or very similar to that of another word. In fact, it is often said that there is no such thing as an absolute synonym for any word, that is, a form that is identical in every aspect of meaning so that the two can be applied interchangeably. According to this extreme view, the only true synonyms are terms having precisely the same denotation, connotation, and range of applicability. As it turns out, these so-called true synonyms are usually named absolute synonyms, which are frequently technical terms and almost always concrete words coming from linguistically disparate sources.

Comprehensive Work

1. The following is a crossword. You are supposed to fill in 14 words according to the clue. Each answer is the antonym of its clue.

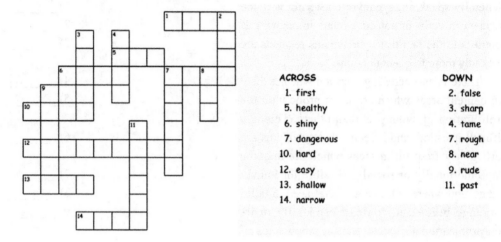

ACROSS
1. first
5. healthy
6. shiny
7. dangerous
10. hard
12. easy
13. shallow
14. narrow

DOWN
2. false
3. sharp
4. tame
7. rough
8. near
9. rude
11. past

2. Writing

There are so many synonyms in English. Take, for instance, the many words that mean "very good": *wonderful, marvelous, incredible, unbelievable, stupendous*, etc. Did these words that mean pretty much the same thing now have separate meanings at one time? Why does English have so many synonyms?

Read More

Text C Hyponymy

Most people are familiar with the terms synonymy and antonymy. Both refer to a relationship between words: synonymy to words having the same meaning, and antonymy to words having the opposite meanings. Fewer people, however, are familiar with a term that refers to an even more important sense relation between words: hyponymy, the relationship between a specific word and a general word when the former is included within the latter.

That relationship is illustrated by the common formula "A is a kind of B." For example, "A dog is a kind of animal," or simply "A dog is an animal." The specific word, *dog*, which is included within, or under, the general word, is known as a hyponym (Greek "under" + "name"). The general word, *animal*, which heads a list of many specific words under it, is a hypernym (Greek "above" + "name"). In this case, those other specific words, or hyponyms, could include, besides *dog*, a vast number of other animal names, such as *bird*, *horse*, and *monkey*. Those specific words under the same hypernym are related to each other as co-hyponyms.

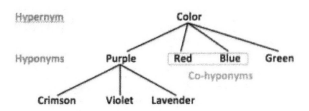

Some words belong to no clear, useful hypernym. Abstract nouns, such as *chaos*, and adjectives, such as *interesting*, are among the words that have only vague general terms, like *state*, as possible hypernyms.

Nevertheless, hyponymy is an important study for at least two major reasons. One of those reasons is that understanding hyponymy helps people define and differentiate many words used in everyday life. Hyponymous relationships form the basic framework within standard dictionaries.

A typical definition of a specific word (hyponym) consists of a general classification word (hypernym) along with modifying details that distinguish the specific word from similar words in the same group (co-hyponyms). For example, a *clarinet* is "a single-reed woodwind instrument having a cylindrical tube with a moderately flared bell." The hypernym is *woodwind instrument*, and among the co-hyponyms are *bassoon, flute,* and *oboe*.

Experienced dictionary users know that they can trace many hierarchical paths of increasingly abstract hypernyms through a dictionary. For example, starting with *cheddar*, one path of hypernyms would be *cheese, food, material, substance, essence*. A different path leading to the same abstract hypernym would be *sapphire, corundum, mineral, substance, essence*.

Another major reason for studying hyponymy is its usefulness in building a vocabulary. The process of learning about sets of hyponyms begins in early childhood, when infants soon recognize both similarities and differences in the meanings of sounds. Later in life people intuitively use the concept of hyponymy to add words to their vocabulary.

For example, most people know that *alligator* and *crocodile* are words denoting similar reptiles, but many people are not sure how to tell the animals apart. Exploring the sense relationship that binds the words together (as co-hyponyms of the hypernym *reptile*) and examining the modifying details that differentiate them, people can add these two clarified words to their permanent vocabulary.

The term hyponymy is relatively new, being recorded only since the mid-1900s. However, the study of hyponymy has quickly proven to be one of the most useful ways of understanding how words relate to each other, an understanding that can lead to clearer communication between users of the English language.

Exercises
1. What is hyponymy?
2. What is the difference between hyponyms and hypernyms?
3. Can a hyponym be a hypernym or vice versa?

4. Provide a hypernym for each group of hyponyms.

Hypernyms	Hyponyms
1)	lily, chrysanthemum, rose, daisy
2)	trumpet, harp, triangle
3)	pen, stapler, notebook
4)	doll, yo-yo, rubber duck
5)	robin, condor, toucan, dove
6)	trunks, cardigan, sari

Text D Oxymoron

Oxymoron is a literary figure of speech usually composed of a pair of neighboring contradictory words (often within a sentence). However, this is not always the case. The Webster Dictionary defines oxymoron as "a combination of contradictory or incongruous words."

Appropriately, the word *oxymoron* is itself oxymoronic because it is formed from two Greek roots of opposite meanings, *oxys* "sharp, keen" and *moros* "foolish," the same root that gives us the word *moron*.

Common Examples of Oxymoron
- open secret
- tragic comedy
- seriously funny
- awfully pretty
- foolish wisdom
- original copies
- liquid gas

The above oxymoron examples produce a comical effect. Thus, it is a lot of fun to use them in our everyday speech.

Oxymoron Examples in Literature

Example #1
Below is an extract from Shakespeare's *Romeo and Juliet*:
"Why, then, O brawling love! O loving hate!
O anything, of nothing first create!
O heavy lightness! Serious vanity!
Misshapen chaos of well-seeming forms!
Feather of lead, bright smoke, cold fire, sick health!
Still-waking sleep, that is not what it is!
This love feel I, that feel no love in this.

Dost thou not laugh?"

We notice a series of oxymoron being employed when Romeo confronts the love of an inaccessible woman. An intense emotional effect is produced to highlight his mental conflict by the use of contradictory pairs of words such as *loving hate, heavy lightness, bright smoke, cold fire,* and *sick health.*

Example #2

The example below is taken from Tennyson's *Lancelot and Elaine*:
"the shackles of love straiten'd him
His honor rooted in dishonored stood
And faith unfaithful kept him falsely true"

We clearly notice the use of oxymoron in phrases *shackles… straiten'd, honor… dishonor, faith unfaithful* and *falsely true.*

Example #3

In Sir Thomas Wyatt's Petrarch's 134th sonnet,
"I find no peace, and all my war is done
I fear and hope, I burn and freeze like ice,
I flee above the wind, yet can I not arise;"

The contradicting ideas of *war…peace, burn…freeze,* and *flee above…not arise* produce a dramatic effect in the above-mentioned lines.

Example #4

Alexander Pope uses oxymoron to develop wit in his poems.
"The bookful blockhead ignorantly read,
With loads of learned lumber in his head,
With his own tongue still edifies his ears,
And always list'ning to himself appears."

The above lines from his *Essays of Criticism* provide fine evidence of his witticism. The oxymora *bookful blockhead* and *ignorantly read* describe a person who reads a lot but does not understand what he reads and does not employ his reading to improve his character.

Function of Oxymoron

Oxymoron produces a dramatic effect in both prose as well as poetry. For instance, when we read or hear the famous oxymoron, *sweet sorrow*, crafted by Shakespeare, it appeals to us instantly. It provokes our thoughts and makes us ponder on the meaning of contradicting ideas. This apparently confusing phrase expresses a complex nature of love that could never be expressed through any other simple expression.

In everyday conversation, however, people do not use oxymoron to make some deep statement like the one mentioned above. Instead, they do it to show wit. The use of oxymoron adds flavor to their speech.

Exercises

1. How is antonym related to oxymoron?
2. Could you find some oxymoron examples in literature other than the examples in the text?
3. Match one word from Column I and one from Column II to form an oxymoron.

Column I	Column II
random	chaos
sweet	order
deafening	estimate
almost	secret
silent	sorrow
open	missing
seriously	silence
controlled	always
found	funny
exact	scream

For Fun

Works to Read

1. *Slap Shot: Synonyms and Antonyms* by Anna Prokos

This book introduces, in a very intriguing way, synonyms and antonyms, including the different forms of synonyms and antonyms and how to properly use each element.

Unit 9 Sense Relations Between Words

2. ***Homonyms, Synonyms & Antonyms*** by Karen Shackelford

Can you explain what a homonym is in one simple sentence? How about a synonym or antonym? Can you give several memorable examples of each? You will be able to confidently read and write using these three types of words once you complete the exercises in this 48-page activity book.

Websites to Visit

1. http://www.firstschoolyears.com/literacy/word/other/synonyms/synonyms.htm

   This site contains free worksheets, flashcards, online activities and other educational resources to help with synonyms and antonyms.

2. http://www.synonym.com/synonyms/

   This is a website intended for synonyms and antonyms. You can type in a word and then search for its synonyms, antonyms or definitions.

3. http://www.sadlier-oxford.com/phonics/synonyms/synonyms.htm

   This is a flash game page about synonyms. When you see the word that is a synonym of the given word, click on the button at the bottom left of the screen. The choices for each synonym will only cycle through twice. The green bar at the right side of the screen tells you how long you have for each question.

Unit 10

Polysemy and Homonymy

> Language is a process of free creation; its laws and principles are fixed, but the manner in which the principles of generation are used is free and infinitely varied. Even the interpretation and use of words involves a process of free creation.
>
> —— Noam Chomsky

Unit Goals

- To understand the difference between polysemy and homonymy
- To know different types of homonymy
- To grasp the rhetorical effects of homonyms in literay works

Before You Read

1. The following are all famous words from commercials or classic dialogues in the movies. Discuss with your partner and give explanations of the sentences. Please pay attention to the italics.

Advertising English	Meaning
1) Seven days without Seven-up make one *weak*.	
2) His back is as *crooked* as politician.	
3) You will go *nuts* for the *nuts* if you get Nux.	

4) A better *stretch* for the long *stretch*.	
5) Try our sweet corn. You'll smile from *ear* to *ear*.	

2. Homophones play an important role in jokes! Read the following jokes and explain where the humor lies. Can you think of any similar Chinese jokes?

— "Waiter!" — "Yes, sir." — "What's this?" — "It's bean soup, sir." — "Never mind what it has been. I want to know what it is now."	
	— "I spent a hot summer in a very pretty city in Switzerland." — "Berne?" — "No, I almost froze."

Start to Read

Text A Polysemy and Homonymy

For convenience we force a uniformity on the world around us. The word *dog* can denote quite different animals. The word *lamb* can denote an animal or a dish. A person's *body* can similarly be alive or dead. The word *play* can denote the activity of a pianist and that of a child. Thus the question arises of how extensive the semantic range of a word or lexeme has to be before we feel that we are dealing with two separate words that have the same form rather than with one word that denotes a variety of things.

In the case of *lamb* we can consider the animal and the dish to be different referents of the one lexeme. In the case of *sound* in the sense of something that one hears and *sound* in the sense of a narrow stretch of water, on the other hand, we are likely to consider that we are dealing with two distinct lexemes that happen to have the same form.

Homonyms are two or more different lexemes which have the same form but are unrelated in meaning. The words which are homonyms usually have different entries in dictionaries. While investigating homonymy one also has to consider homophones and homographs. **Homophones** are lexemes indentical in pronunciation, but different in spelling. **Homographs** are spelled alike but different in pronunciation. When two lexemes happen to be identical both in spelling and pronunciation, they are considered to be **perfect homonyms**.

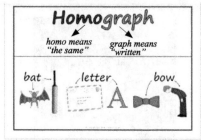

Processes Leading to Polysemy

One of the two main processes in the development of word meaning is radiation. Radiation is the semantic process in which the original meaning of a word is to be considered as the central meaning and the other meanings are derived from it in every direction like rays. These meanings are independent of one another, but can all be traced back to the central meaning. Take the word *hand* for example. It may signify part of the human body beyond the wrist, possession, influence or agency, employee, share in an activity, pointer on a clock, side or direction, handwriting, signature, cards dealt to a player, applause, etc.

The other important process in the development of word meaning is concatenation. Concatenation, meaning "linking together," is the semantic process in which the meaning of a word moves gradually away from its first sense by successive shifts, like the links of a chain, until, in many cases, there is no connection between the sense that is finally developed and that which the term had in it at the outset. For example, the development of the meaning of the word *board* can be shown as follows: a piece of timber → table → council table → councilors → directors of a company.

primary meaning

⟨1⟩ — ⟨2⟩ — ⟨3⟩ — ⟨4⟩ — ⟨5⟩

derived meanings

Sources of Homonyms

One source of homonyms is a phonetic change, which a word undergoes in the course of its historical development. As a result of such changes, words, which were formerly pronounced differently, may develop identical sound forms and thus become homonyms. *Night* and *knight*, for instance, were not homonyms in Old English as the initial *k* in the second word was pronounced. The verb *to write* in Old English had the form *to writan* and the adjective *right* had the form *reht* or *riht*.

Another source of homonyms is borrowing. A borrowed word may, in the final stage of the phonetic adaptation conclude the form either with a native word or another borrowing. In the group of homonyms *rite*, *write*, and *right* (*adj.*), the second and third words are of native origin, whereas *rite* is Latin borrowing (Latin *ritus*). Similarly, *bank* (a shore) is a native word, and *bank* (a financial institution) is an Italian borrowing.

Word building also contributes significantly to the growth of homonymy, the most important type of it being conversion. Such pairs of words as *comb* (*n.*)—*comb* (*v.*); *pale* (*adj.*)—*pale* (*v.*); *make* (*v.*)—*make* (*n.*), etc. are numerous in vocabulary. Homonyms of this type refer to different categories of parts of speech and are called lexico-grammatical homonyms.

Shortening is a further type of word-building, which increases the number of homonyms. For example *fan* (an enthusiastic admirer of some sportsman, actor, singer, etc.) is a shortening produced from *fanatic*. Its homonym is a Latin borrowing *fan* (an element for waving and producing some cool wind).

The noun, for instance, *rep* has 4 homonyms:
   a. rep = repertory
   b. rep = representative
   c. rep = reputation
   d. rep = repetition

Polysemy versus Homonymy

The difference between a polysemous word and a homonym is difficult to determine. The polysemous words should retain the same pronunciation and the same spelling, but have different meanings. Homonyms also have the same spelling and the same pronunciation with different meanings. However, it appears that the different meanings of a polysemous word are related to one another and have the same origin, whereas homonyms are words whose spellings and meanings have separate origins from one another.

As so often, however, the real world does not fall neatly into our categories. Introducing language in the medium of language, the linguist encounters the problem of defining semantic range when talking of semantics. There can be little doubt that in the case of the two referents of the word *sound* that we referred to we are dealing with different lexemes; one is of Latin origin and the other is of Germanic origin. So the word *bill* denoting an account or invoice and that denoting the beak of a bird must be deemed to be different lexemes, the former, a cognate of the French word *billet*, being of Latin origin and the latter being of Germanic origin. But we also have a word *bill* denoting a kind of axe, which may be related to that denoting a beak. Should we treat these as homonyms or as different meanings of a polysemous word? What about *grow* used intransitively, as in *Your tomatoes won't grow well there*, and *grow* used transitively, as in *He grows tomatoes*? The Italian equivalents, for example, are distinct in this case: *crescere* and *coltivare* respectively. Such cases leave the lexicographer with the problem of deciding whether to arrange words under one or several headwords.

After You Read

Knowledge Focus

1. Work with your partner to provide the homograph to each term.

Term	Homograph
1) *n.* 海豹；*v.* 蜂蜡	
2) *v.* 切；*n.* 伤口	
3) *n.* 抽签；*v.* 用铅笔等工具画	
4) *n.* 射线；*v.* 鳐	
5) *n.* 谷物；*n.* 鸡眼	
6) *n.* 箱子；*v.* 拳击	
7) *n.* 账单；*n.*（鸟类的）嘴	
8) *n.* 角；*v.* 钓鱼	
9) *v.* 跌落；*n.* 瀑布	
10) *v.* 下来；*adj.* 点着的	

2. Decide the specific meanings of the following adjectives.

1) blue

   A. He is wearing a blue shirt today.

   B. Her hands were blue with cold.

   C. He's feeling blue all week.

   D. That's a blue joke.

2) green

   A. Wait for the light to turn green.

   B. These apples are too green to eat.

   C. You must be green to believe that!

   D. The passengers turned quite green with seasickness.

3) fast

    A. Who's the fastest runner in the world?

    B. That clock is ten minutes fast.

    C. He led a fast life.

    D. The color is fast.

4) heavy

    A. Her father carried a heavy burden of responsibility.

    B. The going was heavy at the racecourse.

    C. I don't like heavy meals.

    D. It's very heavy—I think there'll be a storm.

5) poor

    A. They were too poor to buy shoes for the kids.

    B. The poor little puppy had been abandoned.

    C. It was raining heavily and visibility was poor.

    D. She's a good teacher but a poor manager.

6) rich

    A. America is a rich country

    B. Oranges are rich in vitamin C.

    C. Indians like rich curries.

    D. They are looking for a rich well-drained soil.

7) short

    A. He is too short to become a police officer.

    B. The hospital is getting short of nurses.

    C. *Ben* is usually short for *Benjamin*.

    D. I'm sorry I was short with you earlier.

8) soft

    A. The grass is soft and springy.

    B. I prefer a soft pink to a harsh red.

    C. A soft breeze rustled the trees.

    D. If you're too soft with these kids, they'll never respect you.

9) strong

    A. Stay indoors in the middle of the day when the sun is strong.

    B. The euro is getting stronger against the dollar.

    C. Strong will is one of the factors to achieve success.

    D. He is a strong candidate for the job.

10) warm

    A. The weather is a bit warmer today.

    B. The host gave me a warm welcome.

    C. The room was furnished in warm reds and browns.

    D. Am I getting warmer?

3. **Find and explain the homonyms in the following statements.**

   1) The bandage was wound around the wound.
   2) The farm was used to produce produce.
   3) The dump was so full that it had to refuse more refuse.
   4) We must polish the Polish furniture.
   5) The apple farmer eats what he can, and cans what he cannot eat.
   6) The soldier decided to desert his dessert in the desert.
   7) Since there is no time like the present, he thought it was time to present the present.
   8) A bass was painted on the head of the bass drum.
   9) When shot at, the dove dove into the bushes.
   10) I did not object to the object.

Language Focus

1. **Fill in the blanks with the following words you have learned in the text. Change the forms where necessary.**

deem	fanatic	uniformity	stretch	concatenation
repertory	tortuous	adaptation	cognate	equivalent

   1) Due to multifarious factors, this movement was slow and _____.
   2) There is a _____ of life in Utopia—of thinking, of ambition, of manners, of dress.
   3) Is there a French word that is the exact _____ of the English word *home*?
   4) The German word *Haus* is _____ with the English word *house*.
   5) He's working on a screen _____ of his latest novel.
   6) Any opera house director would have been delighted to engage this great star to dance the standard ballet _____.
   7) They were told to take whatever action they _____ necessary.
   8) You rarely see boats on this _____ of the river.
   9) Memory is nothing else than a certain _____ of ideas.
   10) Debbie is a big popcorn _____. In fact, one year for her birthday, her husband bought her one of those big popcorn machines like they have in movie theaters.

2. **Proofreading & Error Correction.**

   One source of polysemy and homonymy is the word meaning change. The changes in language will continue forever, but no one knows sure who does the changing. A professor of linguistic at the University of Hawaii explores this in one of his recent books. Sometimes around 1880, a language catastrophe occurred in Hawaii when thousands of emigrant workers were brought to the islands to work for the new sugar industry. These people speaking different languages were unable to communicate with each other or with the native Hawaiians or the dominant English-speaking

   1) _____
   2) _____
   3) _____
   4) _____

owners of the plantations. So they first spoke in Pidgin English—the sort of thing such mixed language populations have always done. A pidgin is not really a language at all. It is more like a set of verbal signals used to name objects and without the grammatical rules needed for expressing thought and ideas. And then, within a single generation, the whole mass of mixed people began speaking a totally new tongue: Hawaiian Creole. The new speech was contained ready-made words borrowed form all the original tongues, but beared little or no resemblance to the predecessors in the rules used for stringing the words together. Although it was generally regarded as primitive language, Hawaiian Creole had a highly sophisticated grammar.

5) _____

6) _____

7) _____

8) _____
9) _____

10) _____

3. Translate the following paragraph into Chinese.

The difference between a polysemous word and a homonym is difficult to determine. In order to be considered a polysemous word, the word has to retain the same pronunciation and the same spelling, but have different meanings. Homonyms also have the same spelling and the same pronunciation with different meanings. However, it appears that the different meanings of a polysemous word are related to one another and have the same origin, whereas homonyms are words whose spellings and meanings have separate origins from one another.

Comprehensive Work
Discussion & Writing

The following is a homonymic poem written by Janet E. Byford. Work in groups of four or five students, pick out the homonyms in the poem and provide a "correct" version of the poem. Discuss the role that homonymy plays in the poem with your group members and write an essay on it.

Take A Bough

An Ode to the Spelling Chequer

Prays the Lord for the spelling chequer
That came with our pea sea!
Mecca mistake and it puts you rite.
Its so easy to ewes, you sea.

I never used to no, was it e before eye?
(Four sometimes its eye before e.)

> But now I've discovered the quay to success.
> It's as simple as won, too, free!
>
> Sew watt if you lose a letter or two,
> The whirled won't come two an end!
> Can't you sea? It's as plane as the knows on yore face.
> S. Chequer's my very best friend
>
> I've always had trubble with letters that double.
> "Is it one or to S's?" I'd wine
> But now, as I've tolled you this chequer is grate
> And its hi thyme you got won, like mine.

Read More

Text B Lexical Relations: Hyponymy and Homonymy

The branch of semantics that deals with word meaning is called lexical semantics. It is the study of systematic meaning related structures of words. Lexical field or semantic field is the organization of related words and expressions into a system which shows their relationship within one another, e.g. *angry*, *sad*, *happy*, *depressed*, and *afraid*. This set of words is a lexical field, in that all its words refer to emotional states. Lexical semantics examines relationships among word meanings. It is the study of how the lexicon is organized and how the lexical meanings of lexical items are interrelated, and its principal goal is to build a model for the structure of the lexicon by categorizing the types of relationships between words.

Hyponymy, homonymy, polysemy, synonymy, antonymy and metonymy are different types of lexical relations. Here hyponymy and homonymy are discussed in brief.

Hyponymy

Hyponymy is a relation between two words, in which the meaning of one of the words includes the meaning of the other word. The lexical relation corresponding to the inclusion of one class in another is hyponymy. A hyponym is a subordinate, specific term whose referent is included in the referent of super-ordinate term. For example, *blue* and *green* are kinds of color. They are specific colors and *color* is a general term for them. Therefore, *color* is called the super-ordinate term, and *blue*, *red*, *green*, *yellow*, etc. are called hyponyms.

A super-ordinate can have many hyponyms. Hyponymy is the relationship between each lower term and the higher term (super ordinate). It is a sense relation. It is defined in terms of the inclusion of the sense of one item in the sense of another. For example, the sense of *animal* is included in the sense of *lion*.

Hyponymy is not restricted to objects, abstract concepts, or nouns. It can be identified in many other areas of the lexicon. For example, the verb *cook* has many hyponyms.

Word	Hyponyms
cook	roast, boil, fry, grill, bake
color	blue, red, yellow, green, black, purple

In a lexical field, hyponymy may exist at more than one level. A word may have both a hyponym and a super-ordinate term. For example,

Word	Hyponyms
being	bird, insect, animal
bird	sparrow, hawk, crow, fowl

Now let's take the word *bird* from above hyponyms. We thus have *sparrow*, *hawk*, *crow*, and *fowl* as hyponyms of *bird* and *bird* in turn is a hyponym of *being*. So there is a hierarchy of terms related to each other through hyponymic relations.

Hyponymy often functions in discourse as a means of lexical cohesion by establishing referential equivalence to avoid repetition.

Homonymy

The word *Homonym* has been derived from Greek term *Homoios* which means "identical" and *onoma* means "name."

Homonyms are the words that have the same phonetic form (homophones) or orthographic form (homographs) but different unrelated meanings.

The ambiguous word whose different senses are far apart from each other and are not obviously related to each other in any way is called homonymy. Words like *tale* and *tail* are homonyms. There is no conceptual connection between its two meanings. For example, the word *bear*, as a verb means "to carry" and as a noun it means "large animal."

There are three types of homonyms.

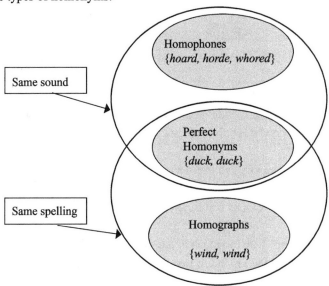

Homophones—Homophones are words identical only in sound but different in spelling and meaning. For example: *no—know, led—lead, would—wood, compliment—complement*, and so on.

Homographs—Homographs are words identical only in spelling but different in sound and meaning. For example, *lead* /li:d/ v. "guide or take"; *lead* /led/ n. "easily melted metal of a dull bluish-grey color." Another example is *desert* (to abandon) and *desert* (arid region).

Perfect homonyms—Perfect homonyms are words identical in both sound and spelling but different in meaning. Examples are *date* (a kind of fruit) — *date* (a boy or girl friend), *bear* (v.) — *bear* (n.), etc.

Questions for Discussion or Reflection
1. What is the difference between hyponymy and homonymy?
2. What are the three types of homonyms?
3. Can you think of some examples of homophones, homographs and perfect homonyms other than the examples given in the text?

Text C Fun with Homonyms

Take a look at the diet slogan—"Are you going the wrong weigh?" Do you identify the twist on the word, *weigh*, which was originally supposed to be spelt *way*? Words that sound the same but have different meanings are called puns. A better way to describe it would be "a play on words." Although such terms render ambiguity to a sentence, it is often added for a humorous or rhetorical effect.

William Shakespeare and Oscar Wilde are masters of the pun. Here are some lines from *Hamlet*:
KING
    Take thy fair hour, Laertes; time be thine,
    And thy best graces spend it at thy will!
    But now, my cousin Hamlet, and my son—
HAMLET
    A little more than kin, and less than kind.
KING
    How is it that the clouds still hang on you?
HAMLET
    Not so, my lord; I am too much in the sun.

More examples are: "It is the unkindest tied that ever any man tied" (from *Richard III*); "Not I, believe me. You have dancing shoes with nimble soles; I have a soul of lead" (from *Romeo and Juliet*).

Oscar Wilde employs puns in his play *Importance of Being Earnest*. Jack Earnest tells Aunt Augusta in Act III: "On the contrary, Aunt Augusta, I've now realized for the first time in my life the vital importance of being Earnest." Similarly, in Act III we see Jack puns his family name again: "I always told you, Gwendolen, my name was Ernest, didn't I? Well, it is Ernest after all. I mean it naturally is Ernest." Here Jack discovers his family name which makes him truly earnest. What's more, Wilde even used puns to make fun of Immanuel Kant, a German philosopher who believed that moral decisions must be based on reason, by saying "Immanuel doesn't pun; he Kant."

Puns fall into two main categories: a. words (or phrases) having two or more distinct meanings are called "perfect homonyms," as they have the same sound and spelling; b. words having the same sound, but differing in form and meaning are called "homophones."

As Walter Redfern rightly put, "to pun is to treat homonyms as synonyms." Making use of this form of speech in our daily language can make it seem more interesting and fun.

Exercises

Find the puns. Are they perfect homonyms or homophones?

1. It's not that he didn't know how to juggle. He just didn't have the balls to do it.
2. —What do you call a woman who stands between two goal posts?
   —Annette.
3. A bicycle can't stand on its own. It's two-tired.
4. Police were called to a kindergarten where a three-year-old was resisting a rest.
5. A pessimist's blood type is b-negative.
6. I used to be addicted to soap, but I'm clean now.
7. A prisoner's favorite punctuation mark is the period (U.S.A.)/ full stop (U.K.). It marks the end of his sentence.
8. —What do you get if you cross a sheep with a kangaroo?
   —A wholly jumper.

For Fun

Works to Read

1. *How Much Can a Bare Bear Bear?* by Brian P. Cleary and Brian Gable

   The best-selling book introduces young readers to different types of words through rhyming verse and illustrations of comical cartoon cats. Offering a lighthearted perspective, each title shows readers the fun and entertaining world of language.

2. ***Eight Ate: A Feast of Homonym Riddles*** by Marvin Terban and Giulio Maestro

This collection of original riddles is unlike any other because the main words in each answer sound exactly alike, but have different meanings. Zany illustrations add to the fun and provide clues to the solutions. And the full-color cover makes the package even more appealing.

Websites to Visit

1. http://learnenglish.britishcouncil.org/en/vocabulary-games

   On this website, you can learn and practice a large number of areas of English vocabulary, obtain some knowledge related to polysemy and homonymy and have some fun as well.

2. http://www.onelook.com

   Type in a word and search many dictionaries at once. Also it has a reverse dictionary and translations.

3. http://www.punoftheday.com/

   This website provides archive of puns in categories such as food, transportation, families, education, and work, plus a one-liner pun every week day.

Unit 11
Semantic Changes

> Almost every word we use today has a slightly different meaning from the one it had a century ago; and a century ago it had a slightly different meaning from the one it had a century before that.
> —— Randolph Quirk

Unit Goals

- To be familiar with the causes of semantic changes
- To grasp the processes of semantic changes
- To learn useful words and expressions and improve language skills

 Before You Read

1. Semantic change describes the evolution of word usage. Please identify the current meanings or original meanings of the following words.

Word	Original Meaning	Current Meaning
pen	feather	
left	weak	
garage	stable	
pool	a card game	
earth		planet on which we live
space		outer space
glad		pleased, joyful
fine		superior in quality

2. Work in groups of four or five students, and list some English words or Chinese ones whose meanings have undergone certain changes over time. Share your word list with other groups and discuss why word meanings change.

Start to Read

Text A　Semantic Changes and the Causes

After a language appears it grows like a child, develops like an adult, changes during its life, due to many linguistic and extra-linguistic factors, and finally it dies, giving birth to other languages. One of the most important phenomena that occur during a language life is semantic change and semantic development. Due to meaning changes, a language develops, enriches and becomes perfect.

The study of semantic change involves studying the etymology of a language. The word *etymology* is derived from Greek *etumologia*, from *étumon* (true meaning of a word) and *-logia* (study). Speaking about etymology, we can't help mentioning history of a language. Historical changes in meaning are unpatterned because derivations are usually idiomatic; the meaning of the whole is not simply the sum of the meanings of the parts. The adjective *sedate* goes back to the Latin verb *sedare* (to settle), which comes from the root *sed-* (sit); hence the basic meaning "(having been) settled." The derived adjective *sedative* is then something that tends to settle someone. However, in Modern English, the adjective *sedate* means "deliberately composed and dignified by one's own character or efforts," not (as *sedative* would suggest) "stupefied by the effects of a drug." The Modern English verb *sedate* is a back-formation from *sedative* and therefore draws on the meaning of *sedative* and not on the meaning of the earlier divergent adjective *sedate*.

The homonymic adjective and verb *sedate* share a common origin in root *sed-*, but have developed such meanings that the ancient adjective cannot suitably describe someone who shows the effects of the recent verb. As the 19th century German philologist Max Muller wrote, "The etymology of a word can never give us its definition."

Even supposedly objective terms like numerals undergo change with the passage of time. Thus, although *only* was originally *one–ly*, it is now an adverb suitable for any quality or quantity, as in the etymological paradox "only twelve." *Combination* is now the mixture of any number of elements, but once it was only of two elements, its base being the Latin *bin-* as in *binary*. *Testimony* is from *tristi*, "the third (person) standing by," but is now evidence given by any person. *Quintessence* was once the fifth and highest essential element (in addition to earth, air, fire, and water), but is now simply the pure example of any thing or person. *September* was once the seventh month (Latin *septem*—meaning "seven"), but is now the ninth; the other months from October to December follow the same pattern. *Dean*, now the head of a group, especially academic, of any number, was once specifically a group of ten (Greek *déka*—meaning "ten," as in *decathlon*); *decimate* once meant "to reduce by a tenth" (compare *decimal*), but now means "to reduce by any substantial amount." *Quarantine* is now a sequestration of any length, but was once of forty days (French *quarante*).

All types of semantic change depend on some comparison of the earlier (whether extinct or still in use) and the new meaning of the given word. This comparison may be based on difference between the concepts expressed or referents in the real world that are pointed out, on the type of psychological association at work, on evaluation of the latter by the speaker, on lexico-grammatical categories, or possibly on some other features.

Specialization of Meaning

Specialization is the narrowing of word meaning. It is a process by which a word of wide meaning acquires a narrower or specialized sense. In other words, a word which used to have a more general sense becomes restricted in its application and conveys a special concept in present-day English.

We can see the following examples: Old English *mete* (meaning "food") changed into *meat* in the Middle English and has acquired a new, more precise one, that of "edible flesh"; Old English *fujol* (meaning "bird") transformed due to the historical evolution of the language into *fowl*—"domestic bird" in Middle English; Old English *deor* became *deer* in Middle English and acquired the meaning of "a wild ruminant of a special species," whereas in Old English it had the meaning of "a beast," which can be proved by the quotation "... rats and mice, and other deer," found in works of the Shakespearean period. The last example proves that it still had the old meaning in Middle English: *hound*—"any kind of dog" from Old English changed its meaning in Middle English, and presently has the meaning of "a hunting dog of a special breed."

Other examples of English words that have undergone specialization include:

Word	Old Meaning
affection	emotion
wife	woman
forest	countryside
girl	a young person
starve	to die

Generalization of Meaning

The process opposite to specialization is called generalization, or extension of meaning. In this case the meaning of a new notion is wider than the old one. In most cases generalization is combined with a higher order of abstraction than in the notion expressed by the previous meaning. *The Oxford Companion to the English Language* gives us the following definition of generalization: "A process of semantic change that widens the meaning of a word, phrase, or lexeme."

In Middle English, *pigeon* meant "a young bird, especially a young dove," but from the late 15th century has come to refer especially to the whole family Columbidae. *Dove* is now generally used for a smaller variety of pigeon. Such shifts in meaning are usually slow and tendential rather than are rapid and absolute. Early usages continue indefinitely alongside later changes that have become dominant, as was true of *pigeon* and *dove* in the 16th century. In the process of change, terms may acquire further meanings within a set of words.

Other examples of English words that have undergone generalization include:

Word	Old Meaning
holiday	a day of religious significance
place	broad street
picture	a painting
journey	a day's walk, or ride
plant	a sprout

It can be noticed that the transfer of meaning is also based on connotative change. Words' meanings get a more elevated connotation (amelioration), or a less pleasant one (pejoration).

Amelioration (Elevation) of Meaning

Amelioration is the process by which a word's meaning improves or becomes elevated, coming to represent something more favorable than it originally referred to.

For example, the word *priest* is descended from the Greek word *presbuteros*, "older man, elder," a comparative form of the word *presbus*, "old man." Because churches of most religions are headed by elders and not youth, and because age is often equated with wisdom, the Greek word gradually acquired the meaning of "church leader, priest."

Other examples of English words that have undergone amelioration include:

Word	Old Meaning
fond	foolish
shrewd	evil, bad, wicked
nice	ignorant
minister	an attendant, a servant
marshal	a horse tender

Pejoration (Degradation) of Meaning

Pejoration is the process by which a word's meaning worsens or degenerates, coming to represent something less favorable than it originally did.

For instance, the word *silly* meant in Old English "blessed." How did a word meaning "blessed" come to mean "silly"? Since people who are blessed are often innocent and guileless, the word gradually came to mean "innocent." And some of those who are innocent might be innocent because they haven't the brains to be anything else. And some of those who are innocent might be innocent because they knowingly reject opportunities for temptation. In either case, since the more worldly-wise would take advantage of their opportunities, the innocents must therefore be foolish, which of course is the current primary meaning of the word *silly*.

Other examples of English words that have undergone pejoration include:

Word	Old Meaning
vulgar	ordinary, common
knave	boy
hussy	a thrifty little woman
criticize	appraise
lust	pleasure

Discussing the process of semantic change, we concentrate upon factors and attempt to find out why the word undergoes change of meaning, how they occur, and what actually was changed. In other words, we compare and describe the difference between them mainly in terms of changes of denotative and connotative meanings.

The factors accounting for the semantic change may be roughly divided into two parts: linguistic and extra-linguistic causes of semantic change.

Linguistic Causes

Linguistic causes are factors acting within a linguistic system. The commonest form is ellipsis. In a phrase made up of two words, one of them is omitted, and its meaning is transferred to its partner. Thus, due to ellipsis, *sale* is used for *cut-price sale*, to *open on* is used in army instead of to *open fire on*, as in: "Today at three a.m. NATO has *opened on* Cosovo's Microwire Plant. There is no information about casualties."

Another linguistic cause of semantic change is differentiation of synonyms, which can be illustrated by the development of a number of words, such as *land* (Old English *land*—"both solid part of earth's surface," and "a territory of a nation"). In the course of the historical development of the language, this word had acquired only the first meaning, that of "solid part of earth's surface," the second one having been lost. Another example is *country* (Old French *countree*). Being borrowed from French, with the meaning of "a territory of a nation," this word had acquired a new meaning, "a village." The word *rapidly* has developed into *immediately*; the verbs to *catch*, to *grasp*, had acquired the meaning of "to understand." An interesting case is the word *tide*, which used to be a synonym for *time* in Old English. Later *tide* took on its more limited application to the periodically shifting waters, and *time* became a general word.

Extra–Linguistic Causes

Extra-linguistic causes of semantic change are those that are connected with development of the human mind and are influenced by science, politics, technical development, etc.

The word *car* goes back to the Latin *carrus*, which used to denote "a four-wheeled wagon." In Middle English, it already meant "a vehicle," in Middle English the word *car* is a general word for any vehicle, without specifying the type. We can also speak about functional change as extra-linguistic cause of semantic change, as in the examples of the words *diesel, ampere, ohm, volt*, etc. Due to the technical evolution of the society, these words started to denote not only proper names but also some physical or chemical terms.

It has to be pointed out that in the majority of cases, meaning shift occurs because of various stylistic devices, which give the context a transferred meaning. They are: metaphor and metonymy (based on association of similarity of contiguity), antonomasia (based on the interplay of logical and nominal meanings of a word), hyperbole (which is an intended exaggeration of the word's meaning), litotes (understatement), irony (based on simultaneity of the dictionary and contextual meaning), euphemism (paraphrasing something unpleasant), etc. Many of these stylistic devices change a word's meaning only in one specific context. However, very often, these words start to be frequently used in a language and become established in speech.

After You Read

Knowledge Focus

1. Match the words in Column A with the terms in Column B.

Column A	Column B
1) shrewd	a. extension
2) journey	b. narrowing
3) cock	c. elevation
4) silly	d. degradation
5) girl	e. historical reason
6) car	f. psychological reason

2. Each of the statements below is followed by four alternative answers. Choose the one that would best complete the statement.

1) The original meaning of *minister* is _____.
   A. head of a ministry   B. a tutor
   C. a farmer   D. a servant

2) The original meaning of *holiday* is _____.
   A. a day of religious significance
   B. Sunday
   C. a period of time when you are not at work or school
   D. a period of time spent travelling or resting away from home

3) In Shakespearean line "rats and mice and such small deer," *deer* obviously designates _____ in general.
   A. a doe
   B. animal
   C. a deer like animal
   D. buck
4) The original meaning of *wife* is _____.
   A. married woman
   B. young woman
   C. woman
   D. widowed woman
5) A process of semantic change that widens the meaning of a word, phrase, or lexeme is _____.
   A. extension
   B. narrowing
   C. elevation
   D. degradation
6) The meaning of *place* changed by mode of _____.
   A. extension
   B. narrowing
   C. elevation
   D. degradation
7) The meaning of *meat* changed by mode of _____.
   A. extension
   B. narrowing
   C. elevation
   D. degradation
8) The meaning of *fond* changed by mode of _____.
   A. extension
   B. narrowing
   C. elevation
   D. degradation
9) The meaning of *vulgar* changed by mode of _____.
   A. extension
   B. narrowing
   C. elevation
   D. degradation
10) _____ is an intended exaggeration of the word's meaning.
    A. Litotes
    B. Irony
    C. Hyperbole
    D. Euphemism

3. The following words have undergone semantic changes. In column A and column B are the meanings before and after the change. Determine whether the process is generalization or specialization.

Word	A Original Meaning	B Current Meaning	Generalization or Specialization
1) maintain	hold in the hand	hold	
2) appetite	a generalized desire	the wish for food	
3) beverage	drink	a kind of drink	
4) campus	field	grounds of college	
5) church	lord's house	house of worship	
6) president	person who presides	head of state	
7) voyage	journey	journey by water	
8) man	the mankind	a male	
9) food	what can be eaten	specific kind of food	
10) son	male child of a parent	a young man	

Language Focus

1. **Fill in the blanks with the following words you have learned in the text. Change the forms where necessary.**

| simultaneity | contiguity | casualty | paradox | sedate |
| sequestration | hyperbole | divergent | stupefy | etymology |

1) He was _____ by the amount they had spent.
2) During their _____, jurors were not allowed to speak to reporters.
3) The wedding was rather a _____ occasion.
4) As an actor, he's a _____—he loves being in the public eye but also deeply values and protects his privacy.
5) It has been the Confucian philosophy to accommodate _____ views
6) Dictionary is a reference book containing an alphabetical list of words, with information given for each word, usually including meaning, pronunciation, and _____.
7) Because of the _____ of the mall to the border, it attracts many shoppers from out of state
8) It was not _____ to call it the worst storm in twenty years.
9) Our aim is to reduce road _____.
10) People found out about the tragedy in near _____, and together watched the story evolve on television.

2. **Proofreading & Error Correction.**

From what has been said, it must be clear that no one can make very positive statements about how language originated. There is no material in any language today and in the earliest records of ancient languages show us language in a new and emerging state.

1) _____
2) _____

It is often said, of course, that the language originated in cries of anger, fear, pain and pleasure, and the necessary evidence is entirely lacking: there are no remote tribes, no ancient records, providing evidence of a language with a large proportion of such cries than we find in English.

3) _____
4) _____
5) _____

It is true that the absence of such evidence does not disprove the theory; but in other grounds, too, the theory is not very attractive. People of all races and languages make rather similar noises in return to pain or pleasure. The fact that such noises are similar on the lips of Frenchmen and Malaysians whose languages are utterly different, serves to emphasize on the fundamental difference between these noises and language proper.

6) _____
7) _____
8) _____

We may say that the cries of pain or chortles of amusement are largely reflex actions, instinctive to large extent, whereas language proper does not consist of signs but of these that have to be learned and that are wholly conventional.

9) _____
10) _____

3. Translate the following paragraph into Chinese.

The process opposite to specialization is called generalization, or extension of meaning. In this case the meaning of a new notion is wider than the old one. In most cases generalization is combined with a higher order of abstraction than in the notion expressed by the previous meaning. *The Oxford Companion to the English Language* gives us the following definition of generalization: "A process of semantic change that widens the meaning of a word, phrase, or lexeme."

Comprehensive Work

1. Work in groups of four or five students. Find three English words that have undergone semantic changes. Do some research and discuss their processes of semantic changes with your group members.

2. Writing

Study the semantic changes of the following word *gay*, and write an essay on how social and cultural factors affect the semantic changes.

Noble, beautiful, excellent	Bright, lively-looking	Carefree, cheerful, merry	
1325	1375	1400	
Dedicated to social pleasures, promiscuous, frivolous	(Woman) leading immoral life	Homosexual	Stupid
1597	1799	1922	1978

gay

Read More

Text B Semantic Shift

Semantic change in the context of words describes the gradual shift in the conventional meaning of words, as people use them in new types of contexts and these usages become normal. Often in the course of semantic change, a word shifts its meaning to the point that the modern meaning is radically different from the original usage. For example, *awful* originally meant "awe-inspiring, filling (someone) with deep awe," as in *the awful majesty of the Creator*. At some point it came to mean "breath-takingly bad; so bad that it fills (a person) with awe and amazement." People began to use the word in contexts where the awe felt was due to something's extreme negative qualities, as in *an awfully bad performance*. But now the intensity of the expression has faded somewhat and *an awful tasting medicine* need not inspire any deep sense of awe. The word in informal usage now just means "very bad." Similar developments are found with *terrible* (inspiring terror) and its onetime synonym *terrific*. The first kept its negative meaning, but lost some of its intensity; the second came to be associated with positive qualities and only then weakened its intensity. The result is that the latter two words have gone from being synonyms to almost exact antonyms.

The following are some examples of semantic change, also known as semantic shift, in English.

- *demagogue*—Originally meant "a popular leader." It is from the Greek *demagogos* (leader of the people), from *demos* (people) + *agogos* (leader). Now the word has strong connotations of a politician who panders to emotions and prejudice.
- *democrat*—At the time of the American Revolution, the term "democrat" had all the negative connotations of the modern usage of the word *demagogue*. A century, the term had shifted in meaning enough that it was viewed favorably as the name of a national political party.
- *egregious*—Originally described something that was remarkably good. The word is from the Latin *egregius* (outstanding) which is from *e-*, *ex-* (out of) + *greg-* or *grex* (flock). Now it means "remarkably bad or flagrant."
- *guy*—Guido (Guy) Fawkes was the alleged leader of a plot to blow up the English Houses of Parliament on November 5, 1605. The burning on November 5 of an effigy of Fawkes, known as a "guy" (at first capitalized as proper name but soon after becoming a common noun), led to the use of the word *guy* as a term of general reference for a man, as in *some guy called for you*. In the 20th century, under the influence of American popular culture, *guy* gradually replaced *fellow, bloke, chap* and other such words throughout the English-speaking world, and is also referred to both genders. For example, *Come on you guys!* could refer to a group of men and women.

Exercises

Fill in the blanks with the words you learned in the text.
1. As a true _____, he has always abhorred that nation's class system.
2. At the end of the film the bad _____ gets shot.
3. That politician is just a _____ who preys upon people's fears and prejudices.
4. I feel _____ about forgetting her birthday.
5. We are shocked by the more _____ examples of calloused indifference.

Text C   The History of Semantic Change

If the history of semantic change had to be summed up as one process, it would be that of specialization. The Anglo Saxons 1,500 years ago made with perhaps 30,000 words in their complete vocabulary, while Modern English has anywhere from 500,000 to a million words, depending on whether or not scientific vocabularies are included.

It could be argued that originally there was one word, from which all others have sprung. The origins of language will never be known, but the first language probably had a vocabulary of a few hundred words, providing a rich enough vocabulary for a primitive people who had few materials and fewer abstract concepts. Many of the words of the first languages had very broad senses of meaning.

If you seek to create a language from an earlier time, you should probably develop a small vocabulary, words having much more overlapping of meaning than the vocabularies of modern languages. Imagine a word *spiratholmos*—an ancient ancestor to Latin *inspirare*—meaning "wind, breath, voice, spirit." A speaker who used the word *spiratholmos* would regard the wind in the trees as the breath of the earth, the voice of God, the spirit animating each of us.

Semantic change is a change in one of the meanings of a word. Every word has a variety of senses and connotations which can be added, removed, or altered over time, often to the extent that words of one time period mean quite different things to the same words as spoken into a previous time.

Questions for Discussion or Reflection
1. Can the process of specialization sum up the history of semantic change? Why or why not?
2. Why should one probably develop a small vocabulary if one seeks to create a language from an earlier time?
3. What does *inspire* mean now?
4. Which do you prefer, the ancient vocabulary where words had much more overlapping of meaning or the modern vocabulary?

Text D Metaphor and Metonymy

Semantic changes involve meaning shift from literal meaning to figurative meaning. Take metaphor and metonymy as examples.

Metaphor

Metaphor is a complex cognitive phenomenon. It is traditionally thought of as a kind of comparison, although how we make instant and internally consistent comparisons between quite disparate things is not really understood. No artificial system, such as models in artificial intelligence, can decode metaphors, and certainly no such system can produce them. Examples of metaphors in everyday language abound. The expression, *You are the sunshine of my life* compares someone's beloved with sunshine; something that is impossible in literal terms unless that person becomes a ball of nuclear fusion. The expression *candle in the wind* likens life to a candle flame that may easily be blown out by any passing draft or gust. The fragility of life is thus emphasized. But metaphor is not just associated with poetic language or especially high-flown literary language. Metaphor is an extremely common and pervasive process in language usage and its results frequently become conventionalized. Thus, the meanings of many words have their origin in metaphor. For example, a cape-like garment that protected against the weather was given the name *cloak*, a word borrowed from French, in which it meant "bell." The garment was given the name for a bell because of its cut: It created a somewhat bell-like shape when draped over the shoulders and allowed to fall vertically to the knees or below, where it *belled* out from the body.

Metaphor is considered by cognitive scientists to be a very powerful conceptual tool because it allows language users to express abstract concepts by reference to more concrete concepts which are more accessible and understandable. For example, many words for concepts without visible correlates, such as temporal terms, are taken from the vocabulary of spatial language. The words *long* and *short* describe a spatial dimension (of, for example, a table), but they also can describe a span of (invisible) time. Metaphors occasionally impede understanding, when people fail to recognize the metaphor. For example, *petrified* literally means "turned to stone," but now figuratively means "terrified" (because of the way that people and animals freeze when in extreme fear). Those who don't know the literal meaning and take the metaphorical meaning as the basic one may wonder why petrified wood has the name it does! Sometimes what was originally a metaphor can completely lose its metaphorical force, when most or all speakers can no longer see the metaphor. Such cases are called "dead metaphors or opaque metaphors." The word *understand*, for example, is a dead metaphor, having its origins in the idea that "standing under" something was akin to having a good grasp of it (another, slightly less dead metaphor) or knowing it thoroughly. Another example is the word *consider* which was originally a metaphor meaning "to consult the stars (using astrological principles) when making a decision," *mantel* once meant "cloak or hood to catch smoke," *gorge* means "throat," and so forth for thousands more.

Metonymy

Metonymy is the use of one word with the meaning of another with which it is typically associated. Metonymy works by contiguity rather than similarity. The name for one thing is applied with the meaning of a different, but spatially and/or temporally associated thing. When someone uses metonymy, they don't wish to transfer qualities as you do with metaphor, but to indirectly refer to one thing with another word for a related thing. The common expression *The White House said today...* is a good example of metonymy. The term *White House* actually refers to the authorities who work in the building called "the White House." The latter is of course an inanimate object that says nothing. Similarly, in a monarchy the expression *the Crown* is used to mean the monarch and the departments of the government headed by the monarch. *Crown* literally refers only to a physical object sometimes worn by the actual monarch. In both of these cases the physical objects referred to by the words used become emblematic of the institutions associated with the object, and so the words for those objects can be applied to the (less concretely visible) institutions.

Metonymy can be seen as a kind of shorthand indirect reference, and people use it all the time, sometimes in very fleeting and non-conventional ways. For example, a doctor or nurse might refer in shorthand to a patient by means of the body part treated (*The broken ankle is in room 2*); a waiter might use a similar metonymy for a customer, this time using the order as an identifying feature, saying *The ham sandwich left without paying*. In both cases, the spatio-temporal contiguity of two things is exploited to use the word for one to refer to the other. The expression *the press* is used not only for an actual printing press but also for the collective institution of the print news media.

Metonymy is a conceptual device of probably equal importance to metaphor when it comes to speakers' strategies for expressing what they want to say in different ways and their hearers' strategies for working out what that is.

Exercises

1. How do you understand that people fail to recognize some metaphors?
2. Why can metonymy be seen as a kind of shorthand indirect reference?
3. What is the difference between metaphor and metonymy?
4. Identify the type of semantic shift that has occurred in each case. Choose either metaphor or metonymy.
    1) barbecue: "a rack for cooking meat over a fire" → "a social event at which food is cooked over a fire"
    2) influence: "something which has flowed in" → "something which affects someone without apparent effort"
    3) mouth: "the body opening through which an animal takes food" → "a person" (e.g. *three mouths to feed*)
    4) solve: "to loosen" → "to clear up something puzzling"
    5) counter "a device for counting" → "a surface on which various devices can be placed"

For Fun

Works to Read

1. ***Current Trends in Diachronic Semantics and Pragmatics*** by Maj-Britt Mosegaard Hansen

    The focus of this volume is on semantic and pragmatic change, its causes and mechanisms. The papers gathered here offer both theoretical proposals of more general scope and in-depth studies of language-specific cases of meaning change in particular notional domains. The volume will be of interest to students and researchers in the fields of semantics, pragmatics, and historical linguistics.

2. ***Regularity in Semantic Change*** by Elizabeth C. Traugott and Richard B. Dasher

    This new and important study of semantic change examines the various ways in which new meanings arise through language use, especially the ways in which speakers and writers experiment with uses of words and constructions. Drawing on extensive research from over a thousand years of English textual history, Traugott and Dasher show that most changes in meaning originate in and are motivated by the associative flow of speech and conceptual metonymy.

Website to Visit

1. http://media.humanities.manchester.ac.uk/humanities/flash/sociolinguistics/exercise05/exercise05.html
   This website provides exercises on semantic change.
2. http://darkwing.uoregon.edu/~l150web/unit3.html
   This website helps you to learn more about semantic change. There are lectures and exercises on it.
3. http://grammar.about.com/od/rs/g/semanticchangeterm.htm
   The website introduces the definition of semantic change and provides some examples of semantic changes.

Unit 12

Figurative Use of Words

> The English language is the sea which receives tributaries from every region under heaven.
> —— Ralph Waldo Emerson
>
> Rhetorical operations are patterns of thought that direct and order our perceptions, ideas, and feelings.
> —— Dorothy M. Guinn and Daniel Marder

Unit Goals

- To understand the definition of figurative language
- To comprehend the distinction between literal language and figurative language
- To explain the figurative use of words in a context
- To raise the awareness of the figurative use of words in the process of language learning

Before You Read

1. Below are all famous lines from commercials. Discuss with your partner and identify the Chinese meanings as well as styles of figurative use of these advertising English.

Advertising English	Chinese Meaning	Figure of Speech
Light as breeze, soft as cloud.		
Something within you is Dior.		
I'm MORE satisfied! Ask for MORE.		
Unlike me, my Rolex never needs a rest.		

2. Figures of speech are frequently used in daily life. Share some examples of figurative language with your classmates.

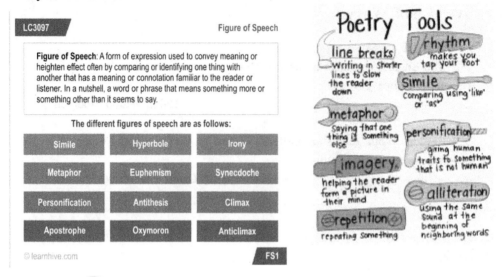

Start to Read

Text A What Is Figurative Speech?

Figurative speech refers to the use of non-literal wording or verbiage to communicate a point. Referred to alternately as figurative language, figurative speech often makes a comparison using verbal images to illustrate the speaker's intention, for effect, and to clarify meaning. "Rhetoric" is a related term that refers to the use of figures of speech and the use of literary language and terms, such as simile and paradox. Read on for examples of some of the most widely used terms of figurative speech.

Metaphor, Simile and Personification

Metaphor makes a comparison by saying something is another thing. Simile, on the other hand, performs the same function, but says something is like another thing. An example of metaphor would be *Life is a bowl of cherries*; a simile would say that *Life is like a bowl of cherries*. An example of personification would be *The cherries smiled up from the bowl*. Personification assigns human characteristics to animals, inanimate objects, or ideas.

Alliteration, Onomatopoeia, Consonance and Assonance

Alliteration, consonance, assonance and onomatopoeia have to do with the sounds of language. Alliteration is the use of a repeated sound or letter in words in close proximity, such as *Limpid light illuminated the lustrous library.* Assonance is the repetition of vowel sounds, such as *The rain in Spain stays mainly on the plain,* and consonance is the repetition of consonant sounds in close proximity, as in the first example. Onomatopoeia is used often in comic books, and refers to the sound something makes, such as in words like *hum, buzz* and *oink*.

Hyperbole, Synecdoche, Metonymy and Euphemism

Hyperbole refers to extreme exaggeration, and is used often in everyday speech. An example would be *I said it a million times*. Synecdoche is the representation of a group or a whole by referring to its parts, such as *I just got a new set of wheels* to refer to an entire vehicle. Metonymy is similar to synecdoche, as it refers to something by singling out an attribute from a whole concept, like *I work with a bunch of suits* to refer to business people. Euphemism is a form of politeness, as it makes reference to something that is socially sensitive or pejorative by substituting another word, such as *to pass away* instead of *to die*.

Understatement and Irony

Understatement, also known as litotes, is a form of expressing an idea by stating its opposite or downplaying its gravity or implications, such as this quote from *The Catcher in the Rye* by J. D. Salinger: "It isn't very serious. I have this tiny little tumor on the brain." Similarly, irony, when expressed verbally, often implies the opposite of what is actually said, or can refer to something said about the coincidence of events or
a situation. Irony can be expressed through such rhetorical figures as antiphrasis (the use of a single, contradictory word), paralipsis (drawing attention to something by pretending to ignore it), or sarcasm.

Oxymoron, Paradox and Antithesis

Oxymoron is the practice of using two apparently opposite terms next to or near one another, such as with the title *The Sounds of Silence* and Erasmus' *Festina lente,* which translates as *Make haste slowly*. Paradox is related to oxymoron, but is less condensed. For example, a paradox is often expressed in a phrase or statement, such as the Biblical paraphrase, "Whosoever loses his life shall find it." Antithesis uses words, often in parallel, that contrast each other. An example of antithesis is found in a quote from Abraham Lincoln, who said, "It has been my experience that folks who have no vices have very few virtues."

Text B Literal and Figurative Language

For analyzing language, traditional systems make a distinction between literal language and figurative language. Literal language refers to words that do not deviate from their defined meaning. The literal meaning of a sentence is entirely determined by the meanings of its component words (or morphemes) and the syntactic rules according to which these elements are combined. Figurative language refers to words and expressions that exaggerate or alter the usual meanings of the component words. Figurative language may involve analogy to similar concepts or other contexts, and may involve exaggerations. These alterations result in figures of speech.

In traditional analysis, words in literal expressions denote what they mean according to common or dictionary usage, while the words in figurative expressions connote—they add layers of meaning. To convert an utterance into meaning, the human mind

requires a cognitive framework, made up of memories of all the possible meanings that might be available to apply to the particular words in their context. This set of memories will give prominence to the most common or literal meanings, but also suggest reasons for attributing different meanings, e.g. the reader understands that the author intended to mean something different.

For example, the sentence, *The ground is thirsty*, is partly figurative. *Ground* has a literal meaning, but the ground is not alive and therefore neither needs to drink nor feels thirst. Readers immediately reject a literal interpretation and confidently interpret the words to mean "The ground is dry," an analogy to the condition that would trigger thirst in an animal. However, the statement, *When I first saw her, my soul began to quiver*, is harder to interpret. It could describe infatuation, panic, or something else entirely. The context a person requires to interpret this statement is familiarity with the speaker's feelings. Other people can give a few words a provisional set of meanings, but cannot understand the figurative utterance until acquiring more information about it.

After You Read

Knowledge Focus

1. Match the figures of speech in Column A with the expressions or sentences in Column B.

Column A	Column B
1) Alliteration	A. Man proposes, God disposes.
2) Simile	B. a dark horse
3) Rhyme	C. differently-abled
4) Oxymoron	D. toss and turn
5) Metaphor	E. like a rat in a hole
6) Antithesis	F. fair and square
7) Synecdoche	G. live by one's pen
8) Euphemism	H. open secret
9) Personification	I. earn one's bread
10) Metonymy	J. Failure is the mother of success.

2. Each of the statements below is followed by four alternative answers. Choose the one that would best complete the statement.

1) *True lies* is an example of _____.
   A. oxymoron B. reiteration
   C. juxtaposition D. rhyme

2) *Spend money like water* is an example of _____.
   A. metaphor B. simile
   C. metonymy D. synecdoche

3) *The salt of the earth* is an example of _____.
   A. simile B. metaphor
   C. metonymy D. synecdoche

4) *From cradle to grave* is an example of _____.
   A. simile   B. metaphor
   C. synecdoche   D. metonymy

5) *Fall into good hands* is an example of _____.
   A. simile   B. metaphor
   C. synecdoche   D. metonymy

6) *The pot calls the cattle black* is an example of _____.
   A. metaphor   B. personification
   C. synecdoche   D. euphemism

7) *Powder one's nose* is an example of _____.
   A. personification   B. euphemism
   C. synecdoche   D. hyperbole

8) *A world of trouble* is an example of _____.
   A. euphemism   B. personification
   C. hyperbole   D. metonymy

9) *Chop and change* is an example of _____.
   A. rhyme   B. repetition
   C. reiteration   D. alliteration

10) *By hook and by crook* is an example of _____.
    A. alliteration   B. rhyme
    C. reiteration   D. repetition

3. **Identify the figure of speech used in each sentence below and rewrite them without using any figurative language.**

   1) The children were covered with dirt from head to toe.
   _____

   2) Susan could run like the wind.
   _____

   3) He was a library of information about basketball.
   _____

   4) The message was as clear as a whistle.
   _____

   5) The grandma insisted that the house be spick and span.
   _____

   6) Mother makes enough dinner to feed an army.
   _____

   7) How could she marry a snake like that!
   _____

   8) I'm trying to imagine you with a personality.
   _____

Language Focus

1. **Fill in the blanks with the following words you have learned in the text. Change the forms where necessary.**

| syntactic | prominence | condense | verbiage | provisional |
| deviate | infatuation | proximity | sarcasm | inanimate |

1) The restaurant benefits from its _____ to several cinemas.
2) Shaw's _____ with the actress is evident in his writing.
3) A rock is a(n) _____ object.
4) "That will be useful," she snapped with heavy _____.
5) This whole chapter could be _____ into a few paragraphs.
6) The speaker lost himself in _____.
7) The study of pragmatic motivations for _____ change in English and Chinese is not only helpful to grammar teaching, but also valuable to translating from English to Chinese and from Chinese to English
8) The Palestinians would then get a _____ state with temporary borders.
9) The newspapers are giving the affair considerable _____.
10) I will never _____ from what I believe to be right.

2. **Proofreading & Error Correction.**

Many students trying to increase their effective reading speed become discouraging when they find that if they try to race through a passage faster, they fail to take what they have read. In the end, they have been so busy "reading faster" but they cannot remember what the passage is about. The problem here is that the material they are practicing on is either too difficult for them in vocabulary or figurative language, nor not sufficiently grasped.

  Figurative language creates figures (pictures) in the mind of the reader or listener. These pictures help convey the meaning faster as well as vividly than words alone, and you should also practice much as you can in your own time. Read things you like reading. Go to the subject catalogue in the library—biography, sport, domestic science, the cinema, and so on. There is bound to be some area that interests you and which you can find books of about your level of ability or just below.

  If you want a quick check on how difficult a book is, read through three or four pages with random. If there are, on average, more than five or six words on each page that are complete new to you, then the book is not suitable for reading-speed

1) _____
2) _____
3) _____

4) _____

5) _____
6) _____

7) _____

8) _____
9) _____

improvement. Incidentally, you should try to read three or four times as much "light" speed reading material like you do close, slow textbook work. You cannot achieve a permanent improvement in your reading speed if most of the time you are practicing reading slowly.

10) _____

3. Translate the following paragraph into Chinese.

    For analyzing language, traditional systems make a distinction between literal language and figurative language. Literal language refers to words that do not deviate from their defined meaning. The literal meaning of a sentence is entirely determined by the meanings of its component words (or morphemes) and the syntactic rules according to which these elements are combined. Figurative language refers to words and expressions that exaggerate or alter the usual meanings of the component words. Figurative language may involve analogy to similar concepts or other contexts, and may involve exaggerations. These alterations result in figures of speech.

Comprehensive Work

1. Use figurative language to rewrite the following sentences with your partner.

1) The grass looks green.

_____

2) The flower smells sweet.

_____

3) Grasshoppers make a high pitched noise.

_____

2. Work in a group. Do some research and find some examples of figurative language on the Bible.

Figures of Speech	Examples	Origin
Simile		
Metaphor		
Personification		
Euphemism		
Hyperbole		
Irony		

3. Writing

Advertising is a device to arouse consumers' attention to a commodity and induce them to buy and use it. In order to enhance the appeal of an advertisement, many advertisers employ figures of speech in their advertisements. Write an essay on the application of the figure of speech in advertising. Use some examples to illustrate your point of view.

Read More

Text C Synecdoche and Metonymy

Synecdoche and metonymy are both figures of speech used in rhetoric. They are not the same thing, though metonymy is often interpreted so widely that synecdoche can be regarded as a special case of it.

We use synecdoche when we speak of a part of something but mean the whole thing. When Patrick O'Brian has Captain Jack Aubrey tell his first lieutenant to "let *the hands* go to dinner," he is employing synecdoche because he is using a part (the hand) for the whole man. We can also reverse the whole and the part, so using a word for something when you only mean part of it. This often comes up in sport: a commentator might say that "*The West Indies* has lost to *England*" when he means that the West Indian team has lost to the English one. *America* is often used as synecdoche in this second sense, as the word refers to the whole continent but is frequently applied to a part of it, the U.S.A..

Metonymy is similar, but uses something more generally or loosely associated with a concept to stand in for it. When Americans speak of *the Oval Office*, for example, they are really referring to the activity within it, the position or function of the

President. It is a linked term, and so a metonym. British writers refer similarly to *the Crown* when they are really discussing the powers, authority and responsibilities of the monarchy, which is symbolized by the crown.

The difference between synecdoche and metonymy is that in metonymy the word you employ is linked to the concept you are really talking about, but is not actually a part of it. Another example is *the turf* for horse racing. But the distinction is not always obvious and often cannot be rigorously applied, and many people use metonymy to mean both.

In his story *Here Lies Miss Groby*, James Thurber wrote about his English teacher's attempts to explain metonymy by talking about "the container for the thing contained." This sounds like synecdoche rather than metonymy, but Miss Groby's examples show she really meant metonymy. For example, when Shakespeare had Antony say in Julius Caesar: "Friends, Romans, Countrymen, lend me your *ears*" he was speaking figuratively of the thing the ears contained — that is, their function, their ability to listen, not some literal component. Thurber recalled that he lay awake that night trying to find an example of the reverse idea and came up with an image of an angry wife about to bash hubby over the head with a bottle of milk, saying "Get away from me or I'll hit you with the *milk*." That is metonymy all right, but you can argue it is also synecdoche because milk is an essential component part of a bottle of milk, not just something associated with it.

Notes

1. **Captain Jack Aubrey:** a fictional character in the Aubrey-Maturin series of novels by the English novelist and translator Patrick O'Brian.
2. **James Thurber:** an American cartoonist, author, journalist, playwright, and celebrated wit. Thurber was best known for his cartoons and short stories, published mainly in *The New Yorker* magazine and collected in his numerous books.

Exercises

1. Decide whether the following statements are True or False.
   1) Both synecdoche and metonymy involve substitution.
   2) Metonymy involves the substitution of the part for the whole, or the whole for the part.
   3) *The pen is mightier than the sword* is an example of synecdoche.
   4) *Her heart rules her head* is an example of metonymy.
   5) *His parents bought him a new set of wheels* is an example of synecdoche.

2. Do you think metonymy is somehow similar to synecdoche? Please make a comparison of these two figures of speech and write an essay on the similarities and differences between these two.

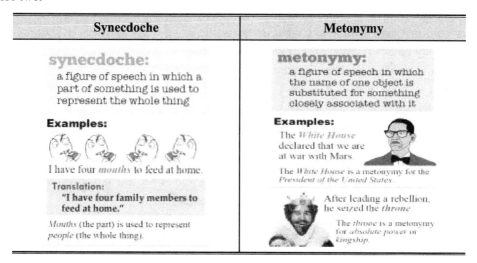

Text D Taboos and Euphemisms

Taboos and euphemisms exist in every language. They play an important part in culture. Dealing with them appropriately enables us to successfully communicate.

A taboo is something forbidden by religions, laws, morals or society and it is a common social phenomenon of every nation. In Western countries, many people consider the date the thirteenth or

Friday to be unlucky. This has its roots in religion. According to the Bible, Judas, who betrayed his master, Christ, was the thirteenth person at Christ's last supper. And Friday was said to be the day Jesus was crucified.

There is also a body language taboo. Taking the distance in social conversation for example, unless they know each other well, British and American people dislike being too close to each other while talking. Westerners of the same sex also do not hold hands, as many people in China do.

There are many taboos in China, too. For example, it is impolite for children to call their parents by name. And a clock should not be used as a gift because in Chinese, "songzhong" (to give sb. a clock as a gift) has the same pronunciation as "songzhong" (to attend upon a dying person), which makes people think of death.

A euphemism is the use of other words or phrases instead of the words required by truth or accuracy. That is, people don't say directly what they mean due to politeness. For example, blind people are sometimes called "sight-deprived" and old people are often called "senior citizens." The euphemistic "sight-deprived" and "senior" are used to avoid offense—people may feel hurt when they are described as old or blind.

In fact, a euphemism is a kind of indirect speech. In such speech the speaker gets the listener to understand what he really means according to the shared background information. When someone says, "Could I ask where the restroom is?" he does not mean to ask a question. It is a request. The speaker makes this request indirectly with a question to say that he wants to use the toilet.

On account of the difference between cultures, taboos and euphemisms are varied according to circumstances and situations. In a certain situation, what is acceptable in one culture may be not in another. For example, Chinese students often begin their talking with foreigners by asking such questions as "How much is your rent?" or "How old are you?" They think it a friendly way to start a conversation and to show friendship. In English, these are considered private questions and Western people feel uncomfortable being asked

questions like these by someone whom they barely know. Another example is "Where are you going?" In Chinese, people say something like this as greeting; while in English it is a real question. If we greet foreigners by saying this, it can cause a misunderstanding.

Generally speaking, both taboos and euphemisms are needed in communication. It is necessary for us to pay attention to such expressions so that we can get along easily with foreigners.

Exercises

Choose the best answer to each of the following questions.

1. What does the euphemism *misspeak* mean?
   A. Stumble or stutter awkwardly on one's words.
   B. Lie about something.
   C. Say a swear word.

2. What does the euphemism *He lost his lunch* mean?
   A. A bully has stolen his lunch.
   B. He was cheeky in class and got detention.
   C. He has vomited.
3. What does the euphemism *I misplaced it* mean?
   A. I found it.
   B. I lost it.
   C. I fixed it.
4. What does the euphemism *His father has bitten the dust* mean?
   A. His father is in a famous music video.
   B. His father has severe allergies towards dust.
   C. His father is dead.
5. What do business bosses sometimes use the euphemism *downsizing* to mean?
   A. Firing employees.
   B. Trying to lose weight.
   C. Trimming down other salaries.

For Fun

Works to Read

1. ***Readings in Rhetorical Criticism*** by Carl R. Burgchardt
   An important collection for scholars and students, this volume surveys major approaches to rhetorical criticism through significant essays that explain and illustrate them. From H. A. Wichelns's groundbreaking "The Literary Criticism of Oratory" to recent criticism of media framing and visual rhetoric, these essays reflect the historical development, diversity, and practice of rhetorical criticism.

2. ***Understanding Figurative Language*** by Sam Glucksberg
   This book examines how people understand utterances that are intended figuratively. Glucksberg's research in this book is concerned with ordinary language: expressions that are used in daily life, including conversations about everyday matters, newspaper and magazine articles, and the media. Metaphor is the major focus of the book. Idioms, however, are also treated comprehensively, as is the theory of conceptual metaphor in the context of how people understand both conventional and novel figurative expressions.

Websites to Visit

1. http://quizlet.com/subject/figurative-language/
   This site has various kinds of quizzes to test your knowledge on figurative language.
2. http://grammar.about.com/od/rhetoricstyle/u/RhetoricStyle.htm
   This site provides some explanations related to figurative language in writing.

Unit 13

Meaning and Context

> Words are like bottles. Their shapes may remain the same, while their contents vary from very bitter to very sweet.
>
> —— Hugh Rawson

Unit Goals

- To understand the different types of context
- To learn how to determine the meaning of a polysemous word in context
- To define unknown words by using context clues

Before You Read

1. Meaning and Context

Is the underlined word in the following sentences important? Do you need to understand the word in order to understand the entire sentence? Read the sentence below and figure out how meaning and context work together in understanding the whole sentence.

> Leo ate so much <u>fettucine</u> that he could not eat another bite. He felt like his stomach would <u>explode</u>.

Questions:

1) Is *fettucine* important or not? What is the meaning of this word? Do you need to know what kind of food it is?

2) Is *explode* important? What can you guess about this word? How does Leo's stomach feel? How would your stomach feel if you ate "so much" of something?

2. How to Guess Word Meanings in Context

What is the meaning of the underlined word in the following sentence?

> The snake <u>slithered</u> through the grass. He was hunting.

A. stopped moving　　　　　　　　B. slept in the grass
C. ate something　　　　　　　　　D. moved or traveled

You must discover what *slithered* means by using logic. Here are the analyses:

A. stopped moving is INCORRECT: The sentence above says THROUGH the grass. *Through* means that there is some movement.

B. slept in the grass is INCORRECT: The sentence above says he is hunting. Snakes don't sleep when they hunt.

C. ate something is INCORRECT: The sentence above says he is hunting. Snakes don't eat when they are hunting. They eat AFTER they hunt.

D. moved or traveled is CORRECT: The sentence above says THROUGH the grass. *Through* means that there is movement.

3. The Polysemous Words and Contexts

Words that have more than one meaning are polysemous words. And these words require many exposures in meaningful text before we feel as if we understand all of the different meanings. Explain the different meanings of the following words in the table and make up a story with these words of the different meanings in it.

Word	Meaning
spell	a. The heartless witch cast a *spell* on the poor little girl.
	b. The pupils learn to *spell* in school.
can	a. If you won't keep quiet you *can* get out!
	b. This *can* holds five liters of water.
mean	a. He that promises too much *means* nothing.
	b. He is a *mean* man.
right	a. She's the sort of woman who always says the *right* things.
	b. We fought for the *right* of access to government information.

Start to Read

Text A Context as the Key to Unlocking Word Meaning

Before you can start thinking critically about what you read, you have to understand the meanings of the words you are reading. You will often come across words whose meanings you do not know. What is the best way to figure out the meaning of a new word? Do you always need to get out a dictionary and spend time looking the word up? First, let's have a clear idea of word meaning.

Types of Word Meaning

Words with forms and meanings are linguistic signs, containing two parts, the signified (a thought that represents an object), and the signifier (the sound or written word). Both the signified and the signifier have a referent (the actual physical object).

Three kinds of words are used on different occasions, that is, common words (stylistically expressing a neutral meaning), formal words (usually used in books, newspapers, documents and serious speeches), and informal words (used in ordinary, familiar, or informal conversation).

The word meaning refers to the thing or idea that a word represents, expresses or conveys. Meaning includes grammatical meaning and lexical meaning.

Grammatical Meaning

Grammatical meaning refers to that part of the meaning of the word which indicates grammatical concept or relations such as part of speech of words, singular and plural meaning of nouns, and tense meaning of verbs and their inflectional forms. The grammatical meaning of a word becomes important only when it is used in actual context. Take this sentence for example, "The monkey is eating a banana." The words *monkey* and *banana* are nouns and both are singular used as subject and object in the sentence respectively; *is eating* is the predicate verb in present continuous tense, and *the* and *a* are determiners, restricting the referent and indicating number.

Unlike lexical meaning, different lexical items, which have different lexical meanings, may have the same grammatical meaning. For example, *pens, apples, trees, cars, policemen* have the same plural meaning; *cake, bag, cup, box, light* have the same singular meaning, and *playing, looking, thinking, teaching* have the same tense meaning. And the same word may have different grammatical meanings, for instance, *think, thinks, thought, thinking* have different tense meanings.

Lexical Meaning

Lexical meaning itself has two components: conceptual meaning and associative meaning.

Conceptual meaning is also called "denotative" or "cognitive" meaning. This refers to the definition given in the dictionary forming the core of word-meaning. For example, in the sentence *The sun rises in the east*, the *sun* here means "a heavenly body which gives off light, heat, and energy", a concept which is understood by anyone.

Associative meaning is the secondary meaning supplemented to the conceptual meaning. It differs from the conceptual meaning in that it is open-ended and indeterminate and comprises affective meaning, collocative meaning, and so on.

Affective meaning refers to that part of meaning which conveys emotions and attitudes of a language user. It indicates the speaker's attitude towards the person or thing in question. It includes appreciative words, i.e., words of positive overtones used to show appreciation or attitude of approval, and pejorative words, i.e., words of negative connotations implying disapproval, contempt or criticism. *Famous, determined, slender* and *notorious, idiot, skinny* fall into the two categories, respectively.

Collocative meaning consists of the association a word acquires in its collocation. It is that part of the word-meaning suggested by the words before or after the word in discussion. For example, *green* in the expression *green hand, green fruit,* and *green with envy* means different things.

Complicated as word meaning seems to be, you may be able to figure out the meaning of a word from its context. No matter how many denotative meanings a word may have, generally there will be no risk of misunderstanding the meaning when it occurs in a particular context.

The Roles of Context

Context refers to what comes before and after a word, phrase, statement, etc. helping to fix the meaning, or refers to circumstances in which an event occurs.

Context is a general term used in linguistics and phonetics to refer to specific parts of an utterance (or text) near or adjacent to a unit which is the focus of attention. It also refers to the features of the non-linguistic world in relation to which linguistic units are systematically used.

Therefore, context can be classified into linguistic context and non-linguistic context. Linguistic context allows learners to refer back and forth through the unfolding text itself. It includes phonological context (intonation, stress, pause which is used to determine different meanings), lexical context (the lexical items combined with a given polysemous word), and grammatical context (either syntactic or lexical, and in some instances rhetorical context).

Non-linguistic context is also named extra-linguistic context which constrains and regulates the application of the shared "ground-rules" for communication. It includes situational context (the background knowledge, actual speech setting, and types of discourse), social context (any kind of relation among human and any contact that concerns the historical background and the background characteristic of times), and cultural context (the cultural background, including beliefs, customs, ideas, value system, religious, history, etc.).

Context plays different roles.

Eliminating Ambiguity

Ambiguity refers to a word, a phrase, a sentence with more than one possible meaning. Ambiguity may be caused by different things, like polysemy, homonymy, grammatical structure as in the following sentences:

This is light. (This is not heavy/easy)

The ball is attractive. (The round object/ dancing party is attractive)

I found her on the roof. (I found her when I was on the roof./ I found her when she was on the roof.)

Ambiguity very often disappears in contexts, linguistic or extra-linguistic. The context often makes the ambiguous meaning so certain that we do not think of the fact that the word or the structure has different meanings.

Shaping Purpose and Constructing Meaning

Context plays an important role in shaping the decisions writers make as they compose a text and that readers make as they construct meaning from a text. For writers, context shapes—some might argue that it actually causes—the purposes for writing. Moreover, context affects the opportunities, requirements, and limitations that affect the choices writers make as they compose their documents.

For readers, context shapes their attempts to construct meaning as they read. Social context can affect the extent to which writers and readers share common experiences and expectations about a text. Cultural context will affect the fundamental assumptions, beliefs, and aspirations that they bring to the reading of a text.

Purposes, influences, representations of readers and writers, and the various levels of context, as relatively distinct as they are, are intimately related with each other. As you consider the role that text plays in the attempts of writers and readers to create shared meaning through text, remember that no single element can stand completely separate from the others.

Providing Clues for Inferring Word Meaning

Writers usually know when they must use a word that will be new to their readers. So they often include other words or phrases to help with the understanding of the new word. These words or phrases are referred to as context clues. They are built into the sentences around the difficult word. If you become more aware of the words around the difficult words you encounter in your reading, you will save yourself many trips to the dictionary. You will be able to make logical guesses about the meanings of many words.

There are a variety of context clues that can be used to infer the meaning of a word.

Definition: Often the writer defines the meaning of the word right in the sentence or gives enough explanation for the meaning to be clear. For example, *Later Congress voted to augment or increase the job training program.* Assuming that the word *augment* may be unfamiliar to some of the readers, the writer explains the meaning by giving a familiar word *increase*.

Examples: Many times an author helps the reader get the meaning of a word by providing examples that illustrate the use of the word. For example, *The lantern illuminated the cave so well that we were able to see the crystal formations on the rocks.* A writer may give just one example or several. Remember that these examples are not synonyms. Look for words or phrases like *such as, including,* or *consists of.* Colons (:) and dashes (—) can also signal examples.

Comparison and Contrast: Comparison and contrast usually show the similarities and differences between persons, ideas, and things. For example, *The Asian gibbon, like other apes, is specially adapted for life in trees.* The phrase *like other apes* indicates that the *Asian gibbon* is a type of ape. In the example *The major points of your plan are clear to me, but the details are still hazy,* the conjunction *but* introduces a clause that contrasts in meaning with the previous one and signal the fact that *hazy* is the opposite of *clear*.

Summary: A summary clue sums up a situation or an idea with a word or a phrase. For example, *Mr. Alonso contributes money to the Red Cross, the Boys Club, and the Cancer Fund; he also volunteers many hours in the emergency ward of the hospital. He is indeed altruistic.* From this account of Mr. Alonso's deeds, the reader may well infer that *altruistic* means "unselfish."

Restatement or Synonyms: Very often the reader can find in the same passage a familiar word that relates to a subject in a manner similar to the way that the unfamiliar term does. For example, *On a March night a girl was attacked by a maniac as she came home from work. The madman took half an hour to murder her, but no one called the police*. From the description of the events in the first and second sentences we know that the words *maniac* and *madman* refer to the same person and are probably synonymous.

Antonyms: Words with opposite meanings may be found in the same context. The author includes an antonym to help the reader understand the meaning of a word. For example, *To be white and not black, affluent and not poor, is enough to provide status in certain social groups*. We note that *white* and *black* are opposites, so when we see the next pair of words in a parallel construction, we can assume that *affluent* is the opposite of *poor*, and must therefore mean "rich."

Inference/General Context Clues: Sometimes a word or phrase is not immediately clarified within the same sentence. Relationships, which are not directly apparent, are inferred or implied. The reader must look for clues within, before, and after the sentence in which the word is used. For example, *The haberdashery was Lou's favorite place. He loved shopping for nice suits. The people who worked there were so kind and helpful*. The first sentence tells us that *haberdashery* is a place. The pronoun *he* and the phrase *shopping for nice suits* in the second sentence imply that *haberdashery* is a place where men can shop for nice suits.

The seven types of context clues do not operate in isolation; two or three types of contextual information are often included in the same sentence.

After You Read

Knowledge Focus

1. Fill in the blanks according to the knowledge you learned.

The word meaning refers to the thing or idea that a word represents, expresses or conveys. We may be able to figure out the meaning of a word from its context. The context often eliminates 1)_____ so that we do not think of the fact that a word or a structure has different meanings. It also shapes purpose and constructs meaning. More importantly, the context provides 2)_____ for inferring word meaning. Often the writer gives the 3)_____ of a word right in the sentence or gives enough explanation for the meaning to be clear. Many times the writer helps the reader get the meaning of a word by providing 4)_____ that illustrate the use of the word.

5)_____ and 6)_____ usually show the similarities and differences between persons, ideas and things. A 7)_____ clue sums up a situation or an idea with a word or a phrase. 8)_____, words with similar meanings, and 9)_____, words with opposite meanings may be included to help the reader understand the meaning of a word. Sometimes a word or phrase is not immediately clarified within the same sentence. The reader must look for clues within, before, and after the sentence in which the word is used to draw 10)_____.

2. **Meaning and context are inseparable from each other. Can you tell the exact meaning of the following sentences? If not, why?**
   1) The table is fascinating.
   2) They're off (adj.).
   3) The girl found a book on Main Street.
   4) The police were ordered to stop drinking by midnight.
   5) Would you care to make up a four with us?
   6) I'm free at last.
   7) Jane was too busy to compose herself.
   8) Go and ask Mr. Wallace who is sitting by the window, please.
   9) He nearly brushed his teeth for twenty minutes every night.
   10) Marta dropped out of school after taking ten courses on Friday.

3. **Try to determine the meanings of the following underlined words based on the context clues in the sentences according to the knowledge you learned.**
   1) Her quiet, <u>timid</u> ways made us guess at her true feelings about the story because she kept her ideas to herself and never spoke in the class.
      A. shy   B. boisterous
      C. kind   D. seriously
   2) He was found running down the street after curfew, and his parents were <u>penalized</u>. The ticket read: "Illegally in the streets at 1:00 a.m." Now he would have to pay the ticket with his own money.
      A. crooked   B. fined
      C. delicate   D. informed
   3) The first review on the Harry Potter movie was <u>favorable</u>. Many people attended and enjoyed the movie. Some people even saw the movie three times!
      A. negative   B. uncertain
      C. positive   D. clear
   4) The woman crossed her fingers as her daughter did the cheer. She was hoping that everything would work out for her daughter as she <u>vied</u> for a position on the squad. Her daughter wanted to be a cheerleader.
      A. shouted   B. enclosed
      C. expanded   D. tried
   5) The boy knew that the lake was <u>teeming</u>, and overflowing with bass, so he brought a big net to help get the fish in the boat.
      A. rare   B. enclave
      C. full   D. sparse

6) It was difficult to listen to Tommy speak because he <u>droned</u> on and on just like a buzzer that won't stop buzzing.
   A. sang   B. talked in the same tone
   C. performed lively   D. shouted
7) The <u>lithe</u> girl was perfect for the basketball team because she was all muscle and could play well.
   A. lean   B. curved
   C. thick   D. eerie
8) Thomas went to the <u>apex</u> of the mountain, and because it was so high, he had to take a tank of oxygen with him.
   A. bottom   B. breathe
   C. top   D. clear
9) The <u>apparatus</u> that Jill used to connect the fabric was similar to a sewing machine, but this one did all of the work while she just pushed a button.
   A. idea   B. zipper
   C. instrument   D. singular
10) The <u>frigid</u> air seemed to suck his breath away as he attempted to finish his first snowman of the season.
    A. deficient   B. sappy
    C. thick   D. cold

Language Focus

1. Fill in the blanks with the following words you have learned in the text. Change the forms where necessary.

| maniac | pejorative | altruistic | parallel | aspiration |
| hazy | adjacent | inference | affluent | indeterminate |

1) Our farm land was _____ to the river.
2) What _____ have you drawn from this evidence?
3) What changes are needed to meet women's _____ for employment?
4) Only those willing to accept jobs with _____ tenure will be employed.
5) What is odd is how fairly quickly the concept of geek has moved from _____ to almost complimentary.
6) He leapt into the car and drove like a _____ to the hospital.
7) The road and the railway are _____ to each other.
8) If he remembers any other country at all, it's at best a few _____ images.
9) Companies that donate books or equipment to schools that collect their tokens are not being entirely _____—after all, you have to buy the products to get the tokens.
10) He is _____ and can afford to send his children to the best schools.

2. Proofreading & Error Correction.

Context means the situation or body of information which causes language to be used. There is a number of different context types, but for our purposes we will concentrate on three: the students' world, the outside world, and formulated information.

The students' world: there are two kinds of students' world, that is, physical surrounding that the students are in (the classroom, school or institution) and the ones the students live (families, friends, and experiences).

The outside world: it provides us for rich context for presentation. For example: there are almost an infinite number of stories we can use to present different tenses. We can also create situations which people speak, or where the writer describes some special information. We can ask students to look at the examples of language which show the new language on operation where these categories can be simulated or real.

Formulated information refers to all that information which is presented in the form of time tables, notes, charts, etc. It can be real and you can design your own. The context we choose will depend on the type of language being introducing.

Another way to categorize types of context is: historic context (current goings on—political leaders/royalty, war, class structure), literary context (what was common among writing at the time—particular genres, style of writing such as poetry, etc.), and author's context (Was the author in an abusive family? Was he/she self-educated?)

1) _____

2) _____

3) _____

4) _____

5) _____

6) _____

7) _____

8) _____

9) _____

10) _____

3. Translate the following paragraph into Chinese.

Writers usually know when they must use a word that will be new to their readers. So they often include other words or phrases to help with the understanding of the new word. These words or phrases are referred to as context clues. They are built into the sentences around the difficult word. If you become more aware of the words around the difficult words you encounter in your reading, you will save yourself many trips to the dictionary. You will be able to make logical guesses about the meanings of many words.

Comprehensive Work

1. **Guess the meaning of each word from the context of the sentences below it. While you are doing the exercises, make sure that you neither use a dictionary nor discuss with other students. Try to describe the meaning of each word in English.**

   1) What does *misogynist* mean?
      a. Mary realized that Mr. Ashman was a misogynist soon after she started working as his assistant.
      b. It is difficult for a woman to work for a misogynist. She is never sure if his criticism is based on her work or on the fact that she is a woman.
   2) What does *foul* mean?
      a. We were all shocked by the foul language the little boy was using.
      b. With the windows closed for so long, there was a foul smell in the room.
   3) What does *soggy* mean?
      a. The window had been left open during the storm, and the papers on my desk were a soggy mess.
      b. We gathered up the soggy towels and bathing suits and hung them all in the sun to dry.
   4) What does *shrink* mean?
      a. I washed the T-shirt in cold water so it wouldn't shrink.
      b. If you want to have enough spinach for dinner, you need to buy a lot. It shrinks to almost nothing when you cook it.
   5) What does *swell up* mean?
      a. Jill's skating accident made her foot swell up until she could no longer wear her shoe.
      b. Poor Simon! After he had his tooth pulled out, the whole side of his face swelled up.

2. **Writing**

   We combine words to form sentences, paragraphs and papers in order to convey meaning and emotion. However, when we read, many times the author doesn't always tell us everything and we must figure things out on our own.

   Take a good look at the picture and study the line at the bottom. Write an essay entitled "What the Teacher Really Means".

"When writing you essays, I encourage you to think for yourselves while you express what I'd most agree with."

Read More

Text B Ambiguity

Although people are sometimes said to be ambiguous in how they use language, ambiguity is, strictly speaking, a property of linguistic expressions. A word, phrase, or sentence is ambiguous if it has more than one meaning. Obviously this definition does not say what meanings are or what it is for an expression to have one (or more than one). For a particular language, this information is provided by a grammar, which systematically pairs forms with meanings, ambiguous forms with more than one meaning.

There are two types of ambiguity, lexical and structural.

Lexical ambiguity is by far the more common. The word *light*, for example, can mean "not very heavy or not very dark." Words like *light, note, bear* and *over* are lexically ambiguous. They induce ambiguity in phrases or sentences in which they occur, such as *light suit* and *The duchess can't bear children*. Everyday examples include nouns like *chip*, *pen* and *suit*, verbs like *call, draw* and *run*, and adjectives like *deep, dry* and *hard*. Consider the sentence, *The tailor pressed one suit in his shop and one in the municipal court*. Evidence that the word *suit* (not to mention *press*) is ambiguous is provided by the anomaly of the "crossed interpretation" of the sentence, on which *one suit* is used to refer to an article of clothing and *one* to a legal action.

The above examples of ambiguity are each a case of one word with more than one meaning. However, it is not always clear when we have only one word. The verb *desert* and the noun *dessert*, which sound the same but are spelled differently, count as distinct words (they are homonyms). So do the noun *bear* and the verb *bear*, even though they not only sound the same but are spelled the same. These examples may be clear cases of homonymy, but what about the noun *respect* and the verb *respect* or the preposition *over* and the adjective *over*? Are the members of these pairs homonyms or different forms of the same word? There is no general consensus on how to draw the line between cases of one ambiguous word and cases of two homonymous words. Perhaps the difference is ultimately arbitrary.

Sometimes one meaning of a word is derived from another. For example, the cognitive sense of *see* seems derived from its visual sense. The sense of *weigh* in "He weighed the package" is derived from its sense in "The package weighed two pounds." Similarly, the transitive senses of *burn, fly* and *walk* are derived from their intransitive senses. Now it could be argued that in each of these cases the derived sense does not really qualify as a second meaning of the word but is actually the result of a lexical operation on the underived sense. This argument is plausible to the extent that the phenomenon is systematic and general, rather than peculiar to particular words. It is also concerned to explain the rich and subtle semantic behavior of common and highly flexible words like the verbs *do* and *put* and the prepositions *at, in* and *to*. Each of these words has uses which are so numerous yet so closely related that they are often described as "polysemous" rather than ambiguous.

Structural ambiguity occurs when a phrase or sentence has more than one underlying structure, such as the phrases *Tibetan history teacher*, *a student of high moral principles* and *short men and women*, and the sentences *The girl hit the boy with a book* and *Visiting relatives can be boring*. These ambiguities are said to be structural because each such phrase can be represented in two structurally different ways, e.g. *[Tibetan history] teacher* and *Tibetan [history teacher]*. Indeed, the existence of such ambiguities provides strong evidence for a level of underlying syntactic structure. Consider the structurally ambiguous sentence, *The chicken is ready to eat*, which could be used to describe either a hungry chicken or a broiled chicken. It is arguable that the operative reading depends on whether or not the implicit subject of the infinitive clause *to eat* is tied anaphorically to the subject *the chicken* of the main clause.

This next sentence is structurally ambiguous: *Put the box on the table by the window in the*

kitchen. Is the box already on the table, and to be put in the kitchen? Or is the box to be put on the table which is in the kitchen? From the sentence alone we cannot tell. It could mean any of the following:

  a. Put the box onto the table that is by the window in the kitchen.
  b. Take the box that is on the table and put it by the window in the kitchen.
  c. Take the box off the table that is by the window and put it in the kitchen.

It is not always clear when we have a case of structural ambiguity. Consider, for example, the elliptical sentence, *Perot knows a richer man than Trump*. It has two meanings that Perot knows a man who is richer than Trump and that Perot knows a man who is richer than any man Trump knows, and is therefore ambiguous. But what about the sentence *John loves his mother and so does Bill*? It can be used to say either that John loves John's mother and Bill loves Bill's mother or that John loves John's mother and Bill loves John's mother, too. But is it really ambiguous? One might argue that the clause *so does Bill* is unambiguous and may be read unequivocally as saying in the context that Bill does the same thing that John does, and although there are two different possibilities for what counts as doing the same thing, these alternatives are not fixed semantically. Hence the ambiguity is merely apparent and better described as semantic under determination.

Although ambiguity is fundamentally a property of linguistic expressions, people are also said to be ambiguous on occasion in how they use language. This can occur if, even when their words are unambiguous, their words do not make what they mean uniquely determinable. Strictly speaking, however, ambiguity is a semantic phenomenon, involving linguistic meaning rather than speaker's meaning. Generally when one uses ambiguous words or sentences, one does not consciously entertain their unintended meanings, although there is psycholinguistic evidence that when one hears ambiguous words one momentarily accesses and then rules out their irrelevant senses. When people use ambiguous language, generally its ambiguity is not intended. Occasionally, however, ambiguity is deliberate, as with an utterance of *I'd like to see more of you* when intended to be taken in more than one way in the very same context of utterance.

There are two types of ambiguous sentence: either there is a local ambiguity (one that is cleared up once you have heard the whole sentence) or it is a global ambiguity (one that remains even after the entire sentence has been heard).

Locally Ambiguous: *The old train... Train* could be a noun (*The old train left the station*) or a verb (*The old train the young*).

Globally Ambiguous: *I know more beautiful women than Julia Roberts*. This could mean that I know women more beautiful than Julia Roberts or that I know more beautiful women than Julia Roberts does.

Topics for Discussion

Sometimes when you read, you find a word whose meaning you do not know. Often you can tell the meaning of the word by the way the word is used in the sentence. This is called understanding word meaning in context. Without a context, word meanings can be ambiguous. And in different contexts, word meanings can be different. What does this sentence mean in

different contexts? How are the meanings different from each other or even completely opposite?

Text C   Context and Context of Situation

We know that it is important not to take a specific passage out of context. Context can erase misunderstandings and expose false doctrine. However, what is context?

Context refers to:

a. the parts of a written or spoken statement that precede or follow a specific word or passage, usually influencing its meaning or effect;

b. the set of circumstances or facts that surround a particular event, situation, etc.

The first definition promotes the limited idea of "surrounding text." The second definition hints there are more than just the surrounding verses. Yet, context has another definition which better explains what we need to understand when reading text.

Malinowski understood that a text written by these people into this language could not be understood by any foreigners or by people living outside this society even if translated into their own languages because each message brought more meanings than those expressed through the words, meanings that could only be understood if accompanied by the situation. Thus, Malinowski introduced the notion of context of situation, meaning the "environment of the text."

Knowledge is transmitted in social contexts, through relationships, like those of parent and child, or teacher and pupil, or classmates, that are defined in the value systems and ideology of the culture. And the words that are exchanged in these contexts get their meanings from activities in which they are embedded, which again are social activities with social agencies and goals.

Context of culture is very important also because it is not only the immediate sight that is important but also the whole cultural history behind the text and determining the significance for the culture. Knowing where, when the text is set will help to understand the text more.

Linguistically, context of situation is the totality of extra-linguistic features having relevance to a communicative act. The three features of the context of situation are:

a. the field of discourse (referring to what is happening, to the nature of the social action that is taking place);

b. the tenor of discourse (referring to who is taking part, to the nature of the participants, their statuses and roles);

c. the mode of discourse (referring to what part the language is playing, what is that the participants are expecting the language to do for them in that situation).

Context includes the experience of the time or place that affects the understanding contained in the text. History can fill in the missing context not included in the text. However, what is taught today as history may be no more than reviewing previous events, within a modern context. Few judge history within the framework of its day including the ambient culture, linguistic understanding, and moral development. Without such examination, it is doubtful that we understand what we read in history. If we neglect this type of context, we have limited understanding and can misjudge the desires of the writer.

Topics for Discussion

Directions: There is no context for the following picture. Discuss with your partner: What is happening in this picture? What might be the context? What does it try to convey?

Text D Decoding Meaning Through Context

A writer might give the meaning of a difficult word in the passage itself. The explanation might follow a comma or a dash after the difficult word. This is especially used for place names, technical terms, and other words that even native English speakers might not be familiar with. For example, in the sentence *New and knew are homophones—words that sound the same but have a different spelling*, *words that sound the same but have a different spelling* is the meaning of *homophones*.

1. In the following sentences, find the words that mean the same as the underlined word.

1) We visited <u>Narvik</u>, a town in the northern part of Norway.
2) When she fell, she broke her <u>ulna</u>, a bone in her arm.
3) When I was in Germany, I enjoyed <u>Schweinebrauten</u>, which is a type of roast pork.

Another way you can guess the meaning of a word is through the relationships of the words around it. For example, in the sentence, *After the heavy rain, the ground was saturated with water*, you should be able to guess that the word *saturated* means "completely wet" because that's what happens to the ground after a heavy rain.

2. Are you able to figure out the meanings of the underlined words?

4) The company <u>lures</u> workers with high salaries and good working conditions.
    A. angers   B. fires   C. attracts   D. organizes
5) In the United States, the <u>transition</u> from one President to the next one is generally smooth.
    A. payment   B. change   C. search   D. understanding
6) The swimmer dived into the pool at one end and swam under water to the other end, where she <u>emerged</u> from the water.
    A. came out   B. dried off   C. sank to the bottom   D. injured herself

The writer may refer to the same thing using a different word in another part of the sentence, or in a later sentence. In that case, if you know the meaning of the second word, that will help you understand the meaning of the word that you don't know. For example, *That vase looks very fragile. With young children in the house, I have to be careful with breakable things.* In these two sentences, *breakable* and *fragile* seem to mean something similar. Therefore, you can guess that something that is fragile must break easily.

3. Are you able to figure out the meanings of the underlined words?
   7) Gary is being paid more than $400,000 per annum. This yearly salary allows him to live very well.
      A. in cash   B. for his services
      C. during the summer   D. each year
   8) The company president's veracity has been questioned, but we do not doubt his truthfulness.
      A. honesty   B. ability
      C. luck   D. finances
   9) Ms. Aaron showed a lot of strength after her daughter died. Everyone admired her fortitude.
      A. sadness   B. courage
      C. niceness   D. appearance

A writer might also contrast the word that you do not know with a word or idea that you already know. In that case, since you can see the opposite of what the word means, you can guess what the word means. For example, *That statue is in a precarious position. Please move it somewhere that it won't fall.* Here, *precarious* is contrasted with *somewhere that it won't fall.* Therefore, *a precarious position* is a position in which something is in danger of falling.

4. Are you able to figure out the meanings of the underlined words?
   10) Most Americans are monolingual, but I don't think that's good. Everyone should learn a second language.
      A. happy   B. speaking one language
      C. very quiet   D. traveling overseas
   11) At first, our problems seemed insurmountable. However, now I think we'll be able to find solutions.
      A. not able to be solved   B. not able to be explained
      C. not able to be discussed   D. not able to be understood
   12) Though the artist has died, her art will be immortal.
      A. forgotten   B. beautiful
      C. eternal   D. damaged
   13) The writing style I used in my report was too colloquial, so my boss asked me to write it in a more formal manner.
      A. casual   B. simple
      C. unusual   D. repeating too much

Your knowledge of cause and effect is useful in helping you understand words that you do not know. For example, *Your statement of purpose is ambiguous, so we don't understand what you intend to do.* If the result is that the reader does not understand, the cause may be that the statement was unclear, so *ambiguous* means "unclear."

5. Are you able to figure out the meanings of the underlined words?
   14) The journey across the mountains was perilous, and several people were killed.
      A. long   B. dangerous
      C. beautiful   D. unnecessary

15) Dean forgot to turn off the water in the bathtub, and the bathroom was <u>inundated</u> with water.
   A. flooded
   B. baked
   C. melted
   D. boiled
16) The insects are so <u>microscopic</u> that you can hardly see them.
   A. ugly
   B. quiet
   C. small
   D. dangerous

A writer might give an illustration related to the word that might help you understand the word. For example, in the sentence *Harry is so parsimonious that he won't spend an extra penny if he doesn't have to, won't spend an extra penny* is an illustration of being *parsimonious*. You can see that *parsimonious* means "too careful with money."

6. Are you able to figure out the meanings of the underlined words?
17) After his long illness, Dave was so <u>frail</u> that he could hardly get out of bed.
   A. fearful
   B. weak
   C. unhappy
   D. thankful
18) Glen belongs to a <u>pacifist</u> religious group, and he is not allowed to join the army.
   A. with many members
   B. with strict rules
   C. opposed to war
   D. well known
19) I really enjoy the <u>solitude</u> of the mountains—being alone with nature.
   A. closeness
   B. height
   C. beauty
   D. privacy

In some cases, the writer will mention the purpose or use of an object, and this tells you what the object is. For example, in the sentence *I used a cherry pitter to remove the seeds from the cherries*, the writer tells you that *a cherry pitter* is something used to remove seeds from cherries.

7. In the following sentences, find the words that tell what the underlined object does.
20) The pilot used the <u>altimeter</u> to see how high the plane was.
21) With a <u>whisk</u>, I stirred the eggs.
22) Use a <u>spatula</u> to turn over the pancakes.

For Fun

Works to Read

1. ***How Words Mean: Lexical Concepts, Cognitive Models, and Meaning Construction*** by Vyvyan Evans

    How Words Mean introduces a new approach to the role of words and other linguistic units in the construction of meaning. It does so by addressing the interaction between non-linguistic concepts and the meanings encoded in language. It develops an account of how words are understood when we produce and hear language in situated contexts of use. It proposes two theoretical constructs, the lexical concept and the cognitive model. These are central to the accounts of lexical representation and meaning construction developed.

2. ***Painless Vocabulary*** by M. Greenberg

The author's friendly, informal narrative style takes the drudgery out of students' vocabulary building, which is a prerequisite for their academic achievement and future success in college and beyond. Each of 24 chapters introduces 15 new words, first placing the words in a brief essay that allows students to comprehend them in a given context. "Brain Tickler" questions that follow challenge students and help them determine whether they have gained some mastery of word usage.

Websites to Visit

1. http://wps.ablongman.com/longlicklidervocabulary1/46/11839.cw/index.html
   On this site you can practice how to use context clues to figure out word meaning.
2. http://www.english-zone.com/vocab/vic01.html
   This offers some learning skills together with the exercises on guessing words in context.
3. http://www.k12reader.com/subject/reading-skills/context-clues/
   The printable worksheets on this site will help you develop the skill in using context clues to comprehend word meaning.

Unit 14

English Idioms

> I do not believe in pure idioms. I think there is naturally a desire, for whoever speaks or writes, to sign in an idiomatic, irreplaceable manner.
> —— Jacques Derrida

Unit Goals

- To grasp the characteristics of English idioms
- To understand the functions of idioms in different situations
- To know the origins of some idioms in daily life
- To be capable of using idioms in communication

 Before You Read

1. Do you know the real meanings of the following idiomatic expressions?

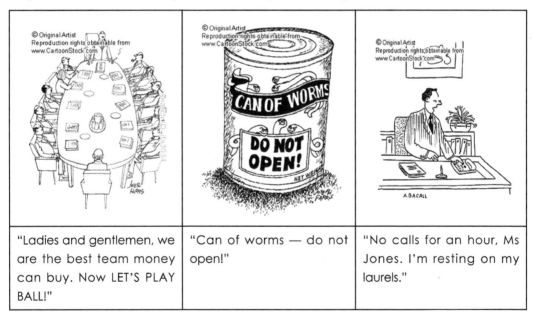

| "Ladies and gentlemen, we are the best team money can buy. Now LET'S PLAY BALL!" | "Can of worms — do not open!" | "No calls for an hour, Ms Jones. I'm resting on my laurels." |

2. **The following is a situation where an idiom is used. Use your imagination to guess the meaning of it.**

   In a fast-food restaurant, a woman genuinely wanted to help a man in trouble, but he made odd requests and used some inappropriate language. "I wasn't sure if he was joking around," she explained. "But really, he might have been *a sandwich short of a picnic*."

3. Choose the right weather idiom.

| rain | wind | thunder | sun |
| cloud | storm | breeze | ice |

1) I think it's all a _____ in a teacup—there's probably no danger to public health at all.
2) Our English exam was a _____. I'm sure I'll get top marks.
3) They threw caution to the _____ and quit their jobs in the heat of the moment.
4) Lily has sprained her ankle, but after a few weeks of rest she should be as right as _____.
5) Don't wear that dress to the wedding; the bride won't like it because you'll be stealing her _____.
6) The project has been put on _____ until our boss decides what to do next.
7) They were both on _____ nine during their honeymoon.
8) This is the best wine under the _____.

4. Share what you know about the following English idioms.

Start to Read

Text A   English Idioms—Cream of the Language

Definition of English Idioms

The English language is abundant in idioms like any other highly developed language. *Longman Dictionary of Contemporary English* defines idioms as "a fixed group of words with a special meaning which is different from the meanings of the individual words."

Idioms are conventionalized multiword expressions. An idiom cannot be translated from the source's language into receptor's because their linguistic wholes are greater than the sum of their parts. For example, in the English expression *to kick the bucket*, a listener knowing only the meaning of *kick* and *bucket* would be unable to deduce the expression's actual meaning, which is "to die." Although it can refer literally to the act of striking a specific bucket with a foot, native speakers rarely use it that way.

Without idioms English would lose much of its variety and humor both in speech and writing. While using it properly, people will not only enhance the ability to express all sorts of ideas but also the ability to appreciate culture, which then improves the linguistic ability. As a specialized form of language, idioms often confuse those unfamiliar with them; students of a new language should learn its idiomatic expressions as well as its other vocabulary.

The Characteristics of English Idioms
A. Semantic Integrity

Each Idiom consists of more than one word, but each is a semantic unity. The various words that make up the idiom have their respective literal meanings, but in the idiom they have lost their individual meanings. Their meanings cannot be recognized in the meaning of the whole idiom. The part of speech of each element is not important any more and quite often the idiom functions as one word. For example, *stir up a hornet's nest* means "to make someone furious and to get into deep trouble." The relationship between the literal meaning of each word and the meaning of the idiom is illogical. Many idioms cannot be explained semantically.

B. Structural Stability

To a large extent, the structure of an idiom is unable to change. Firstly, the constituents of idioms cannot be replaced. Take *look a gift horse in the mouth* for example, we cannot replace the word *gift* with *present*, though the two words have the same meaning. As a free phrase, the form is variable, however, as an idiom, the structure is fixed.

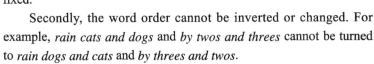

Secondly, the word order cannot be inverted or changed. For example, *rain cats and dogs* and *by twos and threes* cannot be turned to *rain dogs and cats* and *by threes and twos*.

Thirdly, the constituents of idioms cannot be deleted or added to, not even an article. For instance, *out of the question* means "impossible" while *out of question* means "no problem."

Finally, many idioms are grammatically unanalyzable. For example, *(as) sure as eggs is eggs* is grammatically inexplicable, for normally we should put *are* after *eggs* because *eggs* is plural form.

C. Metaphorical Character

English idioms are rich in figure of speech and a large number of idioms are used in their figurative meanings.

Simile is the use of an expression which describes one thing by directly comparing it with another using the word *as* or *like*. Examples are *as busy as a bee*, *sleep like a log*, and *like father like son*.

In metaphor, an implied comparison is made between two unlike things that actually have something in common. Metaphors carry meaning from one word, image, or idea to another. There are many cases in which metaphor is used in the English idioms. Examples are *a dark horse* (a person who tends to keep his activities, feelings or intentions secret), *a new broom* (a person who has newly come to office), and *a wet blanket* (something that spoils the pleasure).

In metonymy, one word or phrase is substituted for another with which it is closely associated. Examples are *from cradle to grave* and *a wolf in sheep's clothing*.

In synecdoche, a part is used to represent the whole (for example, *ABCs* for *alphabet*) or the whole for a part. Synecdoche is often treated as a type of metonymy, but they differ in that metonymy is a case of using the name of one thing for another closely associated with it and synecdoche is that of substituting part for the whole and vice versa. Examples are *two heads are better than one*, *many hands make light work*, and *great minds think alike*.

Euphemism is the substitution of an inoffensive term for one considered offensively explicit. For example, people use terms like *to go to heaven* or *to depart from one's life* to replace the word *to die*.

Text B Major Sources of English Idioms

The most important thing about idioms is their meaning. This is why a native speaker does not notice that an idiom is incorrect grammatically. If the source of an idiom is known, it is sometimes easier to imagine its meaning.

Idioms come from all different sources—from the Bible to horse racing, from ancient fables to modern slang. Sometimes famous authors and storytellers such as Homer, Aesop, Geoffrey Chaucer, or William Shakespeare made them up to add spark to their writings.

Idioms from the Bible

It is a firm concept of western people that God created people. They think that God is omnipotent and sacred. Since the Bible was translated into English centuries ago, many Hebrew or Greek idioms have become part of the English language. However, many idioms have either lost their original meanings or have only vague or loose connection to them now.

Feet of clay: This idiom comes from a story in the Bible. There was a king who saw something in his dreams. The image had a head of gold, breast and arms of silver, legs of iron and feet made of iron and clay. In the dream, a stone fell on the feet, and suddenly, broke the feet and the entire image. Today, we use this idiom to mean that there is a hidden weakness in somebody whom we admire or respect.

There are also many idioms from the Bible that use animals to create an image.

A little bird told me is used when people want to say that they know something but not who gave them the information. This idiom comes from a passage in the Bible that says, "a bird of the air shall carry the voice, and that which hath wings shall tell the matter."

Kill the fatted calf means "to have a large celebration." It comes from a story in the Bible, where a son returned to his family after being gone for a very long time. The son had left home to waste his time and money leading a life of luxury, but later mended his ways and came home. In honor of his return, a calf that had been allowed to grow fat was killed and cooked for a feast.

Another focus of biblical idioms is often food or things related to food.

The apple of their parents' eye means that their parents love them very much and are very proud of them. This comes from the Bible when King David wrote a passage, asking God to remember to take care of him like a child.

The salt of the earth means that a person is very good and honest. Salt was very precious when the Bible was written because it was often used to preserve things. Pure salt will not lose its flavor, but impure salt will. Once the salt loses its flavor, it cannot be used to preserve things any more and should be thrown away. In other words, if you are not honest, then you are worth nothing.

Idioms from Greek and Roman Mythology

Mythologies are ancient stories that are based on popular beliefs or that explain natural or historical events because the people of the primeval society were scared of the nature and longed for the nice future. In Greek mythology there were twelve main Olympian gods and goddesses. And they have many descendants. The following are some major gods and goddesses and their descendants in Greek and Roman mythology that are closely related to some English idioms.

Promethean fire: The fire refers to the fire of life. Prometheus was a son of the Titan Iapetus by Clymene, one of the Oceanids. He was brother to Menoetius, Atlas, and Epimetheus. In spite of Zeus' warning, Prometheus stole fire in a giant fennel-stalk and gave it back to mankind. Prometheus, in eternal punishment, is chained to a rock in the Caucasus, where his liver is eaten out daily by an eagle, only to be regenerated by night, which, by legend, is due to his immortality. Years later, the Greek hero Heracles (Hercules) would shoot the eagle and free Prometheus from his chains.

Pandora's Box: This idiom means a source of unexpected trouble. Pandora was the first woman on Earth. Pandora was created upon the command of Zeus to Hephaestus, the god of craftsmanship. Hephaestus created her using water and earth, while other gods granted her many gifts (for example, beauty from Aphrodite, persuasiveness from Hermes, and music from Apollo). After Prometheus stole fire from heaven, Zeus sought reprisal by handing Pandora to Epimetheus, the brother of Prometheus. At the same time, Pandora was given a box that she was ordered not to open under any circumstances. Despite this warning, overcome by curiosity Pandora opened the jar. Upon doing so, the evils contained within escaped into the world. Scared, Pandora immediately closed the jar, only to trap Hope inside, as was Zeus' will.

Oedipus complex: For Freud, *Oedipus complex* means "the childhood desire to sleep with the mother and to kill the father." Freud describes the source of this complex in his *Introductory Lectures*: "You all know the Greek legend of King Oedipus, who was destined by fate to kill his father and take his mother to wife, who did everything possible to escape the oracle's decree and punished himself by blinding when he learned that he had none the less unwittingly committed both these crimes." According to Freud, Oedipus complex illustrates an individual's psychosexual development, when the young child transfers his love object from the breast (the oral phase) to the mother. At this time, the child desires the mother and resents

"Er...Nice tattoo, Oedipus."

(even secretly desires the murder of) the father.

Idioms from Literary Works

Literature is an art using language as the tool to explain real life and reflects the way of thinking at different stages. As for the words used in the literature, they come from life and contract the life of people. Due the popularity of the literary works, some phrases from literature become idioms.

Shakespeare is regarded as the greatest dramatist and poet in the world. His works, together with Bible, is the major important sources of the western culture. He not only created great works, but also invented many of the widely-used expressions in the language of English and thus greatly enriches the English idioms.

For ever and a day: It means "indefinitely." Of course, *for ever and a day* is a dramatic construct with no literal meaning—for ever is for ever, we can't add days to it. This form of dramatic emphasis has been used many times. Shakespeare coined this and used it in *The Taming of the Shrew*, 1596:

BIONDELLO

I cannot tell; expect they are busied about a counterfeit assurance: take you assurance of her, (cum privilegio ad imprimendum solum:) to the church; take the priest, clerk, and some sufficient honest witnesses: If this be not that you look for, I have no more to say, But bid Bianca farewell for ever and a day.

As pure as the driven snow: It means "entirely pure." *Driven snow* is snow that has blown into drifts and clean. Examples of the precise text *as pure as [the] driven snow* aren't found in print until around the start of the 19th century; nevertheless, we have to thank Shakespeare for this popular simile. The complete phrase *as pure as the driven snow* doesn't appear in Shakespeare's writing, but it almost does, and he used snow as a symbol for purity and whiteness in several plays. In *The Winter's Tale*, 1611:

Autolycus: Lawn as white as driven snow.

In *Macbeth*, 1605:

Malcolm: Black Macbeth will seem as pure as snow.

After You Read

Knowledge Focus

1. Match the following idioms with their meanings.

Idioms	Meanings
1) kick the bucket	a. to sleep very soundly
2) stir up a hornet's nest	b. to refuse or criticize sth.
3) look a gift horse in the mouth	c. a person who has newly come to office
4) a wolf in sheep's clothing	d. a person who is very good and honest
5) by twos and threes	e. to die
6) sleep like a log	f. two or three at a time

Idioms	Meanings
7) a new broom	g. to create a lot of trouble
8) from cradle to grave	h. a person who appears friendly or harmless but is really an enemy
9) feet of clay	i. from birth to death
10) the salt of the earth	j. a failing or weakness in a person's character

2. **Pick up the idioms used in the following dialogue and restore their original forms. Discuss with your partner which way is more appropriate for the dialogue.**

Jeff: This is the worst coffee in town.
Maria: You can say that again.
Cathy: And how!
Maria: We should sound out the boss about getting a new machine.
Jeff: You have got to be kidding. There's no way she'd agree.
Cathy: Someone has to speak up.
Jeff: Let's talk about it at the next staff meeting.
Maria: OK. You say your piece, and then I'll put my two cents in.
Cathy: Excellent! We are definitely on the same wavelength.

3. **Work out the meaning of each phrasal verb below with your partner.**
   1) auction off
   2) cater for
   3) chew over
   4) color up
   5) gear up
   6) kick around
   7) knuckle down
   8) make off
   9) measure against
   10) sleep over

Language Focus

1. **Fill in the blanks with the following words you have learned in the text. Change the forms where necessary.**

| decree | substitute | counterfeit | integrity | omnipotent |
| reprisal | descendant | inexplicable | regenerate | immortality |

1) It would be better to live under robber barons than under _____ moral busybodies.
2) He's a man of _____; he won't break his promise.
3) For some _____ reason, he felt depressed.
4) Fortunately, he died nobly at the Alamo, fighting for Texan independence, and thus secured _____.

5) The court reversed its _____ of imprisonment, and the man went free.
6) They shot ten hostages in _____ for the assassination of their leader.
7) The understudy was _____ when the leading actor fell ill.
8) Many of them are _____ of the original settlers.
9) If the woodland is left alone, it will _____ itself in a few years.
10) This ten-dollar bill is a _____.

2. Proofreading & Error Correction.

Living things grow and change, and so is language. One can readily recognize differences between Shakespeare's English and the English of modern authors, but present-day English is also growing and changing, and these tendencies are not so hard to recognize.

This topic is of great interesting for me because as a linguist I usually have to face different problems connected with the translation of this or that piece of text and very often these problems lie in interpretation of phraseological units or idioms what can not be translated into Russian directly. So they are the real pain in the neck! You should know your enemy in sight, so I decided to study this linguistic phenomenon.

Idioms are always anything special about any language; they build up some distinctive features which differ one language from another. What is more, idioms reflect certain cultural traditions and depict the national character. Since the general tendencies of present-day English are towards more idiomatic usage, it is important that this work in idioms should show the learner how the language is developing.

Idioms are a separate part of the language which one can choose either to use or to omit, but they form an essential part of the general vocabulary of English. A description of what the vocabulary of the language is growing and changing will help to place idioms in perspective. Idioms appear in every language, and English has thousands of them. They are often confused because the meaning of the whole group of words taken together has little, often nothing, to do with the meanings of the words taken one by one.

1) _____
2) _____
3) _____

4) _____

5) _____

6) _____

7) _____

8) _____

9) _____

10) _____

3. Translate the following paragraph into Chinese.

Each Idiom consists of more than one word, but each is a semantic unity. The various words that make up the idiom have their respective literal meanings, but in the idiom they have lost their individual meanings. Their meanings cannot be recognized in the meaning of the whole idiom. The part of speech of each element is not important any more and quite often the idiom functions as one word.

Comprehensive Work

1. **The following piece of discourse was written in highly figurative and idiomatic language. Read the passage, pick out the idioms and explain their meanings. Then rewrite the passage in standard straightforward idiom-free language, keeping the original meaning.**

Lucy is a real cool cat. She never blows her stack and hardly flies off the handle. Furthermore, she knows how to get away with things. Well, of course, she is also getting on. Her hair is pepper and salt, but she knows how to make up for lost time by taking it easy. She gets up early, works out, and turns in early. She takes care of the hot dog stand like a breeze until she gets time off.

2. **Writing**

As John Kennedy was inaugurated, his best speeches were profoundly moving to people. "Ask not what your country can do for you; rather ask what you can do for your country" and phrases like it were a rallying call for generations. Those stirring phrases gave way to more pithy ones: "make love not war," for example. Such political uses of language really did change things for people. Write an essay entitled "An Idiom that Affects Me."

Read More

Text C Animals and English Idioms

Language is the carrier of culture. Idioms are called to be the soul of language and it is like a mirror reflecting the feature of a nation. There are many idioms in the English language which are related to animals' images and they are popularly applied to every area of life. However, if we are not sure about the images' origins and meaning, we can not use them appropriately.

Cats are popular animals for the Europeans. Many families keep them as pets. Cats are a good contributor to some English idioms.

A cat in gloves catches no mice: This expression means that if you are too careful and polite, you may not obtain what you want. For example, "Negotiate carefully, but remember: *a cat in gloves catches no mice!*"

A fat cat: It refers to a rich and powerful person. If you call someone "a fat cat," it means that you disapprove of the way he uses his money or power. For example, "The place was full of *fat cats* on their big yachts."

Cat's whiskers: This expression refers to someone who considers oneself to be better than others in a particular area—beauty, competence, intelligence, sport, etc. For example, "Ever since she got a promotion, she thinks she's the *cat's whiskers*!"

She let the cat out of the bag.
(She gave away the secret.)

Wait for the cat to jump: If you wait for the cat to jump, or to see which way the cat jumps, you delay taking action until you see how events will turn out. For example, "Let's *wait for the cat to jump* before we decide."

Let the cat out of the bag: If you let the cat out of the bag, you reveal a secret, often not intentionally. For example, "When the child told her grandmother about the plans for her birthday, she *let the cat out of the bag*. It was supposed to be a secret!"

Dogs are often regarded as the loyal friends for the human beings, or even family members for the British people. There are a large number of English idioms concerning dogs which manifest their importance and British people's attitude toward them.

Dog's life: People use this expression when complaining about a situation or job which they find unpleasant or unsatisfactory. For example, "It's a *dog's life* working in the after-sales department."

Dog eat dog: This expression refers to intense competition and rivalry in pursuit of one's own interests, with no concern for morality. For example, "The business world is tough today. There's a general *dog-eat-dog* attitude."

Crooked as a dog's hind leg: To say that someone is as crooked as a dog's hind leg means that he is very dishonest indeed. For example, "He can't be trusted—he's *as crooked as a dog's hind leg*."

Every dog has its day: This expression means that everyone can be successful at something at some time in their life. For example, "I didn't win this time, but I'll be lucky one day. *Every dog has its day*!"

There are many other animals closely related with we mankind, such as pig, sheep, goose, hawk, etc.

Make a pig of yourself: If you make a pig of yourself, you eat and drink too much. For example, "Watch what you eat—don't *make a pig of yourself*!"

Black sheep: The black sheep of the family is one who is very different from the others, and least respected by the other members of the family. For examples, "Amy's always been *the black sheep* of the family."

A wild goose chase: If you say that you were sent on a wild goose chase, you mean that you wasted a lot of time looking for something that there was little chance of finding. For example, "They tried to find out who sent the anonymous complaint, but it turned out to be *a wild goose chase*."

Watch someone like a hawk: If you watch someone like a hawk, you keep your eyes on them or watch them very carefully. For example, "Sarah *watches the children like a hawk* when she takes them swimming."

Exercises

1. Complete the sentences with the correct idiom in the correct form.

   a. crooked as a dog's hind leg
   b. wild goose chase
   c. fat cat
   d. let the cat out of the bag
   e. dog's life

   1) "How did you find out about the party?"
      "Well, it was Jeff who _____. I suppose he thought I knew about it."
   2) The report criticized boardroom _____ who award themselves huge pay increases.
   3) Mary says all politicians are _____.
   4) I've got to go to the supermarket, then cook a meal, then pick Dave up from the station—It's _____!
   5) John was angry because he was sent out on _____.

2. Read the sentences and try to guess the meaning of the idioms.

   1) Wow! It's raining cats and dogs today! I wish I'd brought my umbrella to school!
      A. Cats and dogs are falling from the sky.
      B. Cats and dogs are flooding in.
      C. It's raining heavily.

   2) When I told my mom I would be home around 2 am, she had a cow!
      A. she bought a baby cow
      B. she looked really strange
      C. she was really upset
   3) Jean: How did you know it was my birthday today?
      Susan: Oh, a little birdie told me!
      A. nobody told me
      B. an unnamed person told me
      C. a little girl told me

4) Frank: Why didn't your brother ride the roller coaster with us?

   Sam: Oh, he's such a scared cat! He won't get on any fast ride.

   A. he is afraid to ride the roller coaster

   B. he is not interested in the roller coaster

   C. he cannot afford the game

5) I never learned how to use a computer, so I lost my job to a new employee. It's a dog-eat-dog world.

   A. Only the strong or the best survive.

   B. Dogs are eating dogs at the office.

   C. I like to eat dogs for lunch.

Text D   Food and English Idioms

No matter western countries or China, food always has some symbolic meanings, and many idioms come from food culture.

Bread is the main food in western countries, and it is the necessary food for westerners. In the Bible, bread is the staff of life, Jesus said to his followers: "I tell you the truth, it is not Moses who has given you the bread from heaven, but it is my Father who gives you the true bread from heaven. For the bread of God is he who comes down from heaven and gives life to the world."

Bread and butter: The idiom means "the necessities, the main thing." For example, "Just explain *the bread and butter* of your report. You don't have to go into details."

Take the bread out of someone's mouth: The idiom means "deprive someone of his or her livelihood." For example,

    A: It's really terrible!

    B: What happened?

    A: A new supermarket has been built opposite my shop. They're *taking the bread out of our mouth.*

    B: Then you'd better do something.

Milk is consumed all over the world. Meanwhile, milk is a symbol of good and rich. *A land flowing with milk and honey* means "the land is fertile." *The milk of human kindness* means "the good nature of human beings." For example, "Mary is completely hard and selfish—she doesn't have *the milk of human kindness* in her."

Cry over spilt milk: It means that there is no need to keep complaining over the loss. For example, "I know you don't like your new haircut, but you can't change it now. It's no use *crying over spilt milk.*"

Come/go home with the milk: It refers to a person who spent a whole night outside and then came back in the early morning. For example, "Jimmy was scolded by his mother for *coming home with the milk.*"

Honey is an important symbol. It is the supernatural being's and poet's favorite food. And it is related to purity, inspiration, eloquence and bless of God. Meanwhile, honey stands for sweet of love.

You can catch more flies with honey than with vinegar: The idiom means that it is easier to get what you want by flattering people and being polite to them than by making demands. For example,

A: This meal is terrible. Let's get the restaurant manager over here and make a scene unless he gives us our money back.

B: We might have more luck if we ask politely. *You can catch more flies with honey than with vinegar.*

The honeymoon is over: The idiom means that the early pleasant beginning has ended. For example, "I knew *the honeymoon was over* at my new job when they started yelling at me to work faster."

Exercises

Choose the best answer from the four possible choices. You may consult the dictionary if you have difficulties.

1. His father told him not to put all his _____ in one basket, so John studied law as well as graphic design.
   A. fruits   B. eggs
   C. vegetables   D. stone
2. My boss is being nice to me but I know he is only trying to _____ as he wants me to work during the holiday.
   A. bread and butter   B. carrot and stick
   C. butter me up   D. eat humble pie
3. After Mr. Johnson lost his job, his wife started working as someone had to bring home the _____.
   A. sausages   B. bread
   C. pie   D. bacon
4. Look at the little energetic puppy jumping up and running around. He is so full of _____.
   A. milk   B. coffee
   C. beans   D. pees
5. Even though Uncle Barry drinks like a _____, he never looks drunk.
   A. fish   B. crow
   C. giraffe   D. hippopotamus

For Fun

Works to Read

1. ***101 American English Idioms: Understanding and Speaking English Like an American*** by Harry Collis and Mario Russo

   The book is designed to help bridge the gap between "meaning" and "thrust" of American colloquialisms by providing a situation and a graphic illustration of that situation, so that the imagery created by the expression can be felt, rather than simply learned as a stock definition. The book is divided into nine sections. The title of each section reflects a notion or a manifestation of the physical world, the world of behavior, or the world of the senses with which the reader may easily identify.

2. *A Dictionary of American Idioms* by Adam Makkai, M.T. Boatner and J.E. Gates

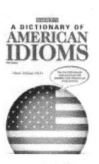

More than 8,000 idiomatic words and phrases that are standard in American English are listed with definitions and sample sentences to clarify their meanings. Earlier editions of this A-to-Z dictionary have proved especially helpful to TOEFL and TOEIC test takers, as well as to other students in North America for whom English is their second language. Idioms undergo constant change in every living language, some falling out of use while new words and phrases become part of the standard vocabulary. This new edition takes account of the latest idiomatic changes and presents a solid background to informal American English.

Websites to Visit

1. http://www.idiomsite.com/
   This website is a comprehensive information resource of English idioms.
2. http://www.voanews.com/MediaAssets2/classroom/interactivelearning/idiomdictionary/deploy/Glossary.html
   The Idiom Dictionary explains idioms used in everyday speech. You can click on a letter, search for a phrase and click to hear. The Sample Dialogue will show you how American idioms are used in conversation.
3. http://www.usingenglish.com/reference/idioms/
   This website provides a dictionary of 3,762 English idiomatic expressions with definitions.

Unit 15

English Vocabulary and Greek Mythology

> No knowledge of a science can be properly acquired until the terminology of that science is mastered, and this terminology is in the main of Greek and Latin origin.
>
> —— Spencer Trotter
>
> The custom of forming compounds from Greek elements prevails in all civilized countries of Europe and America, and if a useful term of this kind is introduced in any one country, it is adopted with great promptitude into the languages of all the rest.
>
> —— Henry Bradley

Unit Goals

- To understand the English words originated in Greek mythology
- To be familiar with Greek roots in the English vocabulary
- To learn some stories of Greek mythology

Before You Read

English Words and Greek Mythology

The following are words derived from Greek mythology. Please identify the meanings and give an account of their origins in Greek mythology.

Word	Meaning	Origin
morphine		
fatal		
hygiene		
chaos		
chronic		
echo		
laureate		
museum		
panic		
phobia		

Start to Read

Text A English Words of Greek Mythological Origins

Ancient Greece is one of the world's four ancient civilizations with a long history and culture origin. The ancient Greece ranged from today's western coast of Asia Minor to the eastern Mediterranean island. Ancient Greeks, inspired by Oriental culture, created a splendid ancient Greek culture. Taking shape around the 8th century B.C., the ancient Greek mythology is the treasure in world literature and has exerted great influence on religion, art, language and astronomy, etc. It is a group of myths, stories or legends about the mythological gods, goddesses, and heroes.

As we all know, modern English is the language of the continuous integration of various ethnic cultures and came into being after a long course of historical development, during which English absorbed the essences of many European languages. The contributions made by Greek mythology are indelible, manifested in the following three aspects.

The Common English Words and Mythology

Owing to their unique characteristics and the extraordinary experiences, the names of the gods, monsters, and heroes in Ancient Greek myth are directly converted into English nouns. The general terms converted generally maintain their original spellings and the symbolic meanings of the mythological figures.

In the myth, Sirens are half human and half bird, singing in such sweet voices that excited the hearts of men, and being so, no sailor or ship had ever been known to pass their island. Accordingly, *siren* means "the charming beauty; good singer; whistle; alarm" in modern English.

Echo is a very beautiful and musical nymph, who could sing and play many instruments. She attracted the hatred of many, whose love she declined, and therefore was killed. Gaia, the Earth goddess, received the pieces of her body and thus Echo, scattered all over the earth, retained her voice and talents answering or imitating every sound. Hence, *echo* signifies "repetition of the sound."

In ancient Greek works of art, Flora is often portrayed as a young woman, holding flowers. Thus, *flora* denotes the meaning of "flower." From the etymological point of view, the name of the U.S. state *Florida* and the Italian city *Florence* are derived from *flora* as well as the words such as *flower, flour, flourish, floral, florist,* etc.

Similarly, as the god of human soul, goodness and protection, Genie made people form characters in varieties. So *gene* means "the determinant of people"; "the talent, nature, characteristics." The meaning of these changes has produced a number of English words, like *genius*.

Eros (Cupid in Roman mythology) was originally portrayed as a handsome young man, the son of Aphrodite (Venus in Roman mythology), and his arrows caused people to fall in love. Nowadays words derived from Eros mean "sexually arousing or pertaining to love or desire." While he himself fell in love with the human maiden Psyche regardless of the constant interference of his mother and plucked up his courage to beg Zeus for justice. Their love story since ancient times is the subject of Western art. During the long evolution of language, the term *psyche* gradually evolved into an abstract noun, meaning "psychological, or spiritual."

In fact, the meaning of English vocabulary varies at different times on different occasions to a different degree. Grappling with the stories behind these words will be conducive not only to the English vocabulary-building but also to the cross-cultural communication.

The English Names of Flowers and Mythology

A large number of names of plants and flowers in Modern English are inextricably linked with ancient Greek mythology. They are either part of God's incarnation or the external manifestations of the soul.

In the west, the Narcissus flower is seen as a symbol of vanity and unrequited love. It dates back to the myth of a tragedy: Narcissus, a young man, because of his beautiful natural good looks, irresistably fell in love with his own reflections in the water, emaciated and finally slipped into the water drowning. The gods felt sorry for him and changed him into a flower growing by the side of water so that he can still  bend his beautiful head and look at the reflection of his own face in the water. There emerge the word *narcissism* (excessive love or admiration of oneself); *narcissist* (someone in love with themselves); *narcissistic* (characteristic of those having an inflated idea of their own importance).

There are flowers from the myth of Adonis. In Greek myth, Adonis was a handsome young shepherd killed while hunting a wild boar. Because he was loved by Aphrodite, Zeus allowed him to be restored to life to the loving embrace of Aphrodite, but when winter came he had to return most reluctantly to the underworld. The anemone flower is said to have sprung from his blood.

Daphne was the beautiful daughter of the river god and fled to the mountains to escape from Apollo's constant pursuit. For the fear that Apollo would ultimately catch her, she called out to Peneus for help. As soon as Apollo approached Daphne, her legs took root, her arms grew into long and slender branches and she finally transformed into a laurel tree. Apollo, distraught by what had happened, made the laurel his sacred tree.

Some Geographic Terms and Mythology

What is noteworthy is that some specific geographical terms were also born in the ancient Greek mythology. Among the names of places, the mountains take the highest percentage. Words enter into English with derivatives produced.

Due to the war and drought, Theseus was among the chosen victims to be sacrificed to the Minotaur and sailed off to Crete, promising to Aegeus, his father, that his ship's black flag would be replaced with a white flag if he is victorious. In returning to Athens, Theseus forgot to switch the black sail with the white one, resulting in his father's death. Aegean Sea was named after him.

And the Turkey's Dardanelles Strait, whose original name was Hellespont Strait, is also related to Greek mythology. Helle is the myth of a teenager. He and his brother were abused by their stepmother and they escaped on a winged, golden ram; however, Helle fell from the animal into the sea that was later named after him (Hellespont).

The Strait of Bosphorus and the Ionia Sea were named in the honour of Io. Io was a princess loved by Zeus, who changed her into a heifer in order to hide her from Hera. During her escape from Hera's gadfly, the Bosphorus, or Ford of the Cow, is named in memory of her passing and all Ionia, or the western coast of Asia Minor, is named after her because she reputedly ran down this coastline.

From the name of Auster, the god of the south wind, comes the adjective *austral*, referring to anything "of, or related to, the southern hemisphere," and thus the southern continent name, *Australia*.

Another important name of the continent *Europe* comes from the legend of Europa. She was the Phoenician princess abducted by Zeus because he disguised himself as a bull, and then carried her on his back to the island of Crete where she bore three sons. Later, Europe bore the same name in her honor.

In English, the term *Atlantic* comes from the myth of Hercules Atlas. He was a Titan punished by Zeus by being forced to support the heavens on his shoulders and his whole body was inserted into the clouds, beautiful mountains and rivers. It is composed of the negative prefix *a* and *tlao* (to endure).

Greek mythology has exerted profound and vast influence upon the western culture. Its influence on the English language can never be overestimated no matter how hard we are working on it. Words deriving from Greek myths entered into English language through early human activities, and they have the far-reaching influence on English language in art, music, literature, and many aspects of the social life of the West. Actually the movements of the words and idioms deriving from Greek myths to English language and culture are permeating till now.

By learning the Greek mythology we get to the core and root of the culture background. It must be borne in mind that the myths, as the earliest crystallization of social order and religious fear, record the incipient history of religious ideals and of moral conduct.

After You Read

Knowledge Focus

1. Tell whether the following statements are true or false according to the knowledge you learned and why.

1) Sirens are half human and half bird and they are so kind that they sing to the sailors so that they can enjoy their journey in the sea. (   )
2) Echo, a beautiful and musical nymph, was envied by Gaia, the Earth goddess. Gaia removed her voice, so Echo could only imitate sounds. (   )
3) The name of the U.S. State *Florida* and the French city *Florence* are derived from *flora*. (   )
4) Eros, the son of Aphrodite, fell in love with the human maiden Psyche against his mother's will. (   )
5) In the west, the Narcissus flower is seen as a symbol of vanity, and narcissism usually refers to a kind of psychological disease. (   )
6) Adonis was restored to life because he was loved by Zeus. (   )

7) *Laureate* derives from the Greek mythology because of the happy reunion of Daphne and Apollo. (   )

8) Aegean Sea was named after Theseus's father. (   )

9) The southern continent name, *Australia* came from the name of Auster, the god of the south wind. (   )

10) Zeus asked Hercules Atlas to support the heavens on his shoulders and *Atlantic* comes from this myth. (   )

2. **Fill in the blanks with the English words of Greek mythological origins you have learned in the text.**

   1) He has no original opinions; he is just his father's _____.
   2) A characteristic of the feminine _____ is to seek approval from others.
   3) If the children are red-haired, one of their parents must have a _____ for red hair.
   4) 3/4 of men say they would love to get flowers and most women love _____ gifts as well.
   5) He is vain almost to the point of _____, unable to resist peeking at himself in every mirror he passes.
   6) The government must resist the _____ voices calling for the sale of weapons to the region.
   7) Streams allowed certain mountain plants to grow and _____.
   8) Einstein was a mathematical _____.

3. **Read the following stanzas taken from "Ode to a Nightingale" by Keats. What Greek myths are mentioned? What do they mean? And why are they used here?**

> My heart aches, and a drowsy numbness pains
> My sense, as though of hemlock I had drunk,
> Or emptied some dull opiate to the drains
> One minute past, and Lethe-wards had sunk:
> 'Tis not through envy of thy happy lot,
> But being too happy in thine happiness,—
> That thou, light-winged Dryad of the trees,
> In some melodious plot
> Of beechen green, and shadows numberless,
> Singest of summer in full-throated ease.
>
> O, for a draught of vintage! That hath been
> Cool'd a long age in the deep-delved earth,
> Tasting of Flora and the country green,
> Dance, and Provencal song, and sunburnt mirth!
> O, for a beaker full of the warm South,
> Full of the true, the blushful Hippocrene,
> With beaded bubbles winking at the brim,
> And purple-stained mouth;
> That I might drink, and leave the world unseen,
> And with thee fade away into the forest dim:

Language Focus

1. Fill in the blanks with the following words you have learned in the text. Change the forms where necessary.

| permeate | indelible | determinant | grapple | inextricably |
| inflated | manifest | incipient | distraught | integration |

1) Social tensions were _____ in the recent political crisis.
2) Physical health is _____ linked to mental health.
3) Relatives are tonight comforting the _____ parents.
4) Her words left a(n) _____ impression on me for years to come.
5) The project is still in its _____ stages.
6) It's a great example of _____ of architecture and landscape.
7) Racism continues to _____ our society.
8) He has a(n) _____ sense of his own importance.
9) He has been _____ with the problem for a long time.
10) The main _____ of economic success is our ability to control inflation.

2. **Proofreading & Error Correction.**

Greek mythology's impact on modern societies can be seen in any clear night. Many constellations are named after characters or monsters from Greek myths, included Cassiopeia, Andromeda, Hercules and Gemini. All of the planets and most of the moons in the solar system are also named after Greek mythological characters, and the planets have been given Roman versions of the Greek names. Even our Earth is named after a Greek myth: Another name for our planet is *Gaia*, the name of the Greek earth mother.

The names of Greek mythology surround us today, sometimes in unusual place. Would Ajax, one of the great Greek heroes of *The Iliad*, be happy knowing he's the namesake for a popular cleaning product? Sometimes, references to Greek mythology are appropriate. The Aegis are the shield used by both Zeus and his daughter Athena. Today, the Aegis Group is an insurance company, and the U.S. navy uses Aegis cruisers. In all of these instances, the reference to Greek mythology is clearly valid in that the insurance company and Navy boats provide protection, just as the Greek shield.

At other times, the connection between Greek mythology and modern products is more

1) _____
2) _____
3) _____
4) _____
5) _____
6) _____
7) _____

tongue-in-cheek. A popular brand of condoms is named *Trojan*, slyly alluding to the Trojan horse who allowed the Greeks to safely penetrate Troy's defenses.

8) _____

Despite our sometimes questionable uses of Greek mythology in contemporary culture, its impact on modern societies cannot be understated. References to Greek myths abound. In fact, Greek myths even influence our maps. A collection of maps is an Atlas, named for the titan who had held up the earth. And Europe, seat of so many societies influenced by Greek myths, is named after Europa, the maiden carrying off by Zeus, who had disguised himself as a bull to trick her.

9) _____

10) _____

3. Translate the following paragraph into Chinese.

Greek mythology has exerted profound and vast influence upon the western culture. Its influence on the English language can never be overestimated no matter how hard we are working on it. Words deriving from Greek myths entered into English language through early human activities, and they have the far-reaching influence on English language in art, music, literature, and many aspects of the social life of the West. Actually the movements of the words and idioms deriving from Greek myths to English language and culture are permeating till now.

Comprehensive Work
Discussion & Writing

Choose one topic to discuss and write a group report after your investigation and exploration.

- Greek myths often attempted to explain mysterious elements of the natural world. Many of the constellations, such as those associated with the astrological signs, are named after characters from Greek myths. What signs of the zodiac can you name? Can you tell the stories behind them?
- Mythological terms are common in contemporary society. For example, an odyssey is a voyage, as well as a minivan! As you learn more about the characters of Greek mythology, you may be surprised to discover many familiar words derived from myths. Explore more deeply the influence of Greek words on our contemporary vocabulary.
- Create an original writing inspired by myth. First, you should choose a character from Greek mythology and tell the character's story looking for a different take, or put the mythical character in a new situation. Before writing, you may discuss how we can make mythology relevant to our own times, and what mythological themes and meanings are still relevant to us now.

Text B The English Word Roots and Mythology

The influence of Greek mythology on the English roots and affixes has been deeply implanted into the English vocabulary.

The English Roots of Gods' Names

Myth names, the root words and word affixes, in accordance with the linguistic point of view, have led the majority of English words to adjectives, followed by nouns and verbs. From the quantitative point of view, the words derived from the names of the goddesses are more than those of the gods.

Eros, the son of the goddess of love, was an archer, and his arrows were responsible for instilling the twists and turns of love and lust in a people's heart. Saying goes, his mother must have the aid from him to spread the so-called human love in the spirit world. So there generate the words *erotic* (of or concerning love and desire or a womanizer); *erotica* (erotic writing and drawings, etc); *eroticism* (a style or quality that expresses strong feeling and fuels love and desire); *erotogenic* (stimulating sexual desire); *erotology* (the study of erotic stimuli and sexual behavior).

Athena is the Goddess of wisdom, knowledge, technology, learning and arts. With the combination of her name *Athena* and the suffix *–um*, we have the word *athenaeum* (an institution, such as a literary club or scientific academy, for the promotion of learning). In the same manner, emerges the word *museum*, in which Muses are goddesses who presided over the arts and sciences. They were believed to inspire all artists, especially poets, philosophers, and musicians.

Eris is the Greek goddess of discord and strife. She was sinister and mean, and her greatest joy was to make trouble. She had a golden apple that was so bright and shiny that everybody wanted to have it. When she throws it among friends, their friendship comes to a rapid end. When she throws it among enemies, war breaks out. Consequently, Eris with the suffix *–tic* becomes *eristic* (of, relating, or given to controversy or logical disputation).

In the history of Western paintings, Aphrodite is the only goddess of beauty that has been demonstrated with the naked body. This ancient Greek myth is unique in its existence. Creative Italian painter Giorgione's "Sleeping Venus (Aphrodite's name in Roman mythology)" typically showed Aphrodite's sensuality and the external side of the vulgar. So Aphrodite turned into English terminology all with "sex or sex-relevant" like *aphrodisiac* (stimulating sexual desire or a drug or other agent that stimulates sexual desire).

There are also gods with super powers, unique abilities or great strength, which can not be neglected.

Tantalus is the root of *tantalizing*. Tantalus was the son of Zeus and was the king of Sipylos. He was uniquely favored among mortals; however, he attempted to kill the gods and was punished by being "tantalized" with hunger and thirst: the gods punished Tantalus by placing him in a clear pool above which grew delicious fruit. Whenever he sought to relieve his thirst or hunger, the water and fruit would always recede just beyond his reach.

Similarly, from Aeolus, custodian of the four winds, came the adjective *aeolian* (of or relating to the wind; produced or carried by the wind). The god of the North Wind Boreas is turned into *boreal* (of or relating to the north or the north wind); likewise, the word *zephyr* (the west wind or a soft or gentle breeze) was born from the god of the West Wind Zephyrus.

Another word, *bacchanalian* meaning "frenzied, orgiastic; drunken; crazy like" comes from the famous Dionysus (Bacchus). He and his followers were often drunk, gay, and they feasted Carnivals. Thus, the other adjective *bacchanal* means "a drunken and riotous celebration or a participant in such a celebration."

The English Affixes of Gods' Names

Such affixes are usually abstract and general that form the majority of the prefixes. Words are mostly from the names of mythological figures with certain power or of certain symbolic significance.

The Greek goddess of the dawn, Eos, was the sister of Helios (sun) and Selene (moon) and the mother of the four winds: Boreas, Eurus, Zephyrus and Notus; and also of Heosphoros and the Stars. She was depicted as a goddess whose rosy fingers opened the gates of heaven to the chariot of the Sun. Evolution of the goddess' name appears as a prefix *eos-*, meaning "dawn, first, original."

The affix *selen-*, meaning "month," evolved from the moon goddess Selene. She resembled a young woman with an extremely white face who traveled on a silver chariot drawn by two horses wearing a half moon on her head. Such words as *selenodesist* (lunar scientist) and *selenology* (studying the lunar surface and science) are related to her name.

Similarly, affix *hebe-*, meaning youth, comes from Hebe, the goddess of youth, who poured the nectar of the gods on the Olympus until Ganymede replaced her. And examples can be found in the word *hebephrenia*, whose medical meaning is "a kind of adolescent disease characterized by withdrawal from reality, illogical patterns of thinking, and delusions."

Ares is the mythological god of war. Observing the strange red-brown Mars, the ancient Greeks assumed this god was making trouble there, so with his Roman name *Mars*, they named the planet. The name *Ares* has evolved into an affix *areo-* (related to planet), such as *areocentric* (Mars-centered); *aerographic* (the Martian surface); *areography* (Mars science).

Another mythological god worth mentioning is Thanatos, the Greek personification of death who dwelled in the lower world. He often brought with him the war, pestilence, floods, as well as death penalty. Therefore, *Thanatos* is changed into a prefix *thanat(o)-* (death) as is in the case of *thanatoid* (resembling death) and *thanatophobia* (fear of incurable disease).

And in the Greek myth, there exist some giants. Mythical giant was produced naturally in people's conquest of the world when the productivity of performance was still low. It was told that once the most gigantic offspring of Uranus and Gaea were a group of creatures, both male and female, who were Titans and Titaness. Titans are a race of godlike giants who were considered to be the personifications of the forces of nature. For that reason, *titan* always refers to the academic or political giant, or people with great strength. The title of the blockbuster *Titanic* is derived from *titan*.

Exercises

1. Match each Greek term with its corresponding definition.

Term	Definition
1) thanatophobia	a. given to controversy or disputation
2) areocentric	b. stimulating sexual desire
3) erotogenic	c. of or relating to youth
4) selenology	d. fear of incurable disease
5) hebetic	e. bout of noisy, drunken merrymaking
6) bacchanal	f. studying the lunar surface and science
7) zephyr	g. a very strong or important person
8) tantalize	h. Mars-centered
9) eristic	i. tease or torment
10) titan	j. a soft or gentle breeze

2. Tell whether the following statements are true or false according to the knowledge you learned and why.

1) *Tantalizing* means "having or exhibiting something that provokes or arouses expectation, interest, or desire, especially that which remains unobtainable or beyond one's reach." The root of the word is *Tantalus*. (   )
2) The prefix *eos-* meaning "sexually arousing or pertaining to love or desire" is originated from the myth of Eros. (   )
3) The affix *hebe-*, meaning herb, comes from the Greek goddess Hebe. (   )
4) Eris is the Greek goddess of conflict and dispute, so *eristic* means "of, relating, or given to controversy or logical disputation." (   )
5) From the quantitative point of view, the words derived from the names of the gods are more than those of the goddesses. (   )

Text C Words in Astronomy of Greek Mythological Origins

The eight planets in our solar system except the earth we live in are all named after the major gods in Greco-Roman mythology. They are listed from the near to the distant against the sun: Mercury, Venus, Mars, Jupiter, Saturn, Uranus and Neptune. There are some other minor planets such as Apollo, Ceres, Clio, Cynosure, Cynthia, Hyades, Vesta, Adonis, Psyche and Pallas.

In 1781, a German-born English astronomer, William Herschel, discovered a new planet more distant than any that were known before. Until that date, all the planets that were known were bright objects in the sky that were easily seen and had been recognized in prehistoric times. The new planet was a very faint object, however, barely visible to the naked eye. Herschel wanted to call the new planet "George's Star" after George III, who was then King of England. Other astronomers suggested it be named "Herschel" after the discoverer. Neither suggestion was adopted. All the other planets had been named after ancient god and goddess and the custom was kept. The new planet was named

"Uranus" at the suggestion of a German astronomer named Johann Bode.

The sixth planet is also the farthest planet from the sun of all the planets known to the Greeks. The sun's gravitation is weak at that distance and the sixth planet moves more slowly than any other planet the Greeks knew. With such a slow and majestic movement, it has seemed to the Greeks that it ought to be symbolized by an old, old god. "Cronus" seemed the natural choice. The Roman naturally called the planet "Saturn" and that is the name that has down to us.

The Greeks named the fifth planet after Zeus. This was a logical choice because the fifth planet was brightest except for the evening and morning stars. The evening star, however, only appeared for a few hours after sunset and the morning star only for a few hours before dawn, while the fifth planet often shines the whole night through. The Roman, of course, used their own version of the name and it is as "Jupiter" that the planet known to us.

In 1846, two astronomers, Britain's John Couch Adams and France's Urbain Le Verrier discovered the eighth planet. It was named "Neptune", not for any particular reasons, but because Neptune was one important god who lacked a planet.

Venus is one goddess whose name given to an important planet. This is the planet commonly called the "evening star" or the "morning star" (depending on which side of the sun it happens to be). It is the brightest and most beautiful object in the heavens next to the sun and moon, and is far brighter than any star.

Now of all the planets in the sky, the one that moves most quickly against the background of the stars was naturally named after the swift-footed Hermes. The Romans identified their own god of commerce, Mercury, with Hermes, and so we know the planet as "Mercury".

The Romans identified their god of war, Mars, with Ares, so we know the planet as "Mars". This planet was named after the god of war because its reddish color reminded people of blood.

Questions for Discussion or Reflection
1. How was the planet Uranus named?
2. What features of the planets Saturn, Mercury and Mars remind people of the gods that they were named after?
3. Which important planet was named after a goddess?
4. Among the eight planets in our solar system, what planets were named after Roman gods? What planets were named after Greek gods?

Text D The Adventures of Odysseus

Odysseus, also known by the Latin name Ulysses, was a legendary Greek king of Ithaca and a warrior renowned for his brilliance, guile, and versatility. His adventures began with the Trojan War which was caused by a golden apple.

Apple of Discord

Zeus held a banquet in celebration of the marriage of Peleus and Thetis. Eris, the goddess of discord, was not invited for her troublesome nature, and upon turning up uninvited, she threw a golden apple into the ceremony, with an inscription that read "For the fairest." Hera, Athena, and Aphrodite all claimed it. Not wanting to get involved, Zeus assigned Paris, prince of Troy, to decide who deserved the apple. Each of the goddesses offered Paris a gift as a bribe in return for the apple: Hera offered to make him the king of Europe and Asia, Athena offered him wisdom and skill in battle, and Aphrodite offered him the most beautiful woman in the world as his wife, Helen of Sparta. Paris chose Aphrodite, a decision that ultimately led to the start of the Trojan war.

Trojan Horse

The ancient Greeks went to war with Troy to regain Helen. During this Trojan War, which lasted ten years, the Greek Odysseus proved himself the shrewdest of the warriors. Odysseus conceived the plan that ultimately enabled the Greeks to defeat the Trojans. He had the Greeks build a huge wooden horse that was hollow inside and then filled it with many of the best Greek warriors. Those Greeks not in the horse then hid from the view of the Trojans.

Seeing only the gigantic horse at their gates, the Trojans thought that the Greeks had departed for their homeland and left the horse as an offering for the gods. They took the horse into their city and celebrated late into the night. When they finally dropped off to sleep, the Greeks emerged from the horse and slaughtered the Trojans.

Odysseus and the Cyclops

However, though the war ended, Odysseus' adventures did not. It took Odysseus another ten years to get home. One of his adventures was filled with a Cyclops, a monstrous one-eyed giant. Odysseus and his men found their way into the Cyclops's cave, but when the Cyclops returned, the giant barred the cave door with a massive boulder that Odysseus and his men could not move. The Cyclops then grabbed two of Odysseus' men, tore off their limbs, and devoured the men, bones and all. Odysseus then devised a plan to get the Cyclops drunk. The intoxicated Cyclops asked Odysseus his name, and Odysseus responded, "My name is Noman." When the Cyclops finally fell asleep from the wine, Odysseus and his men took a sharpened pole and gouged out the giant's eye. Odysseus then tied his men underneath the giant's sheep, which were also in the cave. When morning came, the Cyclops removed the boulder to let out the sheep. The blinded monster felt the back of each sheep for any Greek warriors but never thought to feel underneath. Odysseus, clinging to the underside of the largest ram, and his men thus escaped. Eventually realizing that he had been tricked, the Cyclops called out in agony to his fellow giants, "Noman is killing me." His companions replied that since no man was the cause of his pain, he must be sick and that there was nothing they could do, so they left him alone. Thus, the shrewd Odysseus defeated the Cyclops. The Greek epic the *Odyssey* records many other fascinating adventures.

Penelope's Web

During the twenty years when Odysseus was away, Penelope, his beautiful wife waited faithfully for his return. During this wait, many suitors courted her. They came to her home, insisting Odysseus was dead and would never return. In order to avoid choosing a husband, Penelope came up with a plan. She announced that she was weaving a shroud for her father-in-law, and she said that once she had finished, she would choose among the suitors. Every day she wove the shroud, and each night she unraveled nearly all the day's work. For years, she kept the suitors away until Odysseus finally returned.

Today, any long eventful journey is called "an odyssey." Marco Polo underwent an odyssey by land from Italy to China, Christopher Columbus an odyssey by water from Spain to America, and Neil Armstrong an odyssey through space from earth to the moon.

Exercises

Fill in the blanks with the English words and expressions of Greek Mythological Origins.
1. They departed Texas on a three-year _____ that took them as far as Japan.
2. The removal of poverty is a(n) _____. Everybody is at it.
3. She pretended to be his friend, but she was a(n) _____, sent to find out about his business operations.
4. The right to host the Olympic Games is a(n) _____ between the two countries.

For Fun

Works to Read

1. ***Gifts from the Gods: Ancient Words and Wisdom from Greek and Roman Mythology*** by Lise Lunge-Larsen and Gareth Hinds

    Ancient names come to rich and fascinating life in this lavishly illustrated gift book for mythology fans and word lovers. Where did these words such as *chaos*, *genius*, *nemesis*, *panic*, *echo*, and *narcissus* come from? From the ancient stories of the Greeks—stories that rang so true and wise that the names of the characters have survived for centuries as words we use every day. The brief stories here not only impart the subtle wisdom of these ancient tales, but make us understand the words, and our own world, more deeply.

2. ***The Greek & Latin Roots of English*** by Tamara M. Green

    This book approaches the study of Latin and Greek thematically: vocabulary is organized into various topics, including politics and government, psychology, medicine and the biological sciences, literature, ancient culture, and religion and philosophy. Each chapter of the text concludes with expanded notes, vocabulary, and exercises to help students learn the pleasures of language study.

Websites to Visit

1. http://www.greekmythology.com/

   This site has information on all subjects of Greek mythology.

2. http://www.behindthename.com/nmc/gre-myth.php

   This is an online dictionary of Greek mythology names.

3. http://www.mythweb.com/

   This site is devoted to the heroes, gods and monsters of Greek mythology.